Flying Stars Feng Shui for PERIOD 9
Which Begins Feb 4th 2024

How to enhance prosperity, health and relationships
for the next 20 years

Master Denise Liotta Dennis

Ω

Moon Gate Press
Houston, Texas USA

I dedicate this book to all my wonderful clients

Flying Stars Feng Shui for Period 9
Which Begins Feb 4th 2024
How to enhance prosperity, health and love luck for the next 20 years

Copyright© 2020 by Denise A. Liotta-Dennis
First Edition, First Printing

Photography & Illustrations
Illustrations and charts created by Denise Liotta Dennis. All floor plans provided by Chesmar Homes (Houston, Texas). Photos provided by Unsplash, Pixabay, Flickr, wiki commons, and all creative commons. Thanks to these photographers from *Pixabay and Unsplash*: Erika Wittlieb, Olichel Adamovich, William Kedersha, Solomon Rodgers, Giovanni Gargiulo, Paul Brennan, Andy Giraud, Flash Alexander, Kirk Fisher, Midascode, Arek Socha, James DeMers, Engin Akyurt, David Mark, MikesPhotos, Gretta Blankenship, ddzphoto, Gregory Butler, Skeeze, Wolfields, R H, Quang Nguyen, Vinh, Mschiffm, Jesse Bridgewater, Rita E, Mschiffm, Emlees, Pexels, Debbie Halcomb, Andreas Göllner, Ariesjay Castillo, Steve Siegwalt, Palmettophoto1, F. Muhammad, Ulla Alfons, Karen Arnold, Jonathan Wilkins, Dimitris Vetsikas, Chang Zuo, Quinn Kampschroer, AgE Global Group, Connoman, Jamicc, StockSnap, Katzenfee50, Franckin Japan, Thomas B., AnnaER, Peter H, RD, LH, Andreas Roth, Icewall42, Mike Goad, Javigu33, Ray Miller, Jombbes, and Travel4foodfun, Dan Wayman, Alexandra Seinet, Frank Zhang, Matt Briney, Ling Tang, Stefano Ferrario, WarrenMae Investment Group, Steve Buissinne, Jean van der Meulen, NeONBRAND, Olya Adamovich, Stephen Leonardi, Tookapic, Adheesha Paranagama, k z, Aditya Chinchure, Clifford Photography, ErikaWittlieb, Photo Mix, Roberto Nickson, Andrew Neel, Ahmed Rizkhaan, Daria Nepriakhina, David Monje, khiem tran, cocoparisienne, and Joel & Jasmin Førestbird.

Cover/Book Designer: Denise Liotta Dennis; front cover photo by Josch13 from Pixabay.

Notice of Rights
All rights reserved. No part of this publication may be reproduced, stored in a retrieval system or transmitted in any form, or by any means, electronic, mechanical, photocopying, recording, or otherwise, without the written permission of the publisher. For information in on getting permission for reprints and excerpts, contact: denise@dragongatefengshui.com

Notice of Liability
The information in this book is distributed on an 'as is" basis, without warranty. While every precaution has been taken in the preparation of the book, neither the author nor Moon Gate Press shall have any liability to any person or entity with respect to any loss or damaged caused or alleged to be causes directly or indirectly by the instructions contained in this book.

ISBN-9781983872242
Published in the United States of America

Published by Moon Gate Press (713-897-1719) and Kindle Direct Publishing (KDP)

CONTENTS

Introduction 4

Chapter One: Concepts of Feng Shui 5
Feng Shui's Core Theories
The Five Metaphysical Arts
The Nature of Chi
The Eight Trigrams
Tien Di Ren

Chapter Two: The Origins of Feng Shui 11
He Tu and Luo Shu
The Five Elements
The Two Ba Guas
The Chinese Compass
The Main Branches of Feng Shui

Chapter Three: The San He System 17
Precious Jewel Line Degrees
Water Dragons for Wealth
Five Ghosts Carry Treasure
60 Dragons Method (3 levels)
72 Piercing Dragons Mountain
Earth Mother Transformation Tan Lang
Assistant Star Water Method
Three-Harmony Doorways
Court Official Water Method
Jade Belt Formations
Sky Horse Technique
Five Ghosts Carry Treasure II
120 Gold Divisions
240 Gold Divisions
Eight Roads of Destruction
Peach Blossom Sha
Goat Blade Water
Four Destructions & Six Harms
Death & Empty Lines (DEL)

Chapter Four: The San Yuan System 34
Eight Mansions (BaZhai)
Your Life-Gua Number
The 8 Life Gua Groups & GMY Code
Good & Bad Directions
Advanced Eight Mansions
Life-Gua Personalities

Flying Stars (Xuan Kong Fei Xing)
Natal Flying Star Charts
What are the Stars?
Time Cycles of Flying Stars
Locating the Right Star Chart
Move-In Date
How to Determine the Facing
The 24 Mountains of Flying Stars
Components of a Flying Star Chart
Good and Bad Stars
The 81 Combination of Stars
Annual and Monthly Stars
Xuan Kong Da Gua
Dragon Gate Eight Method
The Castle Gate Method
Peach Blossom Technique for Romance
Pearl and Parent Strings Charts
Combination of Ten Charts
Robbery Mountain Sha
Three Killings
The Five Yellow Star
Grand Duke Jupiter
The Year Breaker
The Great Sun Formula

Chapter Five: Period 9 Charts and Activation 91
Period 9 Charts for all 24 Facings

Chapter Six: Period 8 Charts and Activation 152
Period 8 Charts for all 24 Facings

Chapter Seven: Period 7 Charts and Activation 199
Period7 Charts for all 24 Facings

Glossary 248
Appendix 288
Bibliography 296
Feng Shui Resources 297
Author's Bio 304
Author's Books 305

Introduction

Not only does Flying Stars Feng Shui reveal the energy map of a home, but also how luck will change from year to year. Capital changes occur every 20 years and are milestone markers for this powerful compass-based system.

We will soon enter a milestone marker in Feng Shui. Every 20 years, the world embarks on a major energy shift. In Feng Shui terms, they are known as 'Periods' or Ages. The *Age of 9* promises to be a time of great enlightenment and constant advancement. We all seem to be participating in a great awakening in consciousness. This book is about preparing your home or business for those changes so that you may experience the best this new Period has to offer.

Feng Shui can help improve every area of life that is essential to happiness; prosperity, health and relationships. By making some simple adjustments, you can turn the tides of fortune and opportunities.

What's great about Flying Stars Feng Shui is that it will alert you to non-physical, invisible and inauspicious energies. Unless they are dealt with or cured with appropriate remedial measures, this energy, when aggressive, can cause serious misfortune befalling the householders. Hardships may show up as financial loss, accidents, tragedies or illness. However, when you have the right information about Feng Shui, it makes it possible to reduce the misfortunes in your life.

When you energize the auspicious forces, they can bring unexpected opportunities, good health, and a promotion at work or financial windfalls. Keep in mind that attracting the feel-good energies into your living space are a result of correctly activating the Feng Shui! So, before we embark on making the changes, lets' take a look at the very foundation and roots of Classical Feng Shui.

CHAPTER ONE
Concepts of Feng Shui

Feng Shui's core theories are how the ancients viewed the universe and energy. An extremely diluted version of Feng Shui arrived in America and other Western countries during the 1970's.

The origins of Feng Shui are exceptionally ancient and its concepts of superior living can be traced to the Tang Dynasty. However, oral tradition places it much earlier. This secret knowledge, once obscure to Westerners, is more popular than ever. Even after being in practice for thousands of years, Feng Shui is still viable. In fact, the principles and concepts of Feng Shui are needed as never before. We live in an uncertain world; having this ancient wisdom merits review.

The story of how it came to be is entrenched in ancient philosophies and acute observations that formed the great Chinese culture. The translation of Feng Shui is 'wind' and 'water'. In literal terms, this refers to the topography of the land, the mountains, valleys, and natural water features whose flow, direction, and size, are influenced by the constant interaction of these two powerful forces on earth. To the Chinese people, Feng Shui is a mystical practice that blends ancient wisdom with a body of knowledge that provide guidelines for life's different situations.

It is best to experiment when applying Feng Shui to your home or office. Pay attention to the transformations in personal prosperity, opportunities, relationships and other areas of your life. Is your health improving? Are you attracting better relationships or improving the ones you have? Are opportunities for more wealth or career luck showing up? In short, are things getting better in your life?

Sadly, Feng Shui has fallen in and out of favor throughout its long history. General Mao was the last Chinese leader to forbid its use. As a result, Feng Shui masters were forced to flee to Hong Kong *(then ruled by the British)*, Malaysia, Singapore and Taiwan. It is in these locations that the most sophisticated forms of Feng Shui are practiced today. Americans have rarely heard of Classical Feng Shui, even though high profile billionaires and major institutions such as Oprah, Steve Wynn, Bill Gates, Wells Fargo and Chase Banks use it. Some of these illustrious people and institutions got their first introduction in Hong Kong, which is often called the 'unofficial capital of Classical Feng Shui', while doing business there.

Being born Chinese, either in China, America or elsewhere does not guarantee knowledge of this ancient science. An extremely diluted version of Feng Shui arrived in America during the 1970's. The Asian masters refer to this as faux Feng Shui. This false Feng Shui is featured in 90% of the books and at least 50% on the internet. Therefore, it is difficult to find clear information about Feng Shui's valuable principles. Added to the mix of confusion, is Chinese cultural superstitions which have nothing to do with Feng Shui at all.

Feng Shui is not a religious practice or derived from a religion. It's not magic or rooted in the New Age movement. It has nothing to do with your cat, dog, car, Zen design, phone number, house number, chandeliers, or food arrangement. Westernized Feng Shui was simply the successful commercialization of an ancient, geomantic science.

Genuine Feng Shui considers the exact orientation of the building; birthdates of the occupants; floor plan and design layout; shape of the home/building and the surrounding environment such as roads, canals, mountains, swimming pools, electrical towers, lakes, highways, slopping land, high-rise structures, streams, graveyards, alleys, and nearby parks.

Feng Shui's Core Principles
Feng Shui's basic core theories are how the ancients viewed the universe and energy. Virtually, every book on Feng Shui introduces the famous precepts of the Ba Gua, five elements, yin-yang theory, Luo Shu and He Tu. This often leaves the reader confused as how to apply them.

These tools are *principles* and not stand alone formulas or techniques. If you have several books on Feng Shui, you've already been introduced to the basic concepts. However, you may want to skim over these basic building blocks of Feng Shui even if you are somewhat familiar. If this is your very first Feng Shui book, take a few minutes to peruse these important ideas. This chapter of the book is *not for implementation*, rather to deepen your appreciation of Feng Shui and its roots.

There continues to be a certain mysticism surrounding the practice of Feng Shui. Understanding its many principles and canons requires the acceptance of fundamental theories about the universe. This may, at first glance, seem alien in the context of how the modern world works.

At any rate, Feng Shui is part of Chinese metaphysics which is a huge body of knowledge that is comprised of five major categories of study. All five categories (aka the 'five arts') have their foundation in the same energy tools [the two Ba Guas, five elements, yin-yang and so forth] and then develop into different branches of study. We'll start with the five arts and then briefly discuss them, one by one.

Figure 1: There are five different categories of Chinese metaphysics. Feng Shui is known as physiognomy and one aspect is evaluating the landscape's appearance and shape.

The Five Metaphysical Arts (Wu Shu)

Classical Feng Shui is just one of the five (5) main art-sciences of Chinese metaphysics. Deeply rooted in the I Ching and the Tao, these philosophical tenets—mountain, medicine, divination, destiny, and physiognomy—are the origins of the Chinese culture developed over 5,000 years. It is said that if you are able to master just one of these studies it would be a significant life-accomplishment.

Mountain (Shan or Xian Xue): This category encompasses philosophy (e.g. the teachings of the fourth-century B.C. philosophers Lao Tzu and Zhuang Zi), Taoism, martial arts, Qi Gong, Tai Chi Chuan, meditation, healing, and diet. It also includes the study of Alchemy—the science of prolonging life through specific rituals and exercises, which are deeply rooted in Taoism.

Medicine (Yi): The Chinese follow an integrated, holistic, and curative approach to medicine and healing such as acupuncture, herbal prescriptions, and massage.

Divination (Po): The Chinese are acknowledged for their intuitive skills and abilities to read and interpret symbols. The divination techniques of Da Liu Ren, Tai Yi Mystical Numbers, Qi Men, Mei Hua Xin Yi (Plum Blossom oracle) employ numbers to predict everything from wars or missing persons, to the details of one's past and future.

Destiny (Ming): Most forms of Chinese augury seek to interpret fate and determine the timing of life events. The ancient sages devoted much time and research to this study. The most popular methods of Chinese fortune-telling include Zi Wei Dou Shu (Purple Star Astrology)

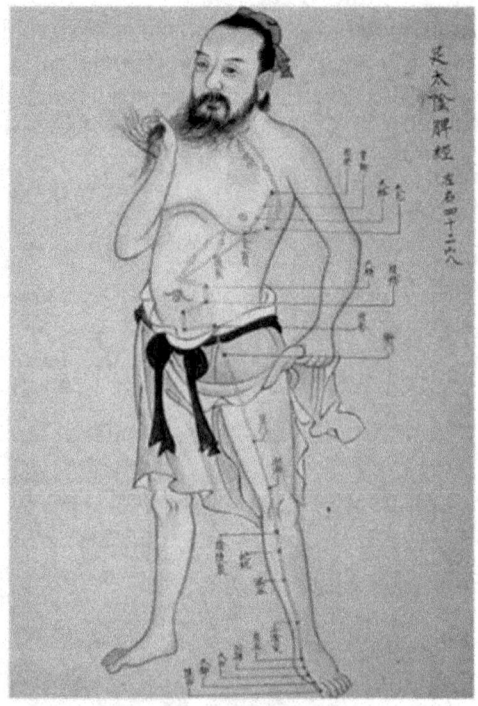

and BaZi (literally means 'eight characters' but is also commonly known as the Four Pillars of Destiny), both of which examine a person's destiny and potential based on their date and time of birth. A complimentary form of Ming is the Science of Divination (Bu Shi), which is analogous to the mathematics of probability.

Physiognomy (Xiang Xue): Grandmaster Yap Cheng Hai refers to this category as *Sow,* and it involves making predictions based on the image, form, and features of the landscape, the human face and palms, architecture, and gravesites. Feng Shui is the fortune-telling of a building by rendering an accurate observation of the structure's appearance, shape, direction, and other surrounding environmental features.

The Nature of Chi

Chi simply means energy. The ancient Chinese was one of the first cultures to discover that humans and our entire universe are comprised of pure energy. Modern-day science now confirms this. Chi also spelled *qi*, (either spelling is pronounced *chee*) is the life-force energy of the universe, heaven, earth, and man. Sometimes it is also referred to as the *cosmic breath*, which is present in every living and non-living entity. It can be auspicious, inauspicious, or benign. Chi is the life-force energy that pervades mankind's existence. It is the unseen force that moves through the human body and the environment.

Feng Shui's main objective is to attract and harness auspicious energy to support people. It is energy that determines the shape and form of the landscape as well as the vitality of all living things. The famous Tai Chi symbol, which resembles two interlocking fish, demonstrates the polarity of energy which is either yin (female) or yang (male).

The Eight Guas or Trigrams

The Guas, also known as Trigrams, date back to Chinese antiquity. These important symbols give a macro, inclusive perspective of our universe, energy and direction. Each of the eight Guas is comprised of three lines either solid or broken. The broken lines indicate yin/female energy while the solid lines represent yang/male energy. The famous Ba Gua includes all eight trigrams; "Ba" means *eight*, and "Gua" means the *result of divination*.

Figure 2: This image is of the Tai Chi (yin-yang) symbol and the eight trigrams.

The eight Guas, in addition to representing the eight directions, have several layers of information that becomes useful in assessing the energy of land, homes or buildings. The Chinese related this information to everyday life, resulting in each Gua representing the father, mother, eldest son, eldest daughter and so forth. In the end, each Gua represents yin or yang energy, relates to a family member, an element, a body part, a possible illness, a season, a number, human personality types, and direction. All the same, these implications and interpretations have great significance in Feng Shui and other Chinese metaphysical studies. The eight Guas are Kan, Gen, Chen, Xun, Li, Kun, Dui, and Chien representing North, Northeast, East, Southeast, South, Southwest, West and Northwest respectively.

In modern-day language, the trigrams are the eight binary numbers of 111, 110, 101, 100, 011, 010, 001 and 000. The *solid lines* represent the 1 digit, while the *broken lines* represent the digit 0; they are read from the bottom up. It's been said that the Chinese were the first to use binary arithmetic. Binary codes are the 'language' of computers.

Tien Di Ren

*"**Heaven Luck** is the boat given to you by God. **Earth Luck** is the wind that fills the sails and the currents of the ocean. **Man Luck** is the way in which you use the wind and the currents to steer your boat."* –Grandmaster Yap Cheng Hai

The three types of luck (opportunities), known as Tien Di Ren, are heaven luck, Earth Luck and Man Luck. Each one of these categories will champion you in a very different way. This aspect of Feng Shui is called the Cosmic Trinity. In other words all three areas will influence your life and living space.

Heaven Luck (Tien)
This category of luck is often referred to as destiny or karma. The Chinese believe that what goes around comes around; that past deeds, for good or evil, will visit you again in this life. They also contend that this area of luck is fixed and may not be influenced; it counts as 1/3 of your overall luck and opportunities in life.

Earth Luck (Di)
This category is the dominion of Feng Shui.
If your home site and living space has auspicious and harmonious energy, you will reap the rewards. Additionally, life will support your efforts, goals, relationships, health and prosperity if this aspect is taken care of. In Earth-luck, you have total control and it can exceed the normal 1/3 associated with it if you have superior energy at home and work. Grandmaster Yap purports that it can be raised to 2/3.

Man Luck (Ren)
This category of luck is another area you have total control over. This is created by you own efforts and the choices you make in life. This may include your education, morals, hard work, beliefs and your ability to seize and exploit good opportunities.

CHAPTER TWO
The Origins of Feng Shui

More than 4,000 years ago, the roots of Feng Shui were being developed. Mathematical diagrams of the He Tu and Luo Shu and ancient lore unlock Feng Shui's secrets.

The He Tu and Luo Shu
These two very distinct mathematical diagrams representing universal energy are so ancient and intrinsic in the Chinese culture that its people are often referred to as the He-Luo culture. Together they form the foundation of Chinese philosophy and are the genesis and origins of Feng Shui. These famous diagrams are frequently mentioned in ancient Chinese literature and are shrouded by legend and mystery. There are a series of lines connected with black and white dots in both diagrams. Most scholars believe the He Tu chronicles the cycle of birth, while the Luo Shu represents the process of death: yin and yang.

Ancient lore surrounding the He Tu began with the reign of the shaman king Fu Xi, who was born in the 29th century B.C., witnessed a mythical dragon-horse bearing strange, unusually patterned markings on its back emerging from the mighty Yellow River. This design became known as the He Tu (pronounced *hur too*). As Fu Xi examined these

markings (see illustration), valuable information pertaining to cosmic laws of the universe was revealed. The dots (black are yin and white are yang) of the He Tu illustrate several concepts; including direction, the five elements of Feng Shui and the flow of chi.

Following Fu Xi's life, succeeding scholars meticulously preserved and passed down the mysteries of the He Tu. Even today, it is found in written texts and ancient scrolls which pervade Eastern ideologies, including traditional Chinese medicine and some of the initial principles of Feng Shui. The five element theory (water, wood, fire, earth, and metal) have its basis in the He Tu. These elements indentify, interpret and predict natural phenomena. Later to arrive on the scene would be the Guas or trigrams. Therefore, the theories and principles of the He Tu gave birth to the first Ba Gua, known as the Early Heaven Ba Gua (Xien Tien Ba Gua).

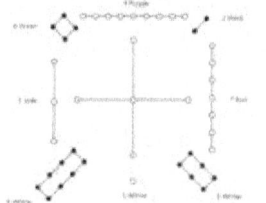

The Luo Shu is also surrounded by legend and myth. Emperor Yu of the Xia Dynasty, while sitting next the River Lo saw a giant turtle emerge in or around 2100 B.C. It too, had a pattern and series of black and white dots on its back. The Luo Shu is a nine square grid containing nine numbers. Each of the nine numbers represents a trigram, body organ, family member, direction, or element and it is either male or female energy. Interestingly, no matter which way you add the numbers in the grid they total 15. The Luo Shu is often referred to as the Magic Square of 15. This arrangement of numbers became part of the Later Heaven Ba Gua (LHB). The Luo Shu is used extensively in all methods and applications of Classical Feng Shui.

The Luo Shu and He Tu are coded maps that represent the cosmology of heaven and earth; they are energy tools which are used to assess buildings, living spaces and land sites. These ancient oracles are considered the backbone of Chinese metaphysics.

Unlocking their mysteries takes many years of study, contemplation and a learned teacher. Please note that South is placed at the top, not North in the He Tu and Luo Shu images. This may take some getting used to.

The Five Elements (Wu Xing)

All categories of Chinese metaphysics explain the world and the universe, in terms of the five elements. As with most brilliant discoveries made by humans, nature served as the inspiration. In ancient China, they paid close attention to the predicable cycles of energy—fire burns wood, and metal comes from the Earth. By associating this information in everyday life and events, the Five Element theory was created.

The Chinese knew that energy was part of everything. Therefore, by placing energy into five different categories offered a viable solution in which to assess their interaction. These five categories or five phases of energy are known as Wu Xing. The five elements are metal (jin-literally the word for gold), wood (mu), water (shui), fire (ho), and earth (tu). Each element is a representation of matter and energy as it coalesces from one form to the next. The Five Element theory simply elucidates the relationship among different types of energy. It is understood as both figurative and literal in Feng Shui applications.

Productive Cycle: It represents the productive force that drives the smooth flow of events in their natural order. This important cycle produces or gives birth to something. Wood feeds fire. Fire produces ash and creates earth. Earth gives birth to metal. Metal melts into a fluid and becomes water, which in turn produces wood.

The Weakening/Reductive Cycle: This cycle represents the retarding force that inhibits and reverses the natural flow of events. This process is the reverse of the productive cycle, because what we give birth to weakens us. Wood stokes fire, therefore, fire weakens wood. Fire generates ash and creates earth, therefore, earth weakens fire. Earth produces metal, therefore, metal weakens earth. Metal melts to a fluid and produces water, therefore, water weakens metal. Water produces wood, therefore, wood weakens water.

The Controlling Cycle: This cycle describes conflict. Constructive conflict is referred to as controlling, while destructive conflict is called killing energy. This process can conquer, control or destroy. Water extinguishes fire, fire melts metal, and metal cuts wood. Wood, in the form of plants or tree roots, controls the Earth by breaking it apart or keeping it together. Earth is big enough to hold water—without earth water would have no boundary.

The Two Ba Guas

Likely the second most recognized image after the Tai Chi symbol is the Ba Gua; however most are not aware that there are two. The Ba Gua literally appears in all Feng Shui books; it is an octagonal map that depicts the eight trigrams. The two Ba Guas are the Early Heaven Ba Gua *(Fu Xi or Xien Tien Ba Gua)* and Later Heaven Ba Gua *(Ho Tien or Wen Wang Ba Gua).* Both are used in the practice of Classical Feng Shui as all formulas, methods, and techniques are born from the two arrangements of the Guas.

The Early Heaven Ba Gua (EHB), which dates back approximately 6,000 years, depicts the polarities in nature. It reflects an ideal world of harmony in which chi is in a constant, perfect state of polarization. The eight Guas, or trigrams, create a conceptual model that marks the changes in energy. The Early Heaven Ba Gua, representing a 'perfect' world, can be commonly seen over doorways to repel negative energy. It is used extensively in Westernized styles of Feng Shui. It has more profound implications and uses in Classical Feng Shui as it is the basis of complex formulas.

The Later Heaven Ba Gua (LHB) was the brilliant work of King Wen, a Chou Dynasty ruler who elaborated on Fu Xi's earlier diagrams. This arrangement was done to represent the cyclical forces of nature. The Later Heaven Ba Gua describes the patterns of environmental changes. Unlike Earlier Heaven Ba Gua, the LHB is dynamic, not static. It represents the ever-changing structure of the universe and the circular nature of life.

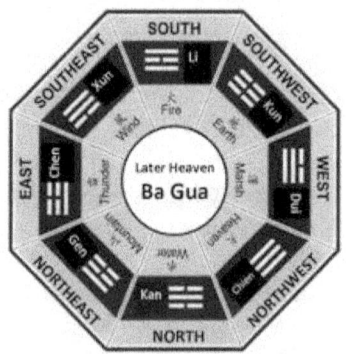

Many Feng Shui applications stem from the understanding of the Later Heaven Ba Gua. For instance, the Luo Shu is the numerical representation of the Later Heaven Ba Gua. Note that South is placed at the top of the images, not North.

The Chinese Compass (Luo Pan)
Hundreds of years before the Europeans, the ancient Chinese discovered the magnetic compass. There is an intriguing legend about how they acquired this enormous gift as part of their culture—it's the ancient legend of the *Warrior-Goddess of the Nine Heavens*. When China's first ruler, the Yellow Emperor Huangdi (2698 to 2598 BC), was asleep one night, there appeared a bright light from heaven in which the goddess emerged.

She held in her hand a 9 by 8 inch jade box. The Yellow Emperor received the jade box from the goddess and found that it contained a magic scroll written on dragon skin. It is said that by following the secrets written on the 'dragon scroll', the Emperor defeated the evil wizard (Chi You) in the famous Battle of Zhuolu. Thus began the start of the great Han Chinese civilization. Other stories tell about Huangdi's unique invention, a compass cart which leads to victory. Either way, the compass/Luo Pan soon became the quintessential tool of the Feng Shui master. Throughout its illustrious and long history, the Luo Pan has been redesigned and refined many times over so that it would align with the latest discoveries relating to landforms, techniques, and directional energy. There are two standard types of Luo Pans—San He and San Yuan—designed to include formulas of these two main disciplines of Classical Feng Shui. The third standard Luo Pan is the Chung He, which combines the most important information of the San He and San Yuan Luo Pans. The purpose of the Luo Pan is the same as a conventional compass—to precisely locate direction. However, the Luo Pan contains some very important differences.

A typical compass may display four or eight directions. A Luo Pan divides up the 360° into 24 sectors. This is derived by dividing the forty-five degrees of the eight directions into three, fifteen degree increments (3x 8=24).

This is very fundamental in Classical Feng Shui, and this ring on the Luo Pan is known as the 24 Mountain ring (not actual mountains, it's just a term). The Luo Pan is an impressive and beautiful instrument, truly a work of art, and well worth the several hundred dollars it commands. Here are the three types of Luo Pans:

Figure 3: The Chinese compass (Luo Pan) was a gift from the *Lady of the Nine Heavens*.

San Yuan Luo Pan: Used in the Flying Stars and the Xuan Kong systems, the San Yuan Luo Pan is readily indentified by the 64 hexagrams of the I Ching ring. It has only one 24 Mountain ring. The first ring of this Luo Pan is always the Later Heaven Ba Gua arrangement of trigrams.

San He Luo Pan: The San He Luo Pan, used for San He (aka San Hup) formulas and schools, is easily identified by its *three* 24 Mountain rings. These rings are used to measure direction, mountains, and water as each of these elements has distinctly different energy. However, these rings also relate to the three harmonies associated with this branch of Classical Feng Shui.

Chung He Luo Pan: Also spelled, or referred to as Zong He, Zhung He, or Chong He. This Luo Pan is an amalgamation of the San He and San Yuan compasses. This is a great instrument for practitioners who employ both systems. Though some rings have been eliminated for size considerations, all essential rings are intact.

This extraordinary instrument is often called the 'universe on a plate' by Feng Shui masters and practitioners. For more information on the Luo Pan and its history, refer to Dr. Stephen Skinner's book entitled *Guide to the Feng Shui Compass*. Thus far, it is the most comprehensive book ever written on the subject.

The Main Branches of Feng Shui: San He and San Yuan

At its core, Feng Shui is based on the keen observations of the heavens (time), earthly forces (exterior environments and interior spaces), and how these elements exchange energy or chi. While the origins of Feng Shui date back thousands of years, the term *Feng Shui* has only been in use for a little more than a hundred years. Its golden era occurred during the Tang Dynasty between the seventh and tenth centuries A.D.

Over time, two main branches of practice emerged, San He and San Yuan. These ideologies form the foundation of Classical Feng Shui. It is important to understand that Feng Shui is highly dynamic and constantly developing, even today. Most modern-day Feng Shui masters will combine these schools into one big body of knowledge. But there are a few who use one or the other exclusively. This is not bad, but rather unusual. Now let's examine these two important and main branches of Feng Shui in more detail. In the next two chapters you will discover a description of each of the numerous formulas and how they work in both San He (external Feng Shui) and San Yuan (internal Feng Shui).

Figure 4: Even though modern-day living is more complex than in ancient times, Feng Shui still has its place in building, developing and designing our living and working spaces using its core principles.

CHAPTER THREE
The San He System

These formulas apply to the exterior of your home/office and *not* the inside or the floor plan design! They are used to evaluate roads, mountains and water near your site.

San He, also known as San Hup, means three harmonies, three unities, or three combinations. It is considered the oldest form of Classical Feng Shui. The San He School gives great importance and consideration to environmental qualities, such as mountains and topography. The direction, shape, flow, and appearance of these features were important issues to evaluate before the construction of a building or when planning a city. In Neolithic China, Feng Shui was first used to select the ideal location for a home, a village, or the perfect gravesite for an ancestor—known as the practice of Yin Feng Shui. By the Tang Dynasty, Feng Shui had blossomed into a science, sophisticated and complex.

Since San He focuses on the environment namely the mountains, rivers, and landforms and it strives to understand how the environment shapes and creates chi. San He techniques are focused on finding the most advantageous or strategic location in which to extract the chi from the environment. This school recognizes that chi is dynamic and that it changes through time. This notion is based on immutable yin energy, such as mountains, to counter fluctuating yang energy, such as time cycles. San He systems do not try to adapt to cycles of chi. Rather, this approach attempts to insulate against and outlive any unfavorable energy cycles by selecting or creating superior landforms.

Figure 5: Roads and mountains are strong purveyors of energy/chi. The *San He* system has extensive methods to evaluate the luck and fortune of both.

San He also relies on extensive systems and formulas to assess formations for disaster, wealth potential, and good luck. San He is the best approach to large-scale Feng Shui projects, such as master-planned communities, city planning, high-rise buildings, hotels, resorts, airports, hospitals, and so forth. Because this system is so highly developed in landforms, it always considers the relationship of mountains (real or tall structures) and water (real water or roads) with the structure. These macro-level considerations should be addressed prior to attempting the micro-engineering design of any structure. San He is not just for large projects, it is perfectly suited for the average home as well, with numerous techniques that address every area of life.

The Best of the San He: *Wealth, prestige, nobility and a happy life. These formulas can be implemented on your site.*

Precious Jewel Lines or Gold Dragons
Exact degrees to bring auspicious events

Precious Jewel Lines (PJL), also known as *Gold Dragons*, are specific compass degrees that can bring great money luck and as the name implies precious things and "jewels" to your life. In any of the eight directions, there are there are six PJLs from which to choose, making a total of forty-eight. An example of a Precious Jewel Line degree is 86.5, which is part of the East direction. PJLs are appropriate for any structure and have various applications. PJLs most commonly apply to doors; generally the main door of a home or business can be set to these auspicious degrees. Driveways, sidewalks, trails, entrance gates, building foundations, important interior doors, desks, and beds can also be angled toward these special degrees.

Water Dragons for Wealth
A formula to bring wealth-luck involving an important door, real water+ exit

In nearly every part of the world, *Water Dragons* are natural to the environment. They are nothing more than a river or stream winding through the landscape, resembling the undulating body of this mythical reptile, hence the name. Man-made *Water Dragons* are quite popular in Southeast Asia but rarely show up in the United States and other Western countries. Taiwanese masters especially find all sorts of applications for these techniques. My teacher, Grandmaster Yap Cheng Hai, is quite famous for his applications of *Water Dragons* in Southeast Asia. He learned this specialized system in Taiwan from his mentor, Master Chan Chuan Huai (also spelled Tan Chuan Hui). It is said that Master Chan's clients are among Taiwan's billionaires, including the Sugar

King, the Cement King, and the Plastics King. *Water Dragon* formulas will bring powerful things in your life, sometimes slowly, sometimes quickly.

Over time, formulas for all possible facings were devised for the purpose of creating man-made *Water Dragons*. A comprehensive body of knowledge came from this study, and many techniques pertaining to wealth were founded on this data. To create a man-made Water Dragon, certain criteria should be met.

Below is the criteria for *Water Dragons*. Keep in mind the formula is compass-based:

- Water Dragons are designed in relationship to the front or main door
- Water Dragons require a fairly flat piece of land
- Water must pass by and be seen from the door
- Water will flow from right to left OR left to right depending on the door degree/facing
- A portion of the water dragon 'stream' can be seen while some portion is underground
- It should be approximately 12 inches wide and about 9 inches deep
- Two sumps will swirl or spin the water (optional)
- The exact degree for the water exit is the real secret to a good Water Dragon
- The heaven plate/ring on a San He or Cheung He Luo Pan should be used to measure the exit
- A different ring/plate is used to measure the front or main door

Water Dragons are expensive, complicated to install, and require constant maintenance. Most Feng Shui masters charge as much as $100,000+ for a *Water Dragon* formula design, depending on the size and the application. Lillian Too offers a good primer on *Water Dragons* in her book *Water Feng Shui for Wealth*. She wrote it in collaboration with Grandmaster Yap Cheng Hai. When it was published in 1995, it became instantly popular with Feng Shui aficionados.

Lillian's own Water Dragon in Kuala Lumpur was designed by GMY as was mine in Houston, Texas. One of my advanced students, who began her studies with Lillian, saw this water dragon in person. I saw GMY's water dragon at his home as well. His and mine were based more on the criteria stated above. They were long, man-made streams surrounding our properties. Lillian's was a shorter version. Either way, they can be effective. If I implemented another one, it would be a shorter version similar to *Figure 6*.

Figure 6: This type of human-made water feature could be a great *Water Dragon* if an exact exit degree were incorporated in the design.

In recent years, the validity of *Water Dragons* has become a hotly debated topic in Feng Shui circles. Some say they are hoax—ineffective and impotent. This is certainly not true. They are a legitimate Classical Feng Shui study, and since they involve real water, they can extract good and bad results. Grandmaster Yap and his teacher, Master Chan, have both experienced their own successes with *Water Dragons*, serving as a wonderful testament to their potential power.

Five Ghosts Carry Treasure
A wealth-luck formula that includes mountain, water and a door

Though the name of this highly guarded secret technique sounds weird and mysterious, it is a powerful wealth-producing formula that delivers, bringing immense good fortune! It is said that when this method is applied correctly, it's like having five ghosts or spirit angels carry prosperity right to your door. Many masters believe that this formula will only last about twelve years or so. However, my research indicates that the luck can extend well past twenty or thirty years. Much depends on the natural mountains surrounding the site.

The *Five Ghosts Carry Treasure* method is technically a water formula. Basically three things need to be in harmony: door direction, water flow, and mountain energy. Wealth is derived by tapping into the combined energy of these great forces. Of course a real mountain and a natural body of water are best, but pools, man-made streams, waterfalls and simulated mountains are excellent substitutes. Mountainous regions offer lots of opportunities to use this energy. In flatter areas, I default to man-made formations, such as out-structures, landscape mounds, large boulders, casitas, two-story detached garages, and pavilions. Yes, even these virtual or simulated mountains work well. Here's an example of how a *Five Ghosts Carry Treasure* could be designed for a north-facing home:

Figure 7: The direction of the *water flow* is very specific in this formula. In the example, it should flow from the direction of North.

- The front door direction is North 1 (337.6 to 352.5 degrees).
- A real mountain is located in the South 1 (specifically chi from 157.5 to 172.5 degrees).
- Water from the North 3 (7.6 to 22.5 degrees).

If you don't have a real mountain in the South, you can simulate a mountain with large boulders (no jagged or sharp edges) or landscape mounds. In either case, the man-made elevation must be three feet or higher to be considered a mountain. You could also create a tall structure in that location, which would also activate the mountain aspect of this formula. The water is fairly simple; a man-made stream could be designed to flow past and in view of your front door. In the example given above, it needs to flow from left to right as you are looking out the door. Each formula will have a different water flow depending on the door direction.

The 60 Earth-Penetrating Dragons Method
Evaluates mountain energy to be auspicious or inauspicious

The *60 earth-Penetrating Dragons* take into consideration the energy of a hillside or mountain immediately behind the house or building, basically evaluating its quality. The 'dragons' cover only 6 degrees, but all 60 dragons are assessed by one of five types of energy being either auspicious or inauspicious. The 60 dragon method was most likely invented by Ts'ai Shin Yu in the 10th century. The energy of the mountain may be likened to an electricity cable that supplies power to a light; the energy fed to the site will 'light it up'.

Remember, in Feng Shui, mountains are closely related to the human body; therefore the energy and quality of a mountain or hill can affect and influence the health. An example would be a mountain or hillside at the rear of the property—with its highest peak between 337.6 to 343.5 degrees; this 6-degree increment may indicate *"Yellow fever, swollen, insanity, and an ill female in the household"*. As ominous as that sounds, even with such a mountain, these inauspicious events may never happen. There are many good 'dragons' as well which support health, wealth, longevity, and good relationships.

The 72 Piercing Dragons Method
Evaluates mountain energy to be auspicious or inauspicious

The *72 Piercing Dragons* are similar to the 60 Dragons; they are also used to examine the energy of a mountain; it covers 5-degree increments. However, the 72 Piercing Dragons is mainly concerned with evaluating the *largest* or main mountain at the back of the property. While the 60 Dragons measure closer, more specific energy fed immediately behind the site. The method for the 72 Dragons is attributed to the famous Master Yang Yun Sung who lived during the Tang Dynasty (618 – 907 AD). He also created the 'Secret Verses' to accompany the 72 possible mountain measurements. These describe what the occupants may expect in the way of fortune and health-- depending on the mountain's degree.

The 72 Dragons also calculates the quality of the mountain into one of five types of energy. Some have seriously negative implications with descriptions like 'fire pits'. An example of this would be a main mountain measuring between 97°-102° and the secret verses explains this 5-degree increment as indicating *"Lonely, death, hunchbacks, bow-legged, and a short life-span."* However many mountain directions are very auspicious, for example if the largest mountain at the back of your property is between 352°-357°, then the secret verse describes it as *"Very auspicious, good children, real estate holdings, very rich and a noble government position."*

Earth Mother Transformation of the Tan Lang Stars
Used to evaluate a near-by mountain

The nine stars have many applications and uses in Classical Feng Shui. When used in the *Eight Mansions* (BaZhai) they are referred to as the Big Wandering Sky. With other applications, they can be referred to as the Small Wandering Sky. The *Earth Mother Transformation of the Tan Lang Stars* is a method used to assess the energy of near-by mountain within a 15-degree increment. The 60 and 72 Dragons use a more precise increment (between 5-6 degrees). These nine stars are *Greedy Wolf* (Tan Lang, 1 Star); *Huge Door* (Jue Men, 2 Star); *Military Arts* (Wu Chu, 6 Star); *Left/Right Assistant* (Tso Fu & Fu Pi, 8 & 9 Stars); *Rewards* (Lu Chun, 3 Star); *Five Ghosts* (Lien Zheng, 5 Star); *Literary Arts* (Wen Qu, 4 Star); and *Broken Soldier* (Tien Kong, 7 Star).

Figure 8: Mountain energy is evaluated using several methods such as 60 and 72 Dragons and the Tan Lang Stars (Earth Mother Transformation).

The Assistant Star Water Method
A formula to bring wealth-health luck involving real or virtual water and door

This technique offers ample and comprehensive choices when it comes to bringing wealth luck to your site via roads or real water, which are used in conjunction with the door direction. A master or practitioner has twenty-four possible door directions and numerous water (virtual and real) directions and exits from which to choose. You will get specific results depending on the choice of water direction. For example, certain water directions bring *wealth from heaven*, a high government position, riches and nobility, and good, filial children. These formulas can determine whether lawsuits, robbery, gambling, loneliness, mishaps, or quarrels are possible based on the placement.

An example of how this technique is applied is the front door faces South 1, South 2 or South 3. A driveway approaches from Southwest 1, 2 or 3. A water exit or drain is located in the Southeast. The formation in our example can indicate the acquisition of a great fortune. But water exiting from the South (e.g. a drain in the front of the house) serves as evidence that your career will be hindered accompanied by serious money loss. I am fond of using the Assistant Star method in new-home construction and when I'm designing a good, wealth-attracting driveway.

Three Harmony Doorway
A formula used to bring harmony-money-nobility luck using a door and virtual water

Despite the name, you don't need three doors to implement this great formula. It involves a door direction a road, driveway or sidewalk. These formulas have what is known as a main harmony and a sub-harmony—when the formula is applied correctly, a brilliant mix of yin and yang energy results. This particular technique attracts lucrative, prosperous, noble, and harmonious chi to the household. They are the most powerful when the road or driveway can also be placed in the actual location that the method calls for. Here is an example of how a *Three Harmony Doorway* can be created:

- The door direction is at Northeast 3 (52.6 to 67.5 degrees).
- A sidewalk comes from South 2 (172.5 to 187.5 degrees).

Figure 9: This house affords a perfect opportunity to install a *Three Harmony Doorway* formula via a sidewalk connecting the driveway to the existing sidewalk leading to the front door.

In our example, the formula becomes very effective if the sidewalk not only begins from the South direction, but also is located in the South of your garden. New homes under construction can easily benefit from this technique as the driveway has not been yet staked and pored. If also combined with a Precious Jewel Line, it can bring double good luck. The *Three Harmony Doorway* formula offers twelve door directions with twelve complementary road directions. Depending on which entrance you choose, these formulas are designed to attract wealth luck or relationship luck, either way it brings harmonious and noble energy. The entrance of the driveway, road, or sidewalk should also activate a good facing star.

Court Official Water Method
A formula used to bring wealth especially for judges, lawyers and CEOs

This technique is named after the importance of the judiciary in Asian cultures. In ancient China, serving as an officer of the court was a prestigious and sought-after post, one that required high intelligence, the mastery of certain skills, and the ability to pass a battery of grueling exams. No wonder these potent formulas were patterned after a government position that brought wealth, opportunities, and status.

Court Official Water Formations are great techniques for those aspiring to take their career or business to new heights. These formulas are particularly useful for people seeking authority and status, such as high-powered lawyers or judges. Court Official formulas have several major indications or predictive results such as high government positions, nobility with high status, huge fame, extreme riches, a world-famous author, and fame and wealth combined.

These formulas draw on a combination of energies from roads or real water, door directions, and nearby buildings. A building could be a towering, stately tree; a pagoda; a high-rise building (twin towers are best); or a tall mountain. A road, real water, electric gates, a curving sidewalk or pathway, or even a door represents water. In some situations, doors and gates denote virtual water—because of this, electric gates are considered auspicious.

Whether real or virtual, *sentimental water*, or water that moves slowly, is the absolute best option when it comes to gaining and retaining wealth. These formulas are even more powerful when combined with San Yuan Flying Stars. The secret to this technique is proper building placement and an excellent water entrance. A cleverly designed *Court Official Water Formation* can double or triple career luck.

The following configuration may attract a lofty position in government:

- Door direction is Northwest 1, Northwest 2, or Northwest 3 (292.6 to 337.5 degrees).
- An eighteen-story high-rise located in the Northwest (not in direct alignment with the door).
- A waterfall that comes from North 1 (337.6 to 352.5 degrees).

For the formula to work correctly, the building must be physically located in the sector indicated by the formulas. In our example above, that means the building could be anywhere in the forty-five degrees of Northwest. A word of warning: A road should not come straight toward the front of the house, or money loss will be the result. A road that comes straight toward the back of the house could indicate losing the family.

Jade Belt Formations
A formation used to bring wealth and prestige

Jade has always been sacred in the long and illustrious history of China. The ancient Chinese believed that jade was the essence of heaven and earth. At one time, rich businessmen and high-ranking officials used jade as money; wealthy Chinese families distinguished their class rank with custom-designed jade tassels. The term Jade Belt comes from the ancient custom of storing jade in a belt and wearing it around the waist. This act represented wealth and no doubt the reason it was adopted as a Feng Shui technique. When the Jade Belt formation is particularly lucrative, it is referred to as an *Emperor's Jade Belt*.

A simple yet powerful method of attracting money luck to your home or business, a Jade Belt formation is a road or driveway that wraps around a site like a belt encircles a waist.

It can also show up as winding water, such as a river that embraces the front of a house—water is an emblem of influence, wealth, and power. In lieu of real water, especially for city dwellers that may not have a nearby waterway, streets and roads can also form natural Jade Belts. Though all these scenarios are auspicious for gaining wealth and recognition, a large piece of land is best to maximize the potential of a good Jade Belt. These formations can be designed on your site if you have sufficient land to do so. But watch out for ever-popular circular driveways; these are unlucky designs.

The Sky Horse Technique
A formula used to speed up the Feng Shui/energy

The expertise and acumen of Grandmaster Yang Yun Song, who lived during the Tang Dynasty, and mentioned in many ancient classics, is still legendary. These accounts describe his powerful Feng Shui skills, which were so potent that he could make a person rich in one hour. Even to this day his methods and techniques are largely a mystery. In fact, many consider these tales are in the realm of myth and magic, beautiful and charming fables. But many lineages have managed to maintain and pass down the secrets that were transmitted orally from master to student. One of these mystical formulae of Grandmaster Yang is called the *Sky Horse Technique.*

The *Sky Horse* strategy conjures up an image of a thoroughbred equine winning the race. This technique attracts money quickly and always implies speed, travel or movement. The Feng Shui of the site must be excellent; it will speed things up—good or bad. In Chinese astrology the term the *Heavenly Sky Horse Star* is used, and this primarily indicates travel for a person, often opportunities abroad.

The *Sky Horse* can be applied to your home or business. This technique is based on the direction of an important exterior door, generally the front door, and the incorporation of a road, pathway, or driveway. For existing homes, the easiest way to design a Sky Horse is by creating a pathway. If you are building a new home, a driveway works great. For large sites and projects, a road is the best foundation for a *Sky Horse.*

The technique is specific to fifteen-degree increments for the door and the road in question. The *Sky Horse* formula includes twelve door directions with four compatible road directions, which are known as the four *traveling houses* or traveling Guas. They are *Northeast 3* (the House of Gen), *Southwest 3* (the House of Kun), *Northwest 3* (the House of Chien), and *Southeast 3* (the House of Xun). Here's an example of a how a Sky Horse may be created: the front door faces South 2 (172.6 to 187.5 degrees) and a road comes from Southwest 3 direction (232.6 to 247.5 degrees)

The Natal Flying Star chart of the house or business should also be considered, because roads, driveways, or pathways act as virtual water. The road should bring in a good facing star with wealth energy (1, 6, 8, or 9)—placing the road on a Precious Jewel Line will attract additional money luck. In our example, this particular *Sky Horse Technique* is meant to bring excellent business relationships and connections.

Five Ghosts Carry Treasure II
A formula used to extract wealth involving real water, mountain and water exit

Many wealth-producing formulae in Classical Feng Shui evolved and developed over time. The *Five Ghosts Carry Treasure II* is one of those that expanded into a completely different approach although it shares the name of the original technique. It is a more advanced application of the first method in that it uses specific water exits. Master Yap told us that the Prime Minister of Taiwan gave him his notebook on this technique, which he treasured. This method is allegedly more secret than the more widely known version of *Five Ghosts Carry Treasure* mentioned earlier. Even the original Five Ghosts formulas have only been revealed in books over the past five years or so. This formula does not use the door direction. Rather, it relies on the sitting or back of the property, the incoming and outgoing directions of water or a road, and a mountain or a tall building. Here is an example of the formula:

- House sits in the *North* (337.6 to 22.5 degrees).
- Water comes from *South 1* (157.6 to 172.5 degrees).
- Water exits *South 3* (187.6 to 202.5 degrees).
- Mountain is in *West 2* (262.6 to 277.5 degrees).

The water or road exit is optional, especially real water. But, if a driveway or road could be designed to exit in the suggested direction, great wealth luck can result. Both of the *Five Ghosts* techniques are designed to bring wealth-luck, and a master or practitioner will design one depending on what is possible at the site before them.

120 Gold Divisions
Used to determine an auspicious facing

There are two rings for the 120 Gold Divisions, *heaven* and *earth* plate on the San He Luo Pan (added in 906-960 CE). These are auspicious dragons for establishing a 'door facing' in order to match a direction that enhances the person's 'element'. The 'facing' element should produce/support the element of the occupants.

240 Gold Divisions
Used to determine an auspicious facing

In some early Luo Pans, the 240 divisions were common. This ring would allow the practitioner to divide each mountain into 10 divisions of 1.5° each. Some authorities suggest that the 240 Fen Chin came chronologically before the 120 Fen Chin. This ring is located among the Heaven Plate rings and does not appear on modern day standard San He Luo Pans. The purpose is the same as for the 120 Gold Divisions.

The Worst of San He: *Destruction, disharmony, money-loss, murder, divorce & affairs. These formulas are for assessment purposes only, not for implementation. If present, they need to be addressed.*

Eight Roads of Destruction
Indicates money-loss, divorce, extreme disharmony, and violence

The *Eight Roads of Destruction* formation is also known as yellow springs. The Chinese refer to the waters of the underworld, or hell, as yellow springs. These devastating scenarios are formed by an important *exterior* door and a *water exit*. An important door would be a front or back door. The water exit could be a road, driveway or sidewalk (virtual water) or real water (drain, stream, ravine, or a natural wash). They involve a 15-degree increment for the door direction and a 15-degree increment for the exit. Driveways and sidewalks are not as detrimental or impactful as a busy road. A huge drain is more serious than a small one. If an *Eight Roads of Destruction* is present, people can encounter bankruptcy, and other catastrophic experiences.

Here's an example of an *Eight Roads of Destruction*; the front door of a home faces *Southwest* (217.6° and 232.5°) and the road is *South* (157.6°-172.5°). Remember they are very specific to 15-degree increments. It won't apply to *all* Southwest-facing homes. The road doesn't include the entire 45 degrees of South either. It only involves a specific 15-degree increment. There are only eight possible formations, one for each direction (N, S, E, W, NW, NE, SE and SW).

Figure 10: This angled driveway, in relationship to the front door, could form an *Eight Roads of Destruction*. If so, it can be cured by tilting the door. See Appendix to learn more about 'door tilts'.

Peach Blossom Sha Formations
Indicating affairs, adultery, incest, and fatal attractions

Figure 11: If this home faces South between 172.6° to 187.5° and a road from the East is between 82.6° to 97.5°, then the home has a *Peach Blossom Sha Formation* and affairs may be an issue.

The *Peach Blossom Sha* formations are extremely negative for relationships, particularly romantic ones. They cause issues with reputation, sexual problems, illicit affairs, adultery, sexting, incest and all types of inappropriate sexual behavior. At a homesite, they are created by an important *exterior* door and a *water/road*. An important door would be a front or back door. The water/road can be real water (pool, stream, lake, pond, or fountain) or virtual water (sidewalk, driveway or an actual road).

The formula includes twelve (12) possible *door* facings with four (4) offending *water/roads*. The door and the water must be in specific 15-degree increments to be a bona fide *Peach Blossom Sha* formation. Here's an example of a *Peach Blossom Sha* formation; the door faces South (172.6° to 187.5°) and the road is from the East (82.6° to 97.5°). These formations should be corrected as they can usher in several of the following results when there is a road or too much water in certain directions or locations can cause the following issues:

- Turns the family upside down and soils the reputation
- Scandals that are made public; disloyalty, incest and exile
- The female runs away, sexual problems, and fatal attractions

It's interesting that nowadays the news is filled with scandalous behavior involving politicians either 'sexting", placing lewd pictures on the internet or sexually harassing women. It's highly probable they have a *Peach Blossom Sha* formation with 'scandals made public'. Tilting the door a few degrees is usually the way a Feng Shui expert will take care of it. Re-angling the door a few degrees forces the door to receive chi or energy differently. Door tilts are hugely popular in Southeast Asia and they take care of the problem very effectively. See photos in the Appendix on page 295.

Goat Blade Water Formation
Indicates adultery, gambling, and drug abuse

A *Goat Blade Water* formation is very similar to The *Peach Blossom Sha* and they can bring a host of harmful events that can drive couples apart. There are eight (8) possible door facings with eight (8) offending roads or virtual water like a road or driveway that will cause a variety of negative results regarding relationships.

For example, if the home faces West between 277.6° to 292.5° and there is water or a road coming from Southwest between 232.6° to 247.5°, then it has a *Goat Blade Water* formation. Just like the *Peach Blossom Sha* formations, if there is too much water in that sector such as a pool, waterfall, river, lake or stream, they render negative events. These features can be human-made or natural and either way they may cause problems for the family. The 'roads' that are the offending *Goat Blade Water* formation is confined to 15-degree increment.

This should be corrected as they can bring on any of the following results:
- Divorce
- Adultery
- Gambling
- Alcohol abuse
- Drug abuse
- Family break-ups
- Overindulgence in sex
- Illegal activities leading to failure in business

Four Destructions and Six Harms
Indicate hassles and no peace

These formations involve a road and door and can bring clashes and hassles in the household and there will be no peace. Not all doors have the same importance or weight; it would involve a well-used, exterior door. This is usually a front or back door. An example of a *Four Destructions* is a door facing North (352.6°-7.5°) and a road from the East (82.6°-97.5°). A *Six Harms* formation is created by a door facing Northeast 52.6°-67.5°) and a road from the Southeast direction (142.6°-157.5°).

Eight Killing Mountain Forces
Death and blood-related accidents

The Eight Killing Mountain Forces *(Pa Sha Hwang Chuen)* is a very serious formation; the energy of the mountain and door are in conflict which causes a host of negative events for the householders including loss of life and blood-related accidents. These formations involve specific 15-degree increments for both the door direction and the mountain. If you live in an area of the world without mountains, tall buildings must be considered as well. Here is an example of the formation: if your door faces Northeast (52.6 to 67.5) and you have a real mountain or tall building also in the Northeast (37.6 to 52.5), you may have an Eight Killings. In this case, the mountain would be in the front.

Figure 12: If this home faces East (82.6° to 97.5°) and the mountain in the rear is Southwest (217.6 to 232.5), then the home has an Eight Killing formation.

Death and Empty Lines or Void Lines
Indicates ghosts, bankruptcy, and discord

A long-time secret of Feng Shui masters was that the facing direction of doors and entrances should never lie exactly on the cardinal lines. These are referred to as Kong Wang or Kun Mang; *Death and Empty Lines* (DEL) or Void Lines. Now, 'death' does not mean dying rather that the property is *void of energy* and will bring all sorts of extreme misfortune and loss such as sickness, bankruptcy, and other forms of bad luck.

These degrees may also explain why some buildings don't sell and languish on the market. There are *lesser* DELs where, for example, West changes to Northwest (292.5) or South ends and Southwest begins (202.5). All DELs are inauspicious degrees and will attract ghost and spirits, which are *never* appropriate for homes or businesses. Benevolent spirits belong in churches and holy places. Listed below are the most serious void/empty lines:

Figure 13: Empty homes that sit on the market almost always have a DEL.

Major Void Lines
90° (East), 180° (South), 270° (West), and 360/0° (North)

Emptiness Lines
202.5°, 247.5°, 292.5°, 337.5°, 22.5°, 67.5°, 112.5°, and 157.5°

When this inauspicious scenario is present, measures should be taken to correct them. A temporary solution is to remove the door from its hinges for an hour, and then re-hang it. This will take a door out of the DEL, at least for a while. A more permanent cure is to re-angle the door within its frame; this will require carpenter skills. Metal on or near the door may also help, but give it some time and then take another compass direction in a month or so. Since compass degrees are based on the *magnetic energies* of the earth, metal can reduce this negative affliction.

Now let's take a look at the other major classification of formulas known as the San Yuan system. It's famous for its timing aspect. The two most popular systems under this umbrella of knowledge and methods for interior Feng Shui is Eight Mansions and Flying Stars. Of course, the Flying Stars system is the focus of this book.

CHAPTER FOUR
The San Yuan System

These formulas apply to the *interior* of your home/office with the exception of water and mountain placement!

San Yuan, known as Three Cycles, is the contemporary cousin of San He. In San Yuan, chi is understood as dynamic with the disposition to cycle. Nothing in our universe is stagnating; everything is constantly in motion. Even so, it is possible to identify certain dependable trends. That's why it is necessary to regularly update your Feng Shui to stay current with the time cycles of energy. Both San Yuan and San He take into consideration the factors of time and form. The main difference between the two systems is that San He gives great credence to *forms* and San Yuan has an extreme focus on *time*.

The *Flying Stars system* (Xuan Kong Fei Xing) and *Eight Mansions system* (Ba Zhai) fall under the San Yuan School. These are two of the more popular Feng Shui systems used today, especially for interior Feng Shui. In Flying Stars, an energy map of the property is derived from calculations and used to determine the quality of chi in each sector of the home. *Eight Mansions*, by contrast, is concerned with harmonizing the occupants with the distinctive energies of the house.

Flying Stars explains why no structure will forever enjoy good or bad Feng Shui as it cycles through time. Every structure has its own unique natal Flying Star Chart, which gives vital clues to the distinct energy held there. Some Flying Star charts are special and indicate exceptional auspiciousness, including *Pearl String Formations* (Lin Cu San Poon Gua), *Parent String Formations* (Fu Mo San Poon Gua), and *Combinations of 10*. All three are famous for bringing great money or relationship luck. Other techniques, such as the *Castle Gate Theory* (Sent Mun Kuet), are used to tap the energy of a natural body of water for greater prosperity.

Other Feng Shui techniques that fall under the San Yuan method include *Zi Bai* (Purple-White Flying Stars); *Xuan Kong Da Gua* (Big 64 Hexagrams Method), which is used for date selection.

The *Dragon Gate Eight* (Long Men Ba Da Ju) method is part of the San Yuan School and is used to attract wealth and enhance career luck. The San Yuan system also developed and adopted techniques from the San He School, which assess annual visiting negative energies. The *Three Killings* (Sam Sart), Grand Duke (Tai Sui) and the *Year Breaker* (Sui Po) can cause disastrous outcomes by disturbing the earth with a digging project, such as a pool construction or major landscaping. The annual visit of the *5 Yellow Star* is also disturbed by digging and construction. The *Great Sun Position* (Tai Yang Dou San Pan) is a technique devised to counter the affect of these negative energies by selecting a good date to begin your construction or digging project and offers protection from harmful results.

The *Robbery Mountain Sha* (Chor San Kibb Sart), the calculation of the daily, monthly and yearly "stars" are other techniques used to assess the Feng Shui, and are part of the San Yuan School.

Eight Mansions Feng Shui (BaZhai)

The Eight Mansions system dates back to the Tang Dynasty. While Eight Mansions is not as complex as Flying Stars, it is amazing. The Eight Mansions system's focus is on the *people* aspect, while Flying Stars' on the *structure*.

When the Eight Mansions formula is applied correctly, it can bring dazzling prospects for love and romance, business opportunities, health, promotions at work, flourishing investments, and money-luck. It can help identify negative energy, which will be apparent when people suffer from disease, poor health, a crippling divorce, bad relationships, accidents, disastrous events, and bankruptcy. In addition, it is the *only* system which has a 'personality type' aspect which is extremely useful for home and working relationships.

Eight Mansions has five (5) aspects: The Life Gua Number; East and West Groups; 4 Good and 4 Bad Directions; Advanced Eight Mansions; and 8 Personality types.

Classical Feng Shui systems, including Eight Mansions, are all compass-based methods. Which means you'll need to take a compass direction of certain things in your space if you wish to use it. This is why compass-based methods are more powerful than the one-size-fits-all types; they are specific to the person and their unique space. Although *Eight Mansions* concern itself with both direction and location, direction is the most important.

Locating Your Life-Gua Number

According to this Feng Shui system, based on your birthday and gender, you will be influenced in positive and negative ways by the eight directions: four will support you and four won't. The lucky directions will augment wealth and money luck, health, good relationships, and stability; the other four can set into motion divorce, bankruptcy, betrayals, lawsuits, cancer, and so forth. To find your personal Life-Gua number, refer to the Eight Mansions chart; make sure you're in the right column as there is one for males and one for females. There is a specific calculation to arrive at this number, but we have included the quick reference chart for ease. If you were born prior to February 4th in any given year, use the previous year to get your Life Gua number. For example, if you were born January 28, 1970, use the year 1969 to get the year's begin-date in order to find the correct Life-Gua number. *See the chart on the next page.*

Life Groups and GMY Codes

Now that you have your personal Life-Gua Number, let's examine the chart on page 38, it has a good deal of information. First, based on your Life-Gua Number, you will be part of the *East Life Group* or the *West Life Group*. Those who are a 1, 3, 4 or 9 Guas are part of the East group, and those who are a 2, 6, 7, or 8 belong to the West group. As opposites attract, it's not unusual for couples to belong to a different group.

Next, notice the GMY Code column. This is the clever creation of Grandmaster Yap Cheng Hai when referring to the good and bad directions without using the Chinese words associated with them. For example your best direction will be +90 which indicate prosperity or wealth luck. The +80 will help you to secure vital health. The +70 direction is your personal direction to and harmony and so forth. We will use the GMY code from now on throughout the book. Once you have located your personal *Life Gua Number* on the chart, just follow down that column to see all good and bad directions and a brief description of what they'll indicate if you use them; below are the detailed indications.

The Life Gua Number is highly significant, not only can you derive the directions that support you but give you important clues about your personality and key relationships. It's also used to determine the capability of spouses, the relationship between parents and children, the dynamic between siblings, work mates and business partners. The following are the Eight Mansions descriptions. They include Grandmaster Yap's code along with a one or two word summary of what they indicate if you activate or use these directions.

1933-1963

Animal	Year	Male ♂	Female ♀
Rooster	1933	4	2
Dog	1934	3	3
Pig	1935	2	4
Rat	1936	1	8
Ox	1937	9	6
Tiger	1938	8	7
Rabbit	1939	7	8
Dragon	1940	6	9
Snake	1941	2	1
Horse	1942	4	2
Goat	1943	3	3
Monkey	1944	2	4
Rooster	1945	1	8
Dog	1946	9	6
Pig	1947	8	7
Rat	1948	7	8
Ox	1949	6	9
Tiger	1950	2	1
Rabbit	1951	4	2
Dragon	1952	3	3
Snake	1953	2	4
Horse	1954	1	8
Goat	1955	9	6
Monkey	1956	8	7
Rooster	1957	7	8
Dog	1958	6	9
Pig	1959	2	1
Rat	1960	4	2
Ox	1961	3	3
Tiger	1962	2	4
Rabbit	1963	1	8

1964-1994

Animal	Year	Male ♂	Female ♀
Dragon	1964	9	6
Snake	1965	8	7
Horse	1966	7	8
Goat	1967	6	9
Monkey	1968	2	1
Rooster	1969	4	2
Dog	1970	3	3
Pig	1971	2	4
Rat	1972	1	8
Ox	1973	9	6
Tiger	1974	8	7
Rabbit	1975	7	8
Dragon	1976	6	9
Snake	1977	2	1
Horse	1978	4	2
Goat	1979	3	3
Monkey	1980	2	4
Rooster	1981	1	8
Dog	1982	9	6
Pig	1983	8	7
Rat	1984	7	8
Ox	1985	6	9
Tiger	1986	2	1
Rabbit	1987	4	2
Dragon	1988	3	3
Snake	1989	2	4
Horse	1990	1	8
Goat	1991	9	6
Monkey	1992	8	7
Rooster	1993	7	8
Dog	1994	6	9

1995-2025

Animal	Year	Male ♂	Female ♀
Pig	1995	2	1
Rat	1996	4	2
Ox	1997	3	3
Tiger	1998	2	4
Rabbit	1999	1	8
Dragon	2000	9	6
Snake	2001	8	7
Horse	2002	7	8
Goat	2003	6	9
Monkey	2004	2	1
Rooster	2005	4	2
Dog	2006	3	3
Pig	2007	2	4
Rat	2008	1	8
Ox	2009	9	6
Tiger	2010	8	7
Rabbit	2011	7	8
Dragon	2012	6	9
Snake	2013	2	1
Horse	2014	4	2
Goat	2015	3	3
Monkey	2016	2	4
Rooster	2017	1	8
Dog	2018	9	6
Pig	2019	8	7
Rat	2020	7	8
Ox	2021	6	9
Tiger	2022	2	1
Rabbit	2023	4	2
Dragon	2024	3	3
Snake	2025	2	4

Eight Mansions Chart: The Magic Life-Gua Numbers

	East Life Group				West Life Group			
	Kan (Water)	Chen (Big Wood)	Xun (Small Wood)	Li (Fire)	Kun (Mother Earth)	Chien (Big Metal)	Dui (Small Metal)	Gen (Mt. Earth)
Good Directions:	**1**	**3**	**4**	**9**	**2**	**6**	**7**	**8**
+90 Best for Money (Sheng Chi)	SE	S	N	E	NE	W	NW	SW
+80 Best for Health (Tien Yi)	E	N	S	SE	W	NE	SW	NW
+70 Relationships (Yen Nien)	S	SE	E	N	NW	SW	NE	W
+60 Stability (Fu Wie)	N	E	SE	S	SW	NW	W	NE
Bad Directions:								
-60 Nothing Goes Smooth (Wo Hai)	W	SW	NW	NE	E	SE	N	S
-70 Lawsuits & Bad Romance (Wu Gwei)	NE	NW	SW	W	SE	E	S	N
-80 Bad Health/Betrayals (Liu Sha)	NW	NE	W	SW	S	N	SE	E
-90 Divorce & Failures (Chueh Ming)	SW	W	NE	NW	N	S	E	SE

Gua 1
SE +90	S +70	SW -90
E +80	**1**	W -60
NE -70	N +60	NW -80

Gua 3
SE +70	S +90	SW -60
E +60	**3**	W -90
NE -80	N +80	NW -70

Gua 4
SE +60	S +80	SW -70
E +70	**4**	W -80
NE -90	N +90	NW -60

Gua 9
SE +80	S +60	SW -80
E +90	**9**	W -70
NE -60	N +70	NW -90

Gua 2
SE -70	S -80	SW +60
E -60	**2**	W +80
NE +90	N -90	NW +70

Gua 6
SE -60	S -90	SW +70
E -70	**6**	W +90
NE +80	N -80	NW +60

Gua 7
SE -80	S -70	SW +80
E -90	**7**	W +60
NE +70	N -60	NW +90

Gua 8
SE -90	S -60	SW +90
E -80	**8**	W +70
NE +60	N -70	NW +80

Work and Health for 3 and 4 Life Gua
Education, philosophy, medicine, pharmaceuticals, print media, publishing, farming, agriculture, Textiles, Fashion, technicians, musicians, broadcast announcers.
Gua 3—Feet
Gua 4—Liver

Work and Health for 1 Life Guas
Sales, finance, banking, freight, shipping, spa, communications, pub/bar, tourism, fishing, firefighting, water produce, police, sex industry, diplomat, painters and artists.
Gua 1—Kidneys

Work and Health for 9 Life Guas
Acting, show business, public speaking, fuel/oil, chemicals, optical, cosmetics, advertising, restaurants, lighting, writers, war correspondence, soldiers, barbers, and hairdressers.
Gua 9—Eyes & Heart

Work and Health for 6 and 7 Life Guas
Engineering, computers, goldsmith, machinery, metal mining, excavation, hi-tech goods, internet, lawyer, judging, white goods, metal jewelry, government service, sports equipment, clocks, & lecturers
Gua 6—Head
Gua 7—Lung, Throat & Mouth

Work and Health for 2 and 8 Life Guas
Property, real estate, construction, earthenware, consultancy, hotel, insurance, architecture, interior design, pottery, recruitment, quarry, HR, handyman, farmer, OB-GYN, monks, & clergyman
Gua 2—Stomach
Gua 8—Hands & Bones

Your Four GOOD Directions:

+90 MONEY! Sheng Chi: Life-giving chi, growing chi and generating breath. Great wealth, great success and millionaire chi. This is the best direction to use for money-luck; also good for timing and opportunities. The Sheng Chi direction is good for the managing director, promotion, wealth, health, and children. Use this direction to set up a high position of power/politics. For wealth-luck set doors, stove knobs, bed direction, and face this direction! Activating this direction with the stove or bed may produce fives sons or lots of children who are very successful and good. *Stove:* If you suppress your Sheng Chi with the stove placement, the women in the household cannot conceive. If you do succeed in having children they will be foolish, and there will be no money. If the firemouth (stove knobs, button or controls) or the bed is to this direction, it will bring great success and harmony!

+80 HEALTH! Tien Yi: Good for wealth and health; the *Heavenly Doctor* protects you. Using this direction brings good friends, the power of speech, social standing and a long life. By activating this direction, a VIP and the government support you. For health-luck set doors, stove knobs, bed direction, and face this direction! You will have gentle and good children; expect three sons when this direction is activated. *Stove:* If you suppress this direction with a stove, you will encounter sickness, disease and there will be no harmony in the household. If the firemouth (stove knobs, buttons or controls) activates this direction, it will bring riches very quickly, a high position of authority and less illness.

+70 RELATIONSHIPS! Yen Nien: The *Yen Nien* direction supports relationships, longevity, health, family, harmonious families, love, romance, and networking. While this direction may indicate a slightly lower income than the +90 or +80, you will have wealthy descendants, conceive children quickly, or children who become specialized, rich and famous; four sons are possible. Place children or young adults in the father's Yen Nien for harmony. Using this direction indicates a very successful, middle class life. This direction may indicate a life less than 70 years, or if exceeding 70 years, the death is celebrated with a party. *Stove:* If you suppress this direction there will be quarrels and a short life. If the firemouth (stove knobs, button or controls) or bed face this direction it indicates lots of harmony, being upper middle class, almost a millionaire, having powerful connections, good relationships, and love.

+60 STABILITY! Fu Wei: Using the *Fu Wei* direction brings stability and peace that can mirror your own energy, moderate happiness/wealth, a middle class family-life, and can protect you from bad luck. Use this direction for adult children living at home so that they may 'move on'. You'll have less children. For stability-luck set doors, stove knobs, bed direction, and face this direction. *Stove:* If you suppress this direction a short life is indicated. If the firemouth (stove knobs, buttons or controls) or bed face this direction brings less sons, living under 70 years, but a good middle class life.

Your Four BAD Directions:

-90 BANKRUPTCY! Chueh Ming: By activating the *Chueh Ming* direction, you will attract the worst things to you! It indicates bankruptcy, divorce, extremely bad health, fatality, business failures, loss of wealth, no harmony, family break-ups, accidents, and no descendants. Using this direction can bring the worst events ever, including death in the family. This is a good location for a toilet or stove. Marriages that are of the –90, the second wife can have two sons. *Stove:* Burning up this area with a stove will bring a long life, lots of money and kids.

-80 BAD HEALTH & BETRAYALS! Lui Sha: The *Six Killings* brings back-stabbing, thievery, injury, loss of wealth, ill health, bad money-luck, accidents, the wife leaves the family, lawsuits by the government, gossip, lingering/ongoing problems, legal issues, couples divorce or separate, no children, bad romance, grievous harm to the family, self-inducing disabilities, being unrecognized in the world, unfortunate accidents (even death), and betrayals. This location is good for a stove or toilet. Old age can be ok or pleasant. *Stove:* Burning up this area with a stove can bring money, children, no lawsuits, and no disasters or sickness.

-70 LAWSUITS & BAD ROMANCE! Wu Gwei: The *Five Ghosts* direction will activate lawsuits, bad romance, difficulty in conceiving, disobedient/rebellious children, fighting, gambling, drug use, petty people, robbery, bad health, fire hazards, career failures, betrayals, bad tempers, annoyances, undermining, no employee support, gossip, hot arguments, no harmony or peace. This is a good location for a stove or toilet. The son is not supporting the family. *Stove:* No fires, no sickness, no money problems, good employers and support.

-60 SETBACKS! Wo Hai: Activating this direction will indicate that *nothing* goes smooth, things turns out badly, irritating events, obstructions, accidents, afflictions, loss of investments, constant set-backs, and mild disasters. You can win a court case but lose money or lose the court case altogether if you use this direction for doors, beds, stove knobs or by facing it. *Stove:* Suppress or 'burn' this sector with a stove and there will be very little sickness in the household.

Advanced Eight Mansions for Fine-Tuning for Opposite Life Groups

What happens if partners belong to different Life Groups? Actually, this happens all the time; opposites attract. However, there is a solution. The Eight Mansions system has two levels; basic Eight Mansions and *Advanced Eight Mansions* (AEM). Here you're allowed to use certain 15-degree increments. This is really important in the 'shared space' (the bed). For more information on how to apply the Eight Mansions system, refer to the book *Feng Shui That Rocks the House* by the author.

The Eight Life Gua Personalities

Now let's explore another aspect of Eight Mansions, the *Life-Gua Personalities*. Since you know your personal Life-Gua number, you now have information on which directions support you and those that can bring trouble. Also, based on your Life Gua, you're assigned certain personality traits, energy, and characteristics. Do keep in mind that they are general and not meant to be definitive. The personality narratives work very similar to astrology; each Life Gua will have an element (water, wood, fire, earth or metal) and this energy will influence the person's behavior, habits, physical looks, health issues, attraction to specific occupations, thinking process, and sexual desires, both negative and positive in all these areas.

1 Life-Gua Personalities

Secretive ● *Emotional* ● *Scholarly*

Famous 1 Guas: Steve Martin, Nicole Brown Simpson, Tom Selleck, Brittany Murphy, Emma Thompson, Kitty Menendez, James Cameron, Ron Howard, Lucy Lui, Jerry Seinfeld, Jet Li, Ashley Judd, Kevin Costner, Mike Meyers, Jeff Bezos, Faye Dunaway, Li Ka-shing, Hugh Bonneville, Brittany Murphy, Greg Kinear, Amanda Bynes, Quentin Tarantino, Mischa Barton, Justin Timberlake, Jackie Chan, Billy Baldwin, David Lee Roth, Lee Shau Kee, Michael Bolton, Amanico Ortega, Ben Affleck, Catherine Bell, Goran Visnjic, Liv Tyler, Yanni, Nora Ephron, Dennis Quaid, Lady Gaga, and Rosanna Arquette.

Personality: The 1 Gua's are highly intellectual and can be studious or even scholarly. To the outside world, they appear calm and cool, however inside they have a rich emotional makeup. As a result, at times they can be overly emotional, moody, anxious and high strung. They are full of brilliant ideas and concepts, and are usually very good at making and holding onto money. The 1 Gua's are skilled at sizing up people using their natural, intuitive abilities. Since their element is water, they can be hard to pin down. They are sensual and can be highly sexual. Tending to keep secrets below the surface, 1 Guas are known to have secret and arcane lives.

2 Life-Gua Personalities
Calm • Reclusive • Dependable

Famous 2 Guas: Nick Nolte, Sharon Tate, Beau Bridges, José Menendez, Madeline Kahn, Ryan O'Neal, Sandra Dee, Stacy Keach, Wesley Snipe, Anjelicia Huston, Lakshmi Mittal, Peter Coyote, Julianne Moore, Wolfgang Peterson, Daryl Hannah, Tom Conti, Bob Dylan, Ashley Greene, Jon Stewart, Paul Simon, Bill Murray, Hilary Duff, William Hurt, David Berkowitz, Gemma Ward, Robbie Cultrane, Katie Holmes, Stephen Cannell, and Katherine Heigl.

Personality: The 2 Gua's exhibit persistence, dependability, and a calm demeanour. They can also be nurturing and supportive to their inner circle. With their calm, relaxed demeanors, 2 Guas are dependable and tend to have developed psychic abilities. They make excellent doctors or practitioners of alternate healing arts such as *chiropractry*, massage therapy, and acupuncture. Since the 2 Guas have the most yin energy of the Guas, they enjoy and feel comfortable in dark spaces, but have a tendency to depression or dark moodiness. Good spelunkers, these grounded people relish activities that focus on the earth—gardening, farming, construction, and agriculture.

3 Life-Gua Personalities
Enterprising • Impatient • Self-Confident

Famous 3 Guas: Charles Manson, Robert De Niro, Erik Menendez, Sharon Gless, Christopher Walken, Lynn Redgrave, Chevy Chase, Penny Marshall, Keith Richards, Isabella Rossellini, Mick Jagger, Annie Potts, Liam Neeson, Meg Ryan, Patrick Swayze, Virginia Madsen, Michael J. Fox, Bonnie Hunt, Laurence Fishburne, Heather Locklear, Eddie Murphy, Rachel Weisz, Matt Damon, Uma Thurman, Rupert Grint, Minnie Driver, Chris O'Donnell, Tina Fey, Ralph Macchio, and Rihanna.

Personality: Three Guas are extremely enterprising and have progressive ideas. They tend to be outspoken, direct, and organized. The 3 Gua's nature is one of nervousness punctuated by lots of energy and steam. Constantly crafting new inventions, new ventures or the latest thing, they love new beginnings and 'start ups'. When in a negative energy, the 3 Guas tend to self-punish, spread their energy too thin leading to collapse, and can be abrasive. However, they are full of surprises; 3 Guas have a sense of vitality and vigor that can overwhelm people.

4 Life-Gua Personalities
Gentle • Malleable • Progressive

Famous 4 Guas: Harrison Ford, Jacqueline Bisset, Marilyn Monroe, Kim Basinger, Paul McCartney, Demi Moore, John Wayne Gacy, Robin Williams, Kelly Preston, Geoffrey Rush, Michelle Yeoh, Steven Segal, Felicity Huffman, Tony Danza, Zooey Deschanel,

Harry Hamlin, Jordana Brewster, Lana Clarkson, Christina Ricci, Colin Firth, Michael Bloomberg, Queen Elizabeth II, Stanley Tucci, Sheldon Adelson, Christina Aguilera, Ice Cube, Matthew McConaughey, Ashton Kutcher and Marcia Cross.

Personality: Malleable, flexible, indecisive, the 4 Gua's may 'blow with the wind' if not grounded, finding it hard to take a stand. In general, they usually are attractive people or may have movie-star qualities. The 4 Gua's are more prone to be sexually controlled by their partners than other Guas. They have progressive ideas and can become famous in writing or rich in the publishing business. The un-evolved 4's may self-destruct by refusing good advice. The 4 Gua's can be somewhat remote and private, but they are also gentle people with an innocent purity.

6 Life-Gua Personalities
Leaders • Solitary • Creative

Famous 6 Guas: Lyle Menendez, Cher, Martin Sheen, Michael Jackson, Sally Field, Liza Minnelli, Chuck Norris, Candice Bergen, Richard Pryor, Dolly Parton, Brian De Palma, Suzanne Sommers, John Lennon, Susan Lucci, Ringo Star, Whoopi Goldberg, Jeff Bridges, Richard Gere, Marisa Tomei, John Belushi, Courtney Cox, Julian Fellowes, Gene Simmons, Christy Walton, Laura Liney, Kevin Bacon, Teri Hatcher, Viggo Mortensen, Prince, Melissa Gilbert, Paul Giamatti, Bridgette Wilson, Jason Statham, Anne Hathaway, Ice-T, and Kristen Dunst.

Personality: The 6 Guas can easily step into positions of power and authority as they are natural leaders that seem to be blessed by the heavens. They make excellent lawyers, judges, and CEO's as their energy commands respect. The 6 Gua's have a regal, royal air that is naturally unpretentious. Clear thinkers, lots of courage, possessing foresight, extremely creative, and they can hold their own in a debate. They need time alone as they often get caught up in over-thinking, which can lead to being sleep-deprived. Oozing with creativity, the 6 Guas are filled with ideas that involve large groups of people, a community or an organization.

7 Life-Gua Personalities
Charming • Excessive • Talkative

Famous 7 Guas: Natalie Wood, Frances Ford Coppola, Phil Hartman, John Clesse, Mark Zuckerberg, Glenn Close, Kim Cattrall, Mike Tyson, Carrie Fisher, Linda Hamilton, Phil Spector, Samuel L. Jackson, Joan Allen, Bo Derek, Billy Crystal, Kyra Sedwick, Phil Hartman, Elizabeth Hurley, Kristin Davis, Ray Romano, Brooke Shields, Bernie Mac, Eva Mendes, Adam Sadler, Cameron Crowe, Kiefer Sutherland, Connie Nielsen, Emily Blunt and Jenna Jameson.

Personality: 7 Guas tend to be youthful in behavior or appearance. They are very attracted to metaphysical studies and arts; they can be talkative, lively, and nervous. The 7 female Guas are often blessed with very good looks, and sensuous beauty. Comfortable with a lot of 'stage', the 7 Gua's are good at acting, speaking, in front of the camera or on the radio. With a strong tendency to over indulge in the pleasures of life such as food, drink, money, and sex, they must keep a balanced life. They can be a fast-talker, smooth talker, or have a razor-sharp tongue. The 7 Guas are very social, charming, and charismatic; they create stimulating, informative conversation wherever they go.

8 Life-Gua Personalities
Successful • *Hoarders* • *Dependable*

Famous 8 Guas: Jon Voight, Princess Kate Middleton, O.J. Simpson, Ali McGraw, Elliot Gould, Lily Tomlin, Michael Dell, Tina Turner, Kevin Kline, Goldie Hawn, James Woods, Mia Farrow, Richard Dreyfuss, Pricilla Presley, Jaclyn Smith, Ted Danson, Deborah Harry, Stephen King, Olivia Newton-John, David Bowie, Lisa Kudrow, Paris Hilton, Vanessa Williams, Cameron Diaz, Dwight Yoakam, Halle Berry, Charlie Sheen, Julia Stiles, Cynthia Nixon, Chris Rock, Jenny McCarthy, Ryan Philippe, Drew Barrymore, Robert Downey Jr., Britney Spears, Kevin James, and Gwyneth Paltrow.

Personality: The 8 Guas have a stubborn, dependable, and steadfast nature. They tend to have a great deal of integrity and are vey attracted to all things spiritual. They can become spiritual seekers, and trek the mountains in search of 'answers' and to find themselves. Hardworking and loving things of the earth, the 8's are talented in construction, real estate, and landscaping. They also have a little of 'save the world' energy. While the 8 Guas tend to resist change, they can deftly handle trouble without falling apart. Un-evolved 8 Guas can become hoarders, self-righteous, and short-tempered. They are geared for success and often become very rich with worldly honors, recognition, and status.

9 Life-Gua Personalities
Adventurous • *Rash* • *Brilliance*

Famous 9 Guas: Anthony Hopkins, Anna Nicole Smith, Jack Nicholson, Meryl Streep, Warren Beatty, Sigourney Weaver, Steven Spielberg, Sissy Spacek, Alan Rickman, Brynn Hartman, Sharon Stone, Annette Bening, Tommy Lee Jones, Michelle Pfeiffer, John Woo, Bruce Willis, Madonna, Kelsey Krammer, Holly Hunter, Russell Crowe, Nicole Kidman, Andi MacDowell, Steve Jobs, Clive Owen, Laura Dern, Rob Lowe, Mira Sorvino, Pamela Anderson, Reese Witherspoon, Yun-Fat Chow, Keri Russell, Carey Mulligan, Lenny Kravitz, Faith Hill, Oliver Stone, Keira Knightley, Danny Glover, Brian Cox, and Bill Gates.

Personality: 9 Guas have a sharp, brilliant intellect; they can also be wise, loyal, and sentimental. Blessed with a fiery spirit and energy, these Guas have a decided adventurous streak. The female 9's are usually beautiful like a diva or goddess but can be argumentative, aggressive, and rash. With concentrated and focused effort, they can reach great height of achievements and standing in the world. The truly un-evolved 9 Guas will exhibit mental illness such as paranoia, or psychotic and unstable behavior. When grounded and evolved, the 9's can light up a room with their radiance.

Flying Stars Feng Shui (Xuan Kong Fei Xing)

When Flying Stars was first introduced to the English-speaking world, most thought it was too mathematical and technical. However, with the passage of time Feng Shui enthusiast are now far less intimidated by the system and there is much more information available. In times past, it was not always clear as how to apply it and was presented as complicated. Nowadays, Flying Stars has garnered international interest and people are avidly looking for information on the potent formulas of *Xuan Kong Fei Xing* (Flying Stars).

While there are an impressive number of Feng Shui formulas and techniques, Flying Stars is, in fact, the most mathematical method as it deals with numbers and the computation of numbers. As a result, many compare it to numerology or astrology, while it is neither, it does have similarities. Flying Stars explains why no structure would forever enjoy good or bad Feng Shui which is why it is sometimes referred to as Time Dimension Feng Shui. The *time* aspect of Flying Stars can work in tandem with or be in conflict with the space design; everyone's Feng Shui needs regular updates.

The Chinese use two calendars, the solar *(based on the cycles of the Sun)* and lunar *(based on the cycles of the Moon)*; because the solar calendar is more accurate, this is exclusively used in Feng Shui because so much depends on accurate timing. Additionally, the New Year usually (99.9% of the time) begins on February 4th. On rare occasions, it starts on the 3rd or 5th.

This is a very interesting time in Flying Stars. It hit a major milestone in energy, worldwide, on February 4, 2004. Another capital change will occur on February 4, 2024 and is the main focus of this book. These milestones have a tremendous impact on the luck transformations of all homes and buildings and will affect them for twenty-year time periods. Many things will happen on the world stage during these times; the idea is to use Flying Stars to safeguard the energy of your homes and workplaces to not just survive, but thrive.

Natal Star Charts

Contingent upon the specific compass direction that a structure faces, it will have a unique natal *Flying Star Chart;* this is like an astrological chart as it identifies strong and weak aspects. Except in this case, it identifies the building's potential and energy map. Once you have identified or flown a Natal Star chart, you will know how to correctly activate the different sectors with auspicious energy.

In general, the practice of Feng Shui lies in how skillfully one analyzes, corrects and enhances the energies as they evolve through time; remember the *nature* of energy is change. In essence, Flying Stars is used to evaluate the invisible life forces that influence the environment/structures and the impact it may have on those who live or work there. While there have been several books on Flying Stars in recent years, most Americans are more familiar with the Westernized styles of Feng Shui such as the Black Hat style. In addition, current books might leave readers a bit confused about this extraordinary and multi-layered system. While it is an advanced, compass-based method, it is not impossible even for a novice, to capture its essence and implement its precise techniques with a little effort.

What are the "Stars"?

The 'stars' are not actual stars in the constellation; rather they are simply the numbers 1 through 9 with energy being expressed in a numerical form. Their purpose is to evaluate the quality of energy in a *building*. This is quite different from other systems that focus more on the *people* aspect such as *Eight Mansions*.

Each "star" has unique qualities and energy that can influence behavior and events. For example some stars indicate wealth, sickness, romance, scholarly pursuits, writing, fame, divorce, and so forth. While the 'stars' are not actual planets located in the sky, the nine stars do however, have an earthly correlation to the seven, real stars of the Big Dipper *(aka the Northern Ladle)* with two imaginary ones. Like many ancient cultures, the Chinese were 'sky watchers' and had an extremely developed sense of *time* based on the movement of the planets.

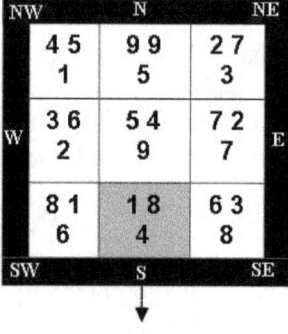

South 2 & 3

Notice the Flying Star chart on this page; it has three stars/numbers in nine boxes.

Time Cycles of Flying Stars Feng Shui

As we discussed earlier, Flying Stars has a time dimension aspect. And it has several key areas regarding the cycles of time and understanding them brings it forward to modern-day Feng Shui. The Flying Star system is based on huge time cycles and planetary alignments. Basically, there are three important blocks of time in Flying Stars 1) the **180 Great Cycle**; 2) **Three 60-year cycles**; and finally 3) there are **nine 20-year increments** known as 'Periods". The last is where we will really focus on in the book, although all are important in the system. Regarding the Great Cycle aka Mega Cycle, according to the ancient Chinese scholars, the planets in our Solar System aligns in a straight line once every 179/180 years. It is believed that the first observation of this phenomenon was around 2500 BC. The Chinese next divided this 180 year cycle into three (3) sixty-year cycles (called Upper, Middle and Lower).

The sixty year cycles were once more divided into 20-year increments which they called Periods or Ages. Each Period is assigned a number (1-9) and a trigram (except the 5, it has no trigram) that has a unique energy that it exhibits for 20 years that affects the world. Why 20-year Periods? It is interesting that they also noted that the Milky Way shifted every 20 years thus affecting the luck of a building/home and human beings. See the chart below giving an example of the nine (9) 20-year Periods comprising the 180-year Great/Mega cycle of time that covers the years of 1864 to 2044.

As you can see we are currently in the Lower Cycle (which is nearing completion) and in Period 8. The next Period will start February 4th 2024; this begins Period 9. The ruling energy or influence is always the number and associated trigram of the Period. For example, in *Period 8,* the 8 Star is king; Period 8 began February 4, 2004 and will end February 3, 2024.

Cycle	Period	Years	Trigram
Upper	1	1864-1884	Kan
	2	1884-1904	Kun
	3	1904-1924	Chen
Middle	4	1924-1944	Xun/Sun
	5	1944-1964	
	6	1964-1984	Qian/Chien
Lower	7	1984-2004	Dui/Tui
	8	2004-2024	Gen/Ken
	9	2024-2044	Li

Locating the Right Star Chart

If you wish to locate a home's unique *Flying Star Chart* you will need the following information. There are two important factors that must be determined, 1) **the move-in date** and 2) the **house facing**. The *house facing* is how the structure receives energy from a specific direction. And the move-in date will tell us which *Period* the structure belongs to; this is where those time cycles come into consideration.

Move-In Date

The move-in date is used to determine the Period of a building. However, not all masters agree with this. Regarding the construction date, is it reasonable to think that a home or building could have the exact same energy after 20, 30 years or more after being built? This rule seems counterintuitive to the whole idea of Flying Stars which rightly suggests that energy does not remain stagnate, it changes! The main thing that changes energy is humans moving in and out of spaces/buildings.

According to Master Yap discussions on the subject between the Asian masters are heated debates. Essentially, masters in Hong Kong prefer the construction date, while those in Malaysia, Singapore and Taiwan use the move-in date. At the end of the day, since I'm in the lineage of Grandmaster Yap, I use move-in date. I find it extremely reliable and accurate in my 20+ years of practice.

Use the following information to determine what Period your home belongs to:

Your home is a **Period 7**, if you moved in between **February 4th, 1984 to February 3rd, 2004**.
Your home is a **Period 8** if you moved in between **February 4th, 2004 to February 3rd, 2024.**
Exceptions for Period 7 homes are if major renovations took place *after* February 4th, 2004.

What constitutes a major renovation? Removing the entire roof (*and some small percentage must be exposed to the open sky at least for a few hours*), major interior remodeling, renovating the front entrance and door, painting the entire inside and outside at the same time, remodeling kitchen or bathrooms, installing a skylight/s, changing all the floors at the same time, adding on a room or adding an attached garage. All of these things will cause a major shift in energy, and therefore your Flying Star Chart will change. So if you did any of these things or a combination of them (*after* February 4th, 2004) and you moved in Period 7, your home will now be a Period 8 chart. If you moved into your house *after* 2004, and have done or are currently doing some renovations, your home is **still** a Period 8.

How to Determine the Facing

You will need a fairly accurate compass to get the correct degree that your home faces. Or you can use your Smartphone with a compass app. A good hiking compass also works very well as it has an actual magnet, whereas Smartphones do not and use GPS.

Let's see the basic rules to determine these two important factors in order to locate the correct chart. Take your compass measurement/degree from the front door if it *faces* to the road. More than 80% of homes will have the door facing the road, and be located in the center of the house. In these homes taking your compass direction will be fairly straight forward. If the door *does not* face the road, then stand in the middle of your front yard/garden to determine the facing degree. Any side doors or angled doors *(even if they seem to face the road)* cannot be used to measure from to determine the facing in *this system*.

The general rule for determining the facing is where the most yang energy (activate and vibrant) is; the truth is almost nothing competes with the energy of a street. For those who live in apartment buildings or condo complex, use the main door/entrance as the facing direction. See page 289 on *How to Take a Compass Direction*.

Determine the Facing Examples: House #1 is how most homes are built, take the compass direction at the door to determine the facing. In house #2, the front door cannot be used to determine the facing, even if this were angled and appeared to face the road. While this door's facing star will be extremely important to the occupants luck, it cannot be used to fly or locate the Star Chart. For house #3, use the door to determine the facing, not the window.

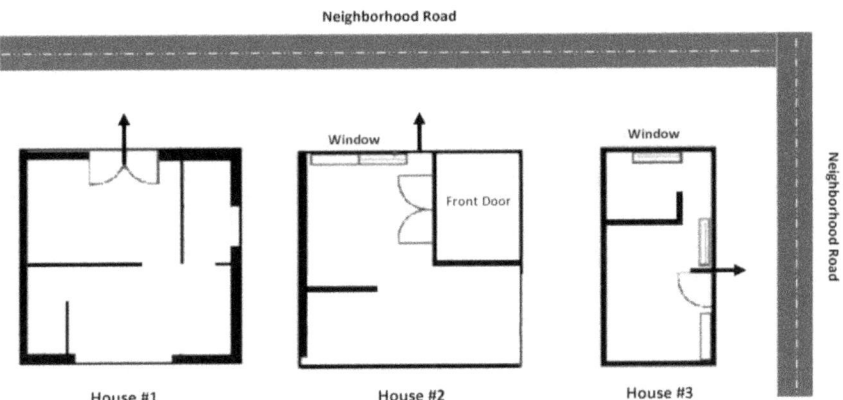

The 24 Mountains

In Classical Feng Shui and in Flying Stars, the 360 degrees of the compass is divided into 24 sections/directions (each comprised of 15 degrees). This famous division is referred to as the *24 Mountains*. According to this understanding, all abodes, buildings/homes can only face one of these 24 directions. The 24 Mountains are not literal mountains, just a term. These 24, 15-degree increments are also referred to as subsectors of a main direction. For example, terms such as South 1, South 2 and South 3 indicate the entire 45 degrees of South, but for Feng Shui purposes, are divided neatly into three subsectors.

The Sub-sectors

Once you have the exact compass degree, you can easily find the right sub-sector on the 24 Mountains Chart. For example, you have measured the facing direction of your property and get a compass reading of 123°. You can see that by referring to the *24 Mountain Chart*, that the structure faces Southeast 1. Or your compass reading may be 110 degrees; according to the chart, this is East 3. Remember this information is needed whether you're simply *locating* the correct Natal Star Chart or if you wish to *fly* a Star Chart.

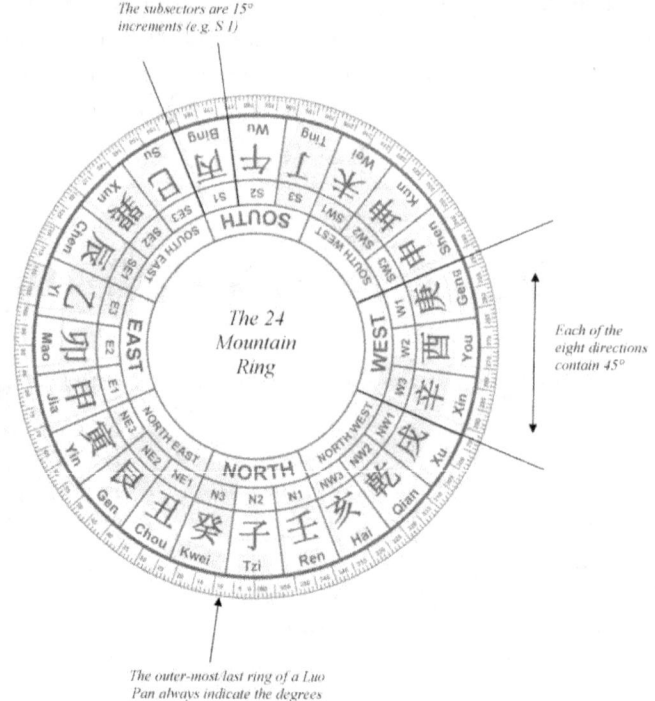

The 24 Mountains Chart: this chart indicates the general **direction** (North, South, East, etc.) and the **sub-sector** with the exact degree range (S1, E2, NW1, etc.). Once you have determined the facing degree, refer to this chart.

General	Exact	Compass Degrees	Name	Energy
SOUTH	S1	157.6--172.5	Bing	Yang Fire
	S2	172.6--187.5	Wu	**HORSE**
	S3	187.6—202.5	Ting/Ding	Yin Fire
SOUTHWEST	SW1	202.6—217.5	Wei	**GOAT**
	SW2	217.6—232.5	Kun	Earth
	SW3	232.6—247.5	Shen	**MONKEY**
WEST	W1	247.6—262.5	Geng	Yang Metal
	W2	262.6—277.5	You	**ROOSTER**
	W3	277.6—292.5	Xin/Sin	Yin Metal
NORTHWEST	NW1	292.6—307.5	Xu	**DOG**
	NW2	307.6—322.5	Chien/Qian	Metal
	NW3	322.6—337.5	Hai	**PIG**
NORTH	N1	337.6—352.5	Ren	Yang Water
	N2	352.6—7.5	Tzi/Zi	**RAT**
	N3	7.6—22.5	Kwei/Gui	Yin Water
NORTHEAST	NE1	22.6—37.5	Chou	**OX**
	NE2	37.6—52.5	Gen/Ken	Earth
	NE3	52.6—67.5	Yin	**TIGER**
EAST	E1	67.6—82.5	Jia	Yang Wood
	E2	82.6—97.5	Mao	**RABBIT**
	E3	97.6—112.5	Yi	Yin Wood
SOUTHEAST	SE1	112.6—127.5	Chen	**DRAGON**
	SE2	127.6—142.5	Xun/Sun	Wood
	SE3	142.6—157.5	Su/Si	**SNAKE**

Components of a Flying Star Chart

So what does a Flying Star chart look like? A Natal Flying Star Chart is not as complex looking as say, an astrological chart. Remember, the Flying Star Chart of a property is simply an **energy map** of a building and its potential for auspicious or negative events. Feng Shui masters use the *Flying Star Chart* to make accurate predictions on relationships, romance potential, success in a career, wealth prospects, when a promotion or marriage may take place, lawsuits—anything that may happen in the human experience. A *Flying Star Chart* is made up of three numbers in a nine-square grid (mimicking the Luo Shu). The chart shown here is a Period 7 house facing South (the arrow indicates the facing direction).

- **Facing Star** *(Shui Xing)*. Also known as *water stars*, these numbers are located in the upper right-hand corner in all nine palaces of the chart.

- **Mountain Star** *(Shan Xing)*. Also known as *sitting stars*, these numbers are located in the upper left-hand corner in all nine palaces of the chart.

- **Time Star** *(Ling Xing)*. Also known as the *base star*, this number indicates the period to which the chart belongs. It is the single star below the facing and mountain stars.

NW	N	NE
4 1 8	8 6 3	6 8 1
5 9 9	3 2 7	1 4 5
9 5 4	7 7 2	2 3 6
SW	S ↓	SE

W — E

Some common terminology about the nine-celled grid is that each 'box' is referred to as a **palace, sector** or **direction**; all are correct and interchangeable. Using the *Flying Star Chart* here, we might say "notice that the North *sector* has an 8 mountain and a 6 facing star" or "the South *direction* has double 7's". To keep things simple and consistent throughout the book, we will use the terms *facing star* and *mountain star*; for purposes of activating a chart, the facing and mountain stars have the most weight and significance.

Facing Stars (aka Water Star)
Always located in the upper right-hand corner in each cell of a natal *Flying Star Chart*, these stars affect money, financial status, growth, business prospects, and career-luck. They symbolize wealth potential and prosperity prospects. Due to the fact that it can indicate riches, having an auspicious *facing star* in important areas (front door, desk-facing, or real water) is said to bring enormous wealth-luck. Good stars indicate wealth luck, while bad stars denote money loss.

Mountain Stars *(aka Sitting Star)*
Always located in the upper left-hand corner in each cell of a natal *Flying Star Chart*, these stars will affect health-luck, romance, people, relationships, family, authority, mental attitudes, career, fertility, and employees. It also symbolizes social status or standing in the community and the family's popularity.

Time Stars *(aka Base Star)*
The time stars are the single star located directly below the facing and mountain stars in each cell of a natal *Flying Star Chart*, they are not activated individually as the mountain and facing stars can be. Time stars are the least potent of all three stars. However, they have significance in the 'special' charts such as the Pearl and Parent Strings and the Combination of Ten charts.

Good and Bad Stars

In order to fully understand the soul of Flying Stars, you must know the meaning each star and what it portends. In this system, the good stars are the 1, 6, 8, and 9 whether they are facing or mountain stars. The 4 Star represents romance/sexual energy, travel, writing/publishing/scholarly pursuits, and fame and supports those who have a public persona. Also, the 3 star is more useable in the later part of Period 8 and more so in Period 9 indicating progressive energy and not so much lawsuits and robbery. However, it must be paired with a good star to be interpreted as such. Please note that the 2, 5, and 7 are very bad stars that can deliver sickness, bankruptcy/cancer, and robbery respectively.

The 5 Star is the worst star and is considered evil and the harbinger of all types of disasters. The bad stars are only good in their period; otherwise, they are considered inauspicious. In other words, the 5 Star is only advantageous in Period 5; remember 'Periods' are those 20-year increments. Same goes for the 2, 3, and 7 stars. When a Flying Star chart is analyzed, there are several important factors—the *nature* of the star (good or bad), your immediate, external environment and the interior layout of your living space. If the external formations (mountains, water, roads and so forth) support the energy of the chart, you will get a positive result. An auspicious formation can bring good fortune, while landforms that do not support the chart can attract misfortune. The chart can only come *alive* and bestow benevolent energy when the interior environment and external landforms support it. Stars exert great influence, both good and bad, on human behavior—they represent energy and potential events/behaviors.

If you wish to learn to 'fly' the stars and generate a Natal Flying Star Chart, refer to the author's book *The Secrets of Mastering Flying Stars Feng Shui*. However, all charts for Period 7, 8 and 9 have been 'flown' and are provided in the book.

How Stars Get Activated

It takes different energy/objects or activity to *set into motion* the facing stars than it does to activate the mountains stars. Naturally, where there is good energy and stars, you'll want to magnify them, and where there is negative, prenicous energy, you'll want to reduce or deactivate it as not to cause harm. The stars do get activated inside and the exterior of a property, however in uniquely different ways. Time stars are not activated individually but are an important component in the special star charts such as the Combination of Ten, Pearl and Parent Strings (details in Chapter Four). The most important stars are the *facing* and *mountain* and the most important star in the entire chart is the *facing ruling star* (in Period 8, the 8 facing star*)*.

In order for a *facing star* to get activated, it will need activity (a well-used door) or moving water (fountain or water fountain). A *mountain star* needs stillness or something that emulates the height and weight of a mountain. An example is brick or stone courtyard walls. Heavy stone or concrete pots/planters or boulders will also activate mountain stars. Whether the stars are good or bad, these are the features or activities that will stimulate them.

How the Flying STARS Get Activated

Mountain Stars (Governs PEOPLE Aspect)	Facing Stars (Governs WEALTH Aspect)
Stillness (Yin)	**Activity (Yang)**
Sleeping	Real water
Real mountains	Doors (interior or exterior)
Landscape mounds	Roads
Huge boulders	Low ground
Heavy planters/pots	Sloping land
Retaining walls	Facing them
Brick or stone walls	Fire
Stoves	Washes
Armories	Canals
Staircase	Sleeping
Fireplace	

Figure 14: In the top photo, the two heavy pots near the door will activate the mountain star. And the photo below has several features that can activate a mountain star—the courtyard walls, the concrete bench and heavy pots/planters.

The 81 Combinations

When the energies of the *facing star* and the *mountain stars* combine, they can invite certain outcomes. More importantly, the ensuing energy will influence human behavior in a household. The combined energies of the nine stars are known as the *81 Combinations* (9 x 9). The *81 Combinations* are extracted from various distinctive Feng Shui classic works; the ancient texts are:

The Purple White Scripts *(Zi Bai Jue)*
Ode of Time and Space *(Xuan Kong Zi Mi)*
Heavenly Jade Classics *(Tien Yu Jing)*
Time Space Mysticism *(Xuan Kong Mi Zhi)*

The following Chinese-to-English translations of the *81 Combinations* are from Grandmaster Yap Cheng Hai. The English has been corrected to make them a little more 'reader friendly'; however the meaning has not been altered. Be forewarned, some of the descriptions sound chauvinist and judgmental. The Chinese culture was, and still is, a strong and traditional patriarchal society. Keep in mind that the *81 Combinations* represent potential energy and does not mean a particular result is present, guaranteed, or even foreseeable. In order for the energy to be activated, requires daily use; doors, bed placement, stoves, fireplaces, bathrooms and desk direction. Equally important are the large environmental features such as water, mountains, driveways, and roads near the property. These features are considered 'big ticket' items in Feng Shui and can determine the quality of a home's energy.

The stars will influence human behavior and events in a home or building. Each star possesses unique characteristics, represents a body part or organ, denotes one of the five elements, and correlates with one of the trigrams (except the 5 star; it has no trigram), thus creating a number of combinations that can influence human behavior and predict events for a building's occupants.

Please note that the mountain star is on the left, while the facing star is on the right. This is why the 1, 4 combination, for instance, reads differently than the 4, 1 combination. The method of activation is dissimilar. The 4, 1 can activate wealth if water is located there, while too much water on the 1, 4 combination can activate bad romance, sexting, scandals and extramarital affairs.

1, 1 Combination
Positive Aspects and Outcomes: This combination supports intelligence, wealth, information, wisdom, travel, recognition, world fame and academic success. It also indicates the philosopher, writing and success in government or professional examinations (e.g. law, doctoral). It is good for academic pursuits. In period 8, this

combination signifies someone protecting you. These stars are also good for young men regarding achievements; they can attain a good reputation and become very well known. These stars form a *Peach Blossom* aka Flower of Romance combo.

Negative Aspects and Indications: This energy carries the possibility of causing alcoholism, especially among men. It signifies both men and women stray and have affairs. It also supports the sex industry, quarrels, and accidents; being gullible and cheated, thievery, loss of reputation, a split personality and drowning in water. It suggests that members of the household may run into problems with the law; possible robberies. In period 7, it may signify residents coming under the influence of gangsters and criminals. Health issues under these stars when untimely are heart disease, ear pain, blood disease, bowels, kidneys, and the bladder.

1, 2 Combination
Positive Aspects and Outcomes: During Period 2, this combination indicates being supported by the public. These stars signify a high position such as a favored and celebrated high prime minister. This energy also supports a king or his son who becomes a president, prime minister or king. These stars will empower women; they may achieve high positions of authority in the government, the health care industry or in corporations.

Negative Aspects and Indications: This combination is very unfavorable to middle-aged men; husband gets humiliated or henpecked by the wife. It indicates no support, rebelliousness, murderers, auto accidents, disputes, divorce and dominating females. As a mountain star and Period star, it suggests feelings of tension and inner antagonism. Illness involves abdominal problems, swollen body, bleeding and an ugly appearance; women activating this energy will suffer from water retention and look fat as a result. Males will get cheated and may develop stomach, intestinal and digestion problems. Women may develop stomach and gynecological problems.

1, 3 Combination
Positive Aspects and Outcomes: These stars indicate wealth, fame, popularity, and new industry or business; industrial empires are formed under their influence. The energy is very progressive creating good luck for family with lots of children; the eldest son will be promoted, get rich, and become very well known. This combination also signifies the possibility of a new baby and in Period 8, lots of traveling.

Negative Aspects and Indications: Leaving home or causing the family to move away. These stars can cause accidents, obstructions, lawsuits, robberies, no sons, bankruptcy, snake bites (when the 7 visits) and lightning strikes. This combination causes arguments, quarrels, disputes or even being cheated by your own family members. Tempers may also flare for anyone affected by this combination.

1, 4 Combination

Positive Aspects and Outcomes: This combination is good for scholarly achievements, media attention, writers, irrigation, the mining business, publicity, study and romance. It's excellent for gold, silver or diamond interests and investments. In good Periods expect promotions and other perks at work when these stars bless you. This is a very strong *Peach Blossom* (romance energy), especially for women.

Negative Aspects and Indications: Too much water may bring scandals made public (e.g. sexting), flirtations, alcoholism, misbehavior, promiscuity and criminals. Also, this energy creates strong sexual appeal, sluttish behavior and forgery of bonds/stocks will be apparent. When the stars are in a malignant position or there is too much water, expect affairs and bad romances.

1, 5 Combination

Positive Aspects and Outcomes: When timely, these stars indicate the scholar and a champion of exams. It also supports a good thinker and wise children. The 5 star is a king-maker in its own Period, brings power and wealth! Out of timing, it's considered the 'disaster' or trouble-making star.

Negative Aspects and Indications: The indications here are water related danger, bankruptcy and being bloated by water. This combination brings a host of health issues such as hearing problems, kidney problems, sex-related diseases, genital disease, boils in private parts, inability to conceive and tubular pregnancies. The negative aspects of the 5 Yellow are highlighted here bringing cancer, toxemia, poisoned by drinking, illnesses, food poisoning and diarrhea. Women may have a miscarriage, uremia, or womb cancer.

1, 6 Combination

Positive Aspects and Outcomes: This combination brings great intelligence and financial skills. It indicates success in the theatrical arts, literary pursuits and writing. It supports the famous teacher or scholar; good astronomer, brilliant career and great professor. These stars can make you very famous; rising to a high rank in the military or FBI, CIA, and the police force. Also happy occasions such as marriages or births can happen with these stars. This combination is good for cultural and artistic activity particularly in Periods 7, 8 and 9.

Negative Aspects and Indications: This combination may cause migraine headaches, bleeding in the brain, mental disorders, concussions, paranoia and brain infections. Fathers and sons fight; this combination also indicates thieves, being jailed, and fear of the cold. When visited by a 5 or 2, it may trigger a nervous breakdown. Metal and water can cause one to feel too sentimental and to be excessively emotional. Metal and water are cold; indications are that men here are mean and egotistical, or even feminine. Accidents that involve knives and blood may also arise, so be careful with sharp metal objects.

1, 7 Combination
Positive Aspects and Outcomes: This was a good combination for wealth in Period 7, not so for all other Periods. These stars signify courtship, romance and love. It also indicates people who are very honest, good linguists and those who are very good with money. This energy is excellent for people in positions of authority. The stars signify lots of travel and are particularly good for the 'traveling salesman'.

Negative Aspects and Indications: This combination supports love affairs, sweet-talking and smooth-talking men who may con you. It's very flirtatious energy, with constant parties and bad-mouthing gossip. It can indicate spending too much money on women and romance; vomiting up blood. Denotes expulsion if the ground is slopping outwards; residents could get relocated or deported and leave under harsh conditions. You can suffer from betrayal and jealousy with this energy; a middle-age man and young girl relationship turning out badly. The 7 star is the gangster, robber or thief. There is also a possibility of attacks from animals, even the house pet or dog. Attacks may also come via robbery by knives or guns. These stars also indicate active or passive termination of pregnancy; leaving home to go to boarding school, work or to jail. This is a negative *Peach Blossom*.

1, 8 Combination
Positive Aspects and Outcomes: This is an excellent combination for great wealth, health, financial intelligence, particularly in water-related businesses such as shipping. It also signifies success in scientific research and in oil exploration, especially offshore. You could get very rich on contracts as it indicates smooth litigations and deal-making.

Negative Aspects and Indications: This combination, when out of timing, will indicate obstructions at work and brothers at each other's throats. It also signifies difficulties with business partnerships; possibly being jailed. Watch out for gall stones, nose infections, back pain and hand injuries. Antagonism among siblings and good friends; the young man hurts the middle aged man and it may suggests generation problems. If the middle son cannot activate this energy, otherwise he may leave home and never come back. This combination may cause hearing problems, especially in the elderly and very young. Painful illnesses such as kidney stones can also crop up from time to time.

1, 9 Combination
Positive Aspects and Outcomes: These stars indicate a high government positions and promotions at work. It supports and fosters honor, peace, lots of children, high social status, great fame, success due to a high intellect, advancements, networking, rank, recognition, exposure to the public, and a studious person.

Negative Aspects and Indications: When untimely, this combination will indicate no mate/partner in life, no harmony, fatal attractions, murdering a spouse, fire disaster, one-sided love, and government lawsuits. Promiscuous men and women will have to be very careful when affected by this combination. There is a possibility of venereal disease as well as sexually transmitted diseases; miscarriages are not uncommon. These stars can support prevalent heart and eye problems, so care must be exercised.

2, 1 Combination
Positive Aspects and Outcomes: This combination indicates fame and great fortunes as a real estate tycoon. It fosters good children and a son who may become a military general. It signifies a good teacher, top industrialist, a chairman and CEOs.

Negative Aspects and Indications: These stars indicate marital disharmony, premature births, untimely deliveries, abortions, bloating, ear and hair problems, diabetics, gastric-related problems, upset bowels and swollen bumps. Males may experience stomach, intestinal and digestive problems, impotence and other problems with their sex lives. There could be land and property loss along with a middle son who leaves and never returns. These stars (2, 1 or 1, 2) are a famous 'divorce' combination.

2, 2 Combination
Positive Aspects and Outcomes: These stars support and foster great doctors, surgeons and all medical professions. It also indicates lots of land and property, strong and powerful females, many children and military officers. When the 2 star is in luck, you may expect windfall gains. However, it can make a person greedy and ill as well.

Negative Aspects and Indications: The 2 star, unless timely, will always bring lots of illness such as skin problems, muscle pain, boils, childbirth problems, abdominal cramps, chronically ill children, stomach, intestinal and digestive problems. This energy indicates an overly aggressive female, greediness, the widow, despair, the family losing their good reputation, attracting female ghosts, feelings of exhaustion or depression. These stars are dangerous in the South or when activated by real water or fire.

2, 3 Combination
Positive Aspects and Outcomes: This combination will bring good charitable deeds and religious status; fosters the Sage or monk who may achieve high religious status.

Negative Aspects and Indications: These stars represent antagonistic energy and is the famous 'bull fight sha' combination indicating gossip, arguments, lawsuits, legal entanglements, bickering, disputes, family break-ups, and bad things fall on you, literally and figuratively; a fatal landslide or getting hurt at work. It signifies greedy people, cheating people, aggressive behavior, court cases, a reversal of fortune, jail time, and very bad family luck.

2, 4 Combination
Positive Aspects and Outcomes: This combination is good for academic pursuits, and making money from property-related fields through intelligence. The 4 star indicates

romance, but could also turn out badly when mixed with the 2 star. This is a bad direction to sleep to as it will cause negative sexual encounters.

Negative Aspects and Indications: This combination of stars is the famous 'cascading wind formation' indicating the wife and mother-in-law fight and argue. The mother gets hurt or injured while the younger woman wins. The older woman leaves and goes to an old folk's home. It also fosters problems with the internal organs, especially the spleen, and may cause mental illness. There is also a danger of illnesses related to the blood. Caution must be taken around animals as this energy indicates attacks from dangerous animals or 'bitten by a tiger'. Also, a lusty man will meet a promiscuous woman.

2, 5 Combination
Positive Aspects and Outcomes: When timely, these stars indicate an abundance of wealth and great fortunes with windfall gains. It is also good for producing a large family. It fosters good judges, even a Supreme Court judge and military personnel. The 5 star is a king-maker in its own Period bringing power and wealth! Out of timing, it's considered to bring catastrophic results. However, during good Periods (Period 8) this combination favors property, real estate and the construction business (2, 5, 8 earth stars) leading to surprising prosperity.

Negative Aspects and Indications: This combination of stars is known as the 'weeping formation' and brings great misfortune and all types of calamites and catastrophes. This energy is the worst possible and indicates lots of illness, death, disease, cancer, bankruptcy, unwanted abortions, appendicitis, divorce and widow-hood. This is an extremely bad combination which harms the owners of house in every way. The house can be haunted by bad spirits and they will especially affect the middle-aged woman. During bad Periods, it can cause older or middle-aged women to fall sick or die of cancerous diseases. This is the most dangerous combination of all, and should not be activated in any way!

2, 6 Combination
Positive Aspects and Outcomes: This combination, when timely, will lead to an affluent and easy life. It brings great wealth and a great family; more good luck and wealth comes in the presence of an 8 visiting star. When a 9 visits, this combination can bring world-fame. A prosperous combination that brings the occupant financial gains, most probably from real estate ventures.

Negative Aspects and Indications: These stars can indicate lung, tongue and throat disease, hot/cold sickness, dysentery, greed, baldness, no property, a miser, and fathers and sons fighting. When a 5 visiting star comes in it could bring apparitions, spirits or ghosts; bad spirits can cause disharmony in the family. The man of the house may be sick all the time, especially if he smokes. The mother may experience breathing problems. This energy may also encourage the making of nuns and monks.

2, 7 Combination
Positive Aspects and Outcomes: These stars will create great judges, doctors, winning money from the lottery, finding money, good investigators or inspectors, and a very rich family with more girls than boys. This combination brings good prospects and opportunities; money will roll in but spend it wisely as it can roll out just as easily. In Period 7, this brings lots of financial prospects and gain.

Negative Aspects and Indications: This combination indicates no sons, bad daughters, stomach illness, fire hazards, diarrhea, abortions, illicit affairs, money loss, and robberies, especially for those who became wealthy in Period 7. There could be affairs that lead to divorce; possible fire hazards when the 9 star flies in. This energy signifies difficulty in producing children, epidemics and incurable diseases, bleeding wounds, and knife injuries.

2, 8 Combination
Positive Aspects and Outcomes: These stars bring great success and riches and affluence in raw land, real estate transactions, property, and in the construction business. It signifies a real estate tycoon; it is rife with financial opportunities and possibilities. This combination is the auspicious sum of ten; it favors the younger man. It is also good for sons and grandsons who may become the gentlemen.

Negative Aspects and Indications: This combination indicates women in the family have indiscreet affairs with young male servants/employees or those close to the family. It encourages or produces nuns or monks. Illness, boastful energy, affairs, and dealing with a minor or lingering illness are also results of this energy. You can get physically fat because of all the wealth; then sick from being too fat.

2, 9 Combination
Positive Aspects and Outcomes: This combination, when timely, favors property, fire and electrical businesses. It indicates many loyal and good children.

Negative Aspects and Indications: These stars signify blindness, stupid children, being unreasonable, superstitious, single-minded, and sluggish. This energy literally chases men away, and in the end, the house has only women left. However there is still plenty of room for romantic affairs; a possible Peach Blossom for women. Heath issues may be diseases of the eye, reproductive issues, mentally ill women and widowhood. It also indicates insanity, instability, and a lack of good judgment.

3, 1 Combination
Positive Aspects and Outcomes: This combination of stars indicates those who are proficient in the law business and legal industry; those with argumentative skills and powers of persuasion; great counselors, lawyers, arbitrators and judges. It also supports the talented sculptor and carver.

Negative Aspects and Indications: These stars indicate bitter quarrels, slander, lawsuits, heated arguments, and money being lost to thieves and unscrupulous third parties. The family may separate and do not keep in contact; hurts the mother. This energy fosters people being attacked or drowning at sea. Heath issues will be mainly related to the liver and chronic dizzy spells.

3, 2 Combination
Positive Aspects and Outcomes: This combination indicates money, fame, a good life and those providing good service. Success in the medical field is supported by this energy; good doctors and surgeons.

Negative Aspects and Indications: These stars represent the famous 'bull fight sha' formation and will bring lots of arguments, quarrels, civil lawsuits, bickering, disagreements, and controversy. It also fosters government lawsuits and punishment/being jailed by the government. Mothers and sons may be constantly bickering, bringing instability to the relationship. Stomach-related illnesses may result in a person feeling starved.

3, 3 Combination
Positive Aspects and Outcomes: These stars indicate analytical and scientific prowess, good reputation, nobility, power in speech and language; the eldest son is very successful. In Period 3, it signifies being very rich and powerful, and new ventures.
Negative Aspects and Indications: This energy fosters physical fighting, robbery, nerve problems, loss of sons, court cases, slander, excessive gossip, disease, being crippled, boss problems, hysteria, becoming mentally ill, abusing or hurting the wife, and being sued by the government. Those activating this combination will be a little cold-hearted and have no mercy. During Period 8, family members steal the family wealth. Eldest son will face robbery and court cases.

3, 4 Combination
Positive Aspects and Outcomes: This combination indicates being very, very rich, as rich as a king; very famous and noble. The family will have bright and smart children who bring honor to the family.

Negative Aspects and Indications: These stars support mental and emotional difficulties, psychological issues, thievery, and begging; men may attract crazy, mentally unstable girlfriends. This is a Peach Blossom for males; they may suddenly find they are the center of attraction for literally every female when this energy is activated. Older ladies must be on their guard.

3, 5 Combination
Positive Aspects and Outcomes: These stars indicate getting rich quick, money and wealth made from real estate, property, or prosperity from industries. This combination

also signifies high government positions and being supported by a VIP in high places. The 5 star is a king-maker in its own Period bringing power and wealth! Out of timing, it's considered to bring catastrophic results.

Negative Aspects and Indications: This combination of stars indicate all types of illness such as cancer, madness, heart disease, infectious disease, car accidents, and weird diseases of the liver, gall bladder, hands or feet. It supports delinquency, negligence and gambling; fortunes can be lost when the 3 and 5 combine primarily through gambling. Also, accidents leading to broken limbs may be very prominent with this combination. There will be antagonism in the family and from outsiders. In Period 8, it brings rebellion, quarrels and harmful aggravation; death or being jailed is indicated caused by money or corruption. The residents can succumb to and be vulnerable to epidemics, cults or Black Magic.

3, 6 Combination
Positive Aspects and Outcomes: These stars indicate growth; great support from government VIPs, business success, a good conductor, success and good political luck.

Negative Aspects and Indications: This combination fosters government lawsuits, fathers and sons fighting, being jailed and a hard and poor life. Headaches are prevalent and accidental injuries, especially from sharp metal objects, which must be guarded against. Money does come in, but you may have a limp; getting shot in the leg or the leg is cut. A person's health is compromised when these two stars combine; a fall from a horse could happen as well.

3, 7 Combination
Positive Aspects and Outcomes: This combination indicates lots of money and wealth in Period 7. It fosters good children and a very rich family. You can also succeed as a government official or military personnel. When a 1 star visits, it could produce a new son; when the 2 visits, you can get rich.

Negative Aspects and Indications: These stars will strongly indicate robbery (especially by a family member), stealing, stubbornness, government lawsuits, thievery, and being betrayed or scammed by a trusted friend or family member. Also, the family breaks apart, feet problems, ghosts in the house, and the eldest son succumbs to alcohol and falls prey to promiscuous women. Be careful of metal-related injuries, drinking alone, and rivals at work.

3, 8 Combination
Positive Aspects and Outcomes: These stars indicate wealth, creditability and status; very good children, especially sons. The family is always in touch with the latest trends of the time and is very shrewd. It also fosters literary talent and success in writing.

Negative Aspects and Indications: This combination suggests that brothers become enemies (two male stars), and fight due to misunderstandings; young males will have to be careful with this combination. Health issues such as miscarriages, heart disease and asthma are likely to occur; families may fall apart.

3, 9 Combination
Positive Aspects and Outcomes: This combination signifies prosperity, glamour and great fame for the occupants. They are also blessed with intelligent, extremely brilliant and gifted children. These stars bring wisdom, happiness, cleverness and mysticism. It signifies that the children will build the wealth for the family.

Negative Aspects and Indications: These stars indicate very smart and cunning people. When they are untimely, fire-related injuries are likely to happen and obesity; indicates success at first, then failure.

4, 1 Combination
Positive Aspects and Outcomes: These stars represent the famous 'literature formation' and fosters success in writing, publishing and all scholarly pursuits. It also supports love and romance. This combination indicates the good ship captain, money, academic success, knowledge and high grades/scores. The 4, 1 is an excellent combination for anyone still studying or academicians. This combination encourages spiritual pursuits such as prayer or meditation. This is a very strong *Peach Blossom* for women.

Negative Aspects and Indications: This combination signifies extra-marital affairs, a bad director. It also indicates useless and good-for-nothing sons that spend money and fight with each other and the family separates due to fighting. With too much water, love affairs may result depending on the annual stars within the area. Young children may suddenly become frightened with this energy.

4, 2 Combination
Positive Aspects and Outcomes: These stars indicate studies in metaphysics, culture and the esoteric. It also signifies the good reporter, astronomer and inspector.

Negative Aspects and Indications: This combination indicates lots of illness such as stomach and gastric problems as well as the spleen and pancreas. It also signifies that the women in the household fight and argue. Mother-in-law and daughter-in-laws are at odds. It is really bad and a threat for older women, so caution needs to be exercised.

4, 3 Combination
Positive Aspects and Outcomes: In good Periods, these stars indicate making money as smooth as a breeze. There will be good and noble sons who may become very famous; money and success to the family.

Negative Aspects and Indications: This combination fosters unfriendly rivals; children becoming thieves or beggars, and unreasonable people. Males under the influence of this combination will find women literally hounding them. Beware though, not all may have the best of intentions. Ladies who are under the influence of these stars may face mental disorders and nervous conditions. It also indicates male aggression against females, most likely by cheating.

4, 4 Combination

Positive Aspects and Outcomes: These stars support fame, a celebrated author, success in government or professional exams, knowledge, intelligence and wisdom. There will be extremely beautiful girls in the family who marry very well increasing social standing and status. The 4 star is good for romance and travel.

Negative Aspects and Indications: This combination indicates suicide by hanging, losing the wife, and sons who leave home and never return. The 4 star fosters romance energy that, with too much water, can turn very bad. It may bring sickness or death; asthma and bad odor form the armpits. This may also be a negative Peach Blossom combo.

4, 5 Combination

Positive Aspects and Outcomes: This combination indicates women in high positions in the business world. It supports a celebrated author, success in exams, and a very famous poet. The 5 star is a king-maker in its own Period bringing power and wealth! Out of timing, it's considered to bring catastrophic results.

Negative Aspects and Indications: These stars are dangerous and will bring lots of serious health issues such as breast cancer, pus and blood from sores, sex-related problems, infectious diseases, leukemia and liver cancer. There could be bankruptcy due to failure in the stock market or shareholdings. The effects also include gang-related problems as well as a nasty gambling habit for the occupants.

4, 6 Combination

Positive Aspects and Outcomes: These stars bring great financial success, fame, very productive women, wealth-luck, family harmony, prosperity, good reputation and always getting promotions. It supports winning money, shares and prizes. There could be lots of fame here through academia and the literary business.

Negative Aspects and Indications: This combination indicates suicide by hanging, lazy females, and failures in the stock market. This energy is very bad for the eldest daughter and middle-age woman. There is a tendency for the father to stray and he loses the wife. Couples will get together in relationships that will be short-lived. Eye and mouth problems, as well as being hurt by metal, are also indicated.

4, 7 Combination
Positive Aspects and Outcomes: This combination of stars supports very smart children, who are gentle and very attractive. It indicates holding power, being honorable with money dealings, romance and honesty.

Negative Aspects and Indications: These stars are notorious for encouraging women in the house to fight; no harmony. It also indicates lawsuits (husband-wife court cases), being wounded by knives, lonely people, sibling rivalries among sisters, marital problems, vomiting, and broken marriages. There is also a danger of violence/death associated with sexual matters.

4, 8 Combination
Positive Aspects and Outcomes: This combination supports and encourages charitable deeds, the dairy industry, good secretaries, philanthropy, the forestry and farming business, land acquisition and horses. Within good periods, expect real estate deals under the influence of the 4-8 combo and excellent financial possibilities. Due to the mother's excellent nurturing of the children, it brings fortune and fame to the family.

Negative Aspects and Indications: These stars signify no harmony among the sons in the family; brother-in-law and sister-in-law have an illicit affair, rheumatism, death from abortions, and nerve pain. This combination supports becoming a solitary nature-lover, hurting young children and problems with small bones.

4, 9 Combination
Positive Aspects and Outcomes: These stars foster very special and intelligent children, women in the family run the family business, good-looking people, successful trade, happy occasions, and very smart girls. This energy indicates a highly respected reputation in society, the birth of a brilliant son, and a celebrated poet or mystic. This is an excellent direction to activate for a gifted, male child.

Negative Aspects and Indications: This combination signifies failure in exams/testing, blood disease, fire hazards, accidental deaths, and being extradited from the country. This energy also encourages abnormal, unusual and peculiar sexual liaisons.

5, 1 Combination
Positive Aspects and Outcomes: When timely, the 5, 1 combo indicates the scholar and a champion of exams. It also supports a good thinker and wise children.

Negative Aspects and Indications: The indications here are water related danger, bankruptcy and being bloated by water. This combination brings a host of health issues such as hearing problems, kidney problems, sex-related diseases, genital disease, boils in private parts, inability to conceive and tubular pregnancies. The negative aspects of the 5

Yellow are highlighted here bringing cancer, toxemia, poison by drinking, illnesses, food poisoning and diarrhea.

5, 2 Combination
Positive Aspects and Outcomes: When timely, these stars indicate an abundance of wealth and great fortunes with windfall gains. It is also good for producing a large family. It fosters good judges, even a Supreme Court judge and military personnel. During good periods (Period 8) this combination favors property, real estate and the construction business (all earth stars) leading to surprising prosperity.

Negative Aspects and Indications: This combination of stars is known as the 'weeping formation' and brings great misfortune and all types of calamites and catastrophes. This energy is the worst possible and indicates lots of illness, death, disease, cancer, bankruptcy, unwanted abortions, appendicitis, divorce and widow-hood. This is an extremely bad combination which harms the owners of house in every way. The house can be haunted by bad spirits; they will especially affect the middle-aged woman. During bad periods, it can cause older or middle-aged women to fall sick or die of cancerous diseases.

5, 3 Combination
Positive Aspects and Outcomes: These stars indicate getting rich quick, money and wealth made from real estate, property, or prosperity from industries. This combination also signifies high government positions and being supported by a VIP in high places.

Negative Aspects and Indications: This combination of stars indicate all types of illness such as cancer, madness, heart disease, infectious disease, and weird diseases of the liver, gall bladder, hands or feet. It supports delinquency, negligence and gambling; fortunes can be lost when the 5 and 3 combine primarily through gambling. Also, accidents leading to broken limbs may be very prominent with this combination. There will be antagonism in the family and from outsiders. In Period 8, it brings rebellion, quarrels and harmful aggravation; death or being jailed is indicated caused by money or corruption.

5, 4 Combination
Positive Aspects and Outcomes: This combination indicates women in high positions in the business world. It supports a celebrated author, success in exams, and a very famous poet.

Negative Aspects and Indications: These stars are dangerous and will bring lots of serious health issues such as breast cancer, pus and blood from sores, sex-related problems, infectious diseases, leukemia and liver cancer. There could be bankruptcy due to failure in the stock market or shareholdings. The effects also include gang-related problems as well as a nasty gambling habit for the occupants.

5, 5 Combination

Positive Aspects and Outcomes: The 5 star, when it is timely, brings extreme wealth, abundance, nobility, important big shots, good consultants, judges and lawyers. You can become as rich and powerful as a king! This energy produces an emperor, great fortunes, power, a good family with lots of children, success, authority, accomplishments, honesty, and sincerity.

Negative Aspects and Indications: These stars indicate complete and total disaster, traumatic and violent deaths, cancer, idiot sons, bankruptcy, natural calamities, ill fortune, freaky accidents, aggressive and abusive behavior, brain-related injuries/comas, bone cancer and impotence. This combination also encourages wars, poisoning, lung cancer, and lawsuits accompanied by scandals. If active, this combination cannot be left unattended.

5, 6 Combination

Positive Aspects and Outcomes: This combination indicates high government positions, well-known authorities, wealth, leadership, military fame, getting very rich with gold, lots of children, sons to carry the family name, money and famous ministers of affairs.

Negative Aspects and Indications: These stars support fatal illness, cancer of the lung, bone or stomach; landslides that could prove fatal, prison (for the man of the house), lawsuits, too much pride, brain infections/dead, headaches, migraines, stress, psychological problems, and head-related issues such as the skull.

5, 7 Combination

Positive Aspects and Outcomes: These stars indicate being famous in the military, money, medical specialists, skilled lawyers, ambassadors, diplomats, orators, and excellent, sharp speakers.

Negative Aspects and Indications: This combination of stars support food poisoning, serious diseases of mouth, perversions, bad-mouthing, throat cancer, drug addiction, heart issues, venereal disease, prostitution, bleeding of the tongue, damaged vocal cords, and problems with the mouth, speech and communicating. Take care of being poisoned; signifies a sharp tongue with cutting and damaging language.

5, 8 Combination

Positive Aspects and Outcomes: This combination supports being loyal to the government; long-time prosperity, lots of money and produces a Sage, Shaman, or holy man.

Negative Aspects and Indications: These stars may bring betrayals, tensions, serious problems, young boys fall sick, issues with the lungs and stomach; broken ribs or tendons, cancer of the bones or nose, and paralysis. Other indications are sweet-talking and flirting.

5, 9 Combination
Positive Aspects and Outcomes: These stars encourage great success in literature and writing, many children, lots of properties, and can reach high positions of power such as a President or King. It indicates a holy person, sage or a savant.

Negative Aspects and Indications: In Period 8, this combination may produce a down-syndrome child or mental retardation. It supports accidents during happy events; joy turns to sorrow. This is a very inauspicious combination that could leave anyone in the immediate area with a fiery feeling (e.g. shingles/herpes-zoster). These stars could also lead to a person developing some very hard-headed and stubborn characteristics. It signifies religious mindfulness morphing into a religious fanatic. The 9 accentuates the negative aspects of the 5; drugs/poisons, injuries, death, accidents, inflammatory situations, sex diseases, leukemia, fire disasters, lawsuits, eye disease and when the annual 7 visits, suicide by drugs or poison is possible.

6, 1 Combination
Positive Aspects and Outcomes: This combination indicates wealth, good career, being accomplished in literary pursuits, good government relations, money, strong athletes, good in all sports and physical activities. These stars support accomplishing high ranks in the military; or anyone in positions of power or in senior management, judges and lawyers. This energy is a Peach Blossom combination, so expect lots of romance in the air.

Negative Aspects and Indications: These stars support lawsuits by the government, fighting over property and land, a revolution, bleeding in the brain, getting hurt with knives, controlling women in the family, and it weakens the father or the head of the family. Metal and water can cause one to feel too sentimental and to be excessively emotional. Metal and water are cold; indications are that men here are mean and egoistical, or even feminine.

6, 2 Combination
Positive Aspects and Outcomes: This combination brings extreme wealth where you can be the richest in the land; great health is also indicated. A distinguished family who are powerful industrialist with lots of sons to run the business. This is a prosperous combination that brings the occupants financial gains, most probably from real estate ventures.

Negative Aspects and Indications: These stars support mental disturbance, hot/cold sickness, one-sided love, greed, miserly, monks, nuns, and expect lots of gastrointestinal problems. With this combination, ladies should be extra cautious as they may find themselves faced with a host of problems relating to their reproductive system. When a 5 visiting star comes in it could bring apparitions, spirits or ghosts; bad spirits can cause disharmony in the family. The man of the house may be sick all the time, especially if he smokes. The mother may experience breathing problems.

6, 3 Combination

Positive Aspects and Outcomes: These stars indicate nobility, good officers, activists, honesty, loyalty and glamour. This combination encourages growth; great support from government VIPs, business success, a good conductor, success and good luck in politics.

Negative Aspects and Indications: This combination fosters government lawsuits, fathers and sons fighting, being jailed and a hard and poor life. Headaches are prevalent and accidental injuries, especially from sharp metal objects, which must be guarded against. Money does come in, but you may have a limp; getting shot in the leg or the leg is cut. A person's health is compromised when these two stars combine; a fall from a horse could happen.

6, 4 Combination

Positive Aspects and Outcomes: These stars bring great financial success, a rich family, fame, military intelligence and power such as the FBI, CIA or generals. There could be lots of fame and recognition through one's intelligence, academia and the literary business.

Negative Aspects and Indications: This combination indicates affairs, suicide by hanging, lazy females, and failures in the stock market. This energy is very bad for the eldest daughter and middle-age woman and hurts the wife. There is a tendency for the father to stray with this energy; he loses the wife. Couples will get together in relationships that are short-lived; separations are indicated here. Eye and mouth problems, being hurt by metal and miscarriages are possible.

6, 5 Combination

Positive Aspects and Outcomes: This combination indicates high government positions, wealth, leadership, military fame, getting very rich with gold, lots of children, sons to carry the family name, money and famous ministers of affairs.

Negative Aspects and Indications: These stars support headaches, migraines, lung cancer, too much pride, being stubborn, bone cancer, brain infections, anxiety, mental pressure, disloyalty at work, mental illness, misfortune and collapse of a business or power. In waning Periods, it can cause impotence, and in really extremes cases, going into a coma. Men may find their career paths difficult and may even be retrenched/laid-off.

6, 6 Combination

Positive Aspects and Outcomes: These stars support good careers, authority, fame, plenty of government support, extremely powerful military leaders, excellent physical prowess and good sportsmen. It also signifies lots of good sons/children, great wealth, and illustrious careers. Scholars will gain recognition and reap great rewards; unexpected windfalls.

Negative Aspects and Indications: This combination indicates lawsuits, rumors, foolish sons, lung disease, abusing the wife, loneliness, employee or labor problems, liver issues and family feuds and quarrels.

6, 7 Combination
Positive Aspects and Outcomes: This combination indicates high political power, good judges and lawyers, success, fame, and powerful military officers and leaders.

Negative Aspects and Indications: These stars represent the famous 'sword fighting sha' formation or the 'double metal clash' and it will promote robbery by knives; jealousy, cheating, a man being controlled by his mistress, metal-related injuries, and brothers of the household constantly fighting and at each other's throats. It signifies combat, conflict, and competition between males. This energy is that of an old man with a young wife which causes misfortune where one of them dies. For the family, it is more girls than boys; young adults may die with this combination.

6, 8 Combination
Positive Aspects and Outcomes: These stars portend great wealth and fortunes, especially through real estate; great authority, fame, achievements, accomplishments, success in the military, money, distinguished careers, and excellent reputations. It also indicates sons and fathers getting rich together; a very wealthy family with children and grandchildren inheriting.

Negative Aspects and Indications: This combination could indicate losing a spouse (widows and widowers), no children or descendants, being ignored and loneliness. It also signifies mental illness, instability, gangsters, and attaining wealth and money by illegal means.

6, 9 Combination
Positive Aspects and Outcomes: These combination of stars support riches, happiness, success, world-famous authors and editors, being honored by the government (given the 'purple cloth' which means accolades, recognition, titles and so forth); and respected authority. Living long, healthy lives are also indicated.

Negative Aspects and Indications: This combination is the famous 'fire burning heaven's gate' and indicates sons challenging fathers and violent revolts against authority or the government; especially when there is sharp, jagged mountains in the immediate environment. It brings numerous health issues such as leukemia, breathing and lung problems, blindness, brain disease, vomiting, high fevers, and high blood pressure. This energy will hurt the father of the house; children will misbehave and be hard to control. These stars also encourage sex scandals, masochism, and accidents after a happy event or occasions.

7, 1 Combination
Positive Aspects and Outcomes: These stars signify getting rich in the hunting and fishery business, a famous sculptor, beautiful children, very good fortune for young women, glamorous lifestyles and travel; and those who are litigation experts. This combination of stars is good for anyone whose career requires them to travel. These stars are also a *Peach Blossom* and romance can go very well or bring scandals, affairs depending on the overall energy of the home.

Negative Aspects and Indications: This combination of energy support abortions, brothels, flirting, lots of parties with too much wine, women and song; stammering, stuttering, kidnapping, alcoholism, and being expelled from the country. Romance is also very prevalent with this combination, however by the same token, these romances could also be affairs, so married men should be careful. Robberies are possible with the criminals being armed with guns or knives, and it could get fairly violent when these stars come together.

7, 2 Combination
Positive Aspects and Outcomes: This combination of stars signify good doctors, surgeons, officers, good health, very intelligent men, a supportive family, wonderful children, good for medical studies, and excellent for sports and sportsmen of all types.
Negative Aspects and Indications: These stars support abortions, miscarriages, fire hazards, women fighting in the family, vomiting up blood, difficulties in conceiving, and a young wife prematurely becoming a widow. Mothers-in-law and daughters-in-law may also find themselves in constant discord.

7, 3 Combination
Positive Aspects and Outcomes: These stars support making lots of money, talented business men and women, success in the military, great success in writing and literature; and making a fortune on sports books. It also indicates an unexpected gain in business.

Negative Aspects and Indications: This combination signifies bad health, internal injuries and bleeding requiring surgery, hot tempers, fraud, financial troubles due to lawsuits, stealing, burglaries, and eye-related injuries or illness. The 7 and 3 are both robbery stars; expect trouble in this area when they are activated.

7, 4 Combination
Positive Aspects and Outcomes: This combination of stars indicate beautiful children, success in journalism, a respected newspaper business, a magazine producer, good

newspaper boss, and a famous, prestigious publisher. These stars are an excellent combination for anyone who intends to travel.

Negative Aspects and Indications: These stars encourage madness, panting and respiratory-related problems, leg and thigh issues, arguing, bickering, coughing fits, hurting the older woman, no family harmony, and lawsuits depending on the annual or monthly visiting stars. This energy is more feminine and women in the house may fight; could bring bad romance depending on the overall energy of the home. This is a negative *Peach Blossom* combo.

7, 5 Combination

Positive Aspects and Outcomes: These stars support being very famous in the military sector, making lots of money through public speaking, ambassadors, diplomats, lawyers, orators, and getting very rich on medical lecture and speeches.

Negative Aspects and Indications: This combination of stars indicate communication break-downs, bad eating habits, drug addiction, mouth or throat cancer, and aggressive or impatient behavior. Other health issues are venereal disease, mental illness leading to madness, death by a drug overdose, no peace of mind, and heart disease. The 7, 5 combination gets worse in Period 8; if active, this energy must be addressed.

7, 6 Combination

Positive Aspects and Outcomes: This combination indicates high political power, good judges and lawyers, success, fame, and powerful military officers and leaders who could enjoy an unexpected windfall. It also supports world-famous army officers and authors, excellent secretaries, respected professors, celebrated sculptors and those who are famous for writing sharp and cutting papers or reports.

Negative Aspects and Indications: These stars represent the famous 'sword-fighting sha' formation and signify serious rivals at work, illicit affairs, kidney problems, an older man with a very young wife, fierce competition, illegal marriages (a polygamist or bigamist), skin-related diseases; and fights that involve metal such as swords, spears and knives. Due to all the metal energy, it supports combat, conflict, armed robbery, death by metal, and women leaving or going astray.

7, 7 Combination

Positive Aspects and Outcomes: These stars indicate money, wealth, riches, metaphysics, great prosperity, good sons, very smart girls, famous military officers and beautiful, celebrated and famous actresses. This energy favors women over men.

Negative Aspects and Indications: This combination of stars signify fire hazards, armed robbery, loss of the wife, accidents, death, small talk, quarrels, slander, sex scandals, unfavorable affairs for men, superficiality, risk of road accidents, surgical operations, and men in the house may be seduced by sweet-talking women.

7, 8 Combination
Positive Aspects and Outcomes: These stars support wealth, commercial success, harmony in the family, smart children and riches (jewels, gold, jade, land and silk) known as the *10,000 Boxes of Treasure*; can get rich at a very young age. It signifies good, honest and loyal girls that make a famous marriage bringing great wealth and status. This combination is extremely auspicious for money with numerous opportunities for windfall gains if exploited cleverly. Good romance and career success is also supported by these stars.

Negative Aspects and Indications: This combination, when untimely, indicate women leaving their husbands (jumping over the wall), misbehaving and out of control children, and under-nourished young people.

7, 9 Combination
Positive Aspects and Outcomes: This combination of stars indicate innovation, inventors, very clever and bright people, progression, a good marriage, an activist for human rights or fighting against a corrupt government (Gandhi, Nelson Mandela, Martin Luther King), good family luck, light and playful behavior, and good love and romance energy. A *Peach Blossom* combo.

Negative Aspects and Indications: These stars support flirting, sexual abuse, venereal disease, seductions, fire hazards, heart disease, eye issues, illicit seductions, and can be very serious when combined with a visiting 5 star. When another 9 star visits, expect fires or large blazes.

8, 1 Combination
Positive Aspects and Outcomes: These stars support being recognized in the world, fame, getting rich in the fishery or farming business, a prestigious career, a good educator, money-luck, a celebrated professor or dean, good judges, excellent writers and talented curators.

Negative Aspects and Indications: This combination indicates middle sons leave home and never return, sons die, bladder-related illness, young children with chronic ear infections, and disease or issues with the reproductive system; older men should be careful with this energy.

8, 2 Combination
Positive Aspects and Outcomes: These stars bring rank, great success, riches and affluence in raw land, real estate transactions, property, and in the construction business. It signifies a real estate tycoon; it is rife with financial opportunities and possibilities.

This combination can make you rich as a country!

Negative Aspects and Indications: This combination signifies illness with the reproductive organs, gastrointestinal issues, young males servants/employees mixing with the girls in the family, the youngest and brightest son gets hurt, and possible financial ruin. This energy is best suited for a temple or monastery.

8, 3 Combination

Positive Aspects and Outcomes: These stars indicate a very long life, wealth, creditability and status; respectful children, especially sons. The family is always in touch with the latest trends of the time and is very shrewd. It also fosters literary talent, success in writing and success in government exams.

Negative Aspects and Indications: This combination signifies young sons die, the loss of all money and property, no harmony in the family, possible divorce, suicide, and being childless. The children of the house may become difficult and run into problems at school. Singles who desire to marry should avoid this combination at all costs.

8, 4 Combination

Positive Aspects and Outcomes: This combination encourages literary prowess, financial intelligence, land acquisition, and estate planning. Within good periods, expect real estate deals under the influence of the 8-4 combo; excellent financial possibilities. These stars also signify great success in industry-related businesses, honest people, textile mills, and very sharp lawyers.

Negative Aspects and Indications: These stars indicate kidney-related diseases, gallstones, young people in the household die and other illnesses. It encourages reclusive behavior or aspiring to be the 'hermit in the mount'. Since this combination is known to cause lots of marital discord, newlyweds and couples should avoid activating this energy or direction.

8, 5 Combination

Positive Aspects and Outcomes: This combination supports being loyal to the government; long-time prosperity, lots of money and produces a sage, shaman, or holy man.

Negative Aspects and Indications: These stars indicate accidents involving bones, nerve and bone disease, dislocation of bones, nose and stomach cancer, humpback people, midgets, sweet-talkers, paralysis, idiots, and being childless.

8, 6 Combination

Positive Aspects and Outcomes: This combination of stars indicate illustrious bankers, fame, notable preachers of moral ethics, wealth through real estate, good reputation, learning, success in all military arts, impressive career luck and very profitable army books and manuals.

Negative Aspects and Indications: These stars signify being childless, accidents, loss of wealth, no sons or descendants, mental instability, and the dislocation of the joints or bones.

8, 7 Combination
Positive Aspects and Outcomes: These stars promote financial success and getting rich at a young age, prosperity, passion, good romance, an excellent marriage, advancement in relationships; talented, humble and honest business people.

Negative Aspects and Indications: This combination of stars encourage couples to fight constantly, illness, a weak appearance, loss of money, under-nourished children, being selfish and becoming a leech and using people.

8, 8 Combination
Positive Aspects and Outcomes: This combination of stars support being rich and noble, honor in the family, loyalty, long-term prosperity particularly for the youngest son, splendid wealth and the accumulation of assets, financial gain, illustrious children, and all holy people.

Negative Aspects and Indications: These stars can bring nose disease, bone fractures of the arm and legs, tendon injuries, sprains, being bloated or puffed up, and young sons leave and never return.

8, 9 Combination
Positive Aspects and Outcomes: These stars represent and foster celebrations, extreme wealth, promotions, happy events, weddings, family harmony, parties, high positions in the government, festivities and in Period 8, great windfalls if activated.

Negative Aspects and Indications: This energy signifies being too attached to property, fire hazards, losing one's way in the material world, hands getting burned and getting into debt catches up with you.

9, 1 Combination
Positive Aspects and Outcomes: This combination indicates promotions at work or trading up for a better job, lots of sons, romance, honors and high positions, being very famous and successful; academic achievements and a studious person. This is a good *Peach Blossom* combo.

Negative Aspects and Indications: These stars can bring ill health, heart disease, talking too much or being silent, skin disease, eye problems, miscarriages, and venereal disease or bad romance when negative stars visit. Women can rule the house with this combination; couples fight.

9, 2 Combination
Positive Aspects and Outcomes: These stars signify lots of children, always getting promotions, and a skilled Feng Shui master. This combination, when timely, favors property, fire and electrical businesses. It indicates many good children.

Negative Aspects and Indications: This combination of stars indicate widows, foolish people, gynecological problems, a Feng Shui master becomes suddenly stupid, gynecological problems fires, and cerebral impediments.

9, 3 Combination
Positive Aspects and Outcomes: This combination signifies prosperity and great fame for the occupants. They are also blessed with intelligent, extremely brilliant and gifted children. These stars bring illustrious judges and wise advisors.

Negative Aspects and Indications: These stars indicate very cunning and wicked people, being jailed bitten by animals, and liver disease. With the exception of lawyers, this combination should be avoided. It leads to lawsuits and other legal disputes. Practices that may be a little shady may see a person end up in jail with this energy.

9, 4 Combination
Positive Aspects and Outcomes: These stars foster prosperity, peace, good children, success in exams, a world-famous author, good-looking people, successful trade, happy occasions, and very smart girls. This energy indicates a highly respected reputation in society, the birth of a brilliant son, and a celebrated poet or mystic. In Periods 7 and 8, the 9 mountain star supports excellent health.

Negative Aspects and Indications: This combination indicates the wife leaving (jumping over the wall), no support at work, failing exams, fire disasters and a selfish family. These stars can lead to very abnormal and inappropriate sexual encounters, even incestuous relationships.

9, 5 Combination
Positive Aspects and Outcomes: These stars encourage great success in literature and writing, many children, lots of properties, and can reach high positions of power such as a president or king. It indicates a holy man, sage or a savant.

Negative Aspects and Indications: This combination signifies stress, mental pressure, a religious fanatic, cancer, money loss and lawsuits. The 9 star accentuates the negative aspects of the 5; drug overdoses, poisons, injuries, death, accidents, inflammatory situations, sex diseases, leukemia, fire disasters, eye disease and when the annual 7 visits, suicide by drugs or poison.

9, 6 Combination
Positive Aspects and Outcomes: These set of stars support riches, intelligence, happiness, success, world-famous authors and editors, being honored by the government (given the 'purple cloth' which means accolades, recognition, titles and so forth); and respected authority. Living long, healthy lives are also indicated.

Negative Aspects and Indications: These stars signify sons leaving home or becoming violent towards the father, the wife murders or hurts an old man or her older husband, fatal attractions (for women in particular), challenging authority, ill health, and brain-related and lung disease.

9, 7 Combination
Positive Aspects and Outcomes: This combination signifies lots of money, media publicity, promotion and being rich and powerful. It also indicates being innovative, clever and bright.

Negative Aspects and Indications: These stars promote women trouble, being over-sexed, fire hazards, AIDS, bad reputation, tuberculosis, couples fight, too many parties with women, wine and song, fire-related accidents, and people with heart issues should not activate this direction and this combination.

9, 8 Combination
Positive Aspects and Outcomes: These stars signify a famous mountain climber, wealth, lots of children, good reputation, a successful trading company, a good ambassador, success in exams, celebrations, festivals and weddings. It also indicates that newlyweds, couples, and even older couples find great happiness as a result of this combination. Although romance may not be overly passionate, there is still room for nuptial bliss.

Negative Aspects and Indications: This combination encourages an idiot, difficulties in conceiving, difficult or dangerous childbirths, a man dies while climbing a mountain or dies in a huge, catastrophic avalanche.

9, 9 Combination
Positive Aspects and Outcomes: This combination indicates a great diplomat, celebrated chefs, a holy man or sage, famous jewelry designers, the cosmetic industry, successful smelting businesses for steel or gold, pottery or earthenware ventures, spiritual development, boutiques, meditation, and mind power.

Negative Aspects and Indications: When untimely, the 9 star indicates working too hard, thinking too much, eye problems, heart disease, heart disease, blindness, losing your mind, the wife dies young, a man hurting himself or his wife and lots of violence.

Annual and Monthly Stars

Not only does the *Flying Stars* reveal the energy map of a home or business, it offers information on how the energy changes from year to year and even month to month. In other words, in order to ensure continual good fortune, you must be aware that this is a dynamic and changing practice that requires some attention each year.

This is one of the 'time' dimension aspects of the *Flying Stars* system. While the annual stars are not a capital change or a milestone marker such as leaving one Period and going into another, they are important to consider. Annual stars should always be factored in as they can greatly impact everyday events and affect your overall luck. Monthly stars are not as significant as yearly ones, but they should be noted as well. Neither, the monthly or annual stars are of the same importance as the natal *Flying Star Chart*.

The purpose of the annual and monthly stars is to alert you to dangerous or pernicious energy that may bring trouble. When you're able to identify these afflictions, you can take action to mitigate their influence. It also signals where additional prosperous energy may visit for the year.

Best of San Yuan: *Formulas that Bring Wealth, Prestige, and Harmony. These formulas can be implemented on your site.*

Xuan Kong Da Gua or the Big Sixty-four Hexagrams

Xuan Kong Da Gua (*Mysterious Void Wind/Water School of Great Divinatory Symbols*) is also known as the Big Sixty-four Hexagrams or I Ching Method of Feng Shui. It is based on the sixty-four hexagrams of the ancient text of Taoist divination, the *I Ching*. This particularly potent set of formulae, appropriate for residential and commercial applications, describes ideal settings for the location and the orientation of a building in relation to its surroundings. Each configuration, or *formation*, described in the formulae has the potential to deliver great wealth and success to the occupants under certain circumstances. The formulae are complex and contain an enormous body of information, as anyone who has read the *I Ching* or sought to understand the meanings of the hexagrams can appreciate.

To activate a formation, four factors must be perfectly aligned. These include the *facing* and the *sitting* directions of a building in relation to an *incoming dragon* (a mountain or ridge) and a body of *water* (or river). Naturally occurring environmental features are best and the most potent messengers of luck. The degree of success will depend on the size, proximity, and beauty of the mountain and the water relative to the building. The system is most commonly used as a means of date selection for the auspicious timing of important events, such as the opening of a business, the moving of a household, or a wedding.

Dragon Gate Eight Formations

In Taiwan this set of formulas is known as Chien Kun National Treasure *(Qian Kun Guo Bao)*. Technically, these, too, are water formulas, but unlike the Five Ghosts technique, this method makes use of specific water exits. The following three considerations must be in harmony when designing a Dragon Gate formation: water entrance, water exit, and incoming dragon or mountain. First and foremost, the design process begins by using the *sitting* direction—or back—of the site or structure. Next, it is important to determine from which direction the water will enter: one direction brings wealth, while the other attracts nobility and success. The mountain direction will indicate who in the family receives the benefit, and there are six, fifteen-degree increments from which to choose.

Here's an example of how a formation might be designed if the building sits in Southeast 1, Southeast 2, or Southeast 3 (112.6 to 157.5 degrees):

- Water enters from West 1, West 2, or West 3 (247.6 to 292.5 degrees)
- Water exits from Northeast 2 (37.6 to 52.5 degrees)
- Incoming mountain from South 1, South 2, or South 3 (157.6 to 202.5 degrees)

This formation (a house sitting Southeast and facing Northwest) brings overall family wealth but will benefit the eldest child or son when he or she is of age. The following two other key considerations must be accounted for when designing a Dragon Gate: the Natal Flying Star chart of the house, and the proper flow of the water.

If water flows past the front door, basic water rules must be followed. Water will flow left to right or right to left depending on the door direction. This applies to *all* water formulas. Even though the Dragon Gate formations are not based on the door direction, if water can be seen or flows by the front door, the flow must be correct. In our example above, the house faces Northwest and sits in the Southeast. If water begins in the West and exits in the Northeast—it will have to pass the front door. Otherwise, serious money loss is possible if the basic principles of water flow are violated.

Grandmaster Yap does not consider these as potent as the Five Ghosts Carry Treasure formations. I agree, but I have had excellent results when it comes to jump-starting a career, particularly with a natural mountain or high ridge nearby. Don't hesitate to collaborate with a landscape architect: these techniques are simple to include in your landscape design. In the end, it will look like a gorgeous man-made stream incorporated into the schematic.

Dragon Gate Eight formations are also perfectly suited for large-scale projects, such as urban planning and development, shopping malls, and master-planned communities.

Castle Gate Formations

Castle Gate Formations—or in Chinese *Cheng Men Jue*—offer two approaches, both of which are under the auspices of Classical Feng Shui. I learned both styles from two different teachers. These formations are highly prized and can bring prosperity and wealth to every area of your life. Technically they are water formulas designed to manipulate energy for wealth luck. Traditional Castle Gate Formations are the most sophisticated water techniques offered in the San Yuan/Xuan Kong system.

The traditional method for this technique is to surround three sides of a building with mountains—often referred to as *land embrace*—while leaving a gap or opening at the front of the site. The best scenario is mountains with a natural space between them, which creates a concentrated form of energy. This opening becomes the gateway of chi, and it is captured when real water is placed in the front of the site, bringing wealth to the recipients. Buildings, however, can be substituted in place of real mountains, but this becomes a little trickier. As you may have guessed by now, natural mountains near a home site allow for numerous wealth-producing formulas. In fact, a gap between mountains may also be used in the Five Ghosts Carry Treasure and the Dragon Gate Eight formations.

The other popular method is known as *Castle Gate Theory*, *Sent Mun Kuet*, or *He Tu Castle Gate*, and it works best with big water near or in the front of the house. With this well-known technique, it is said that one *steals chi from heaven* by manipulating the Flying Star Chart of the house. The current prosperity energy is activated by real water when a door to a natural body of water, such as a lake, pond, or ocean, is opened. This door or gate is only good for the Period in which you create it.

The Peach Blossom Technique
'Peach Blossom' (Tao Hua) or the 'Flower of Romance' Direction

The Peach Blossom or aka the Flower of Romance is a Feng Shui technique that uses direction (*a specific 15-degree increment*) and is based on the animal year in which you were born. This is not the Peach Blossom Sha that we discussed earlier in Chapter Three. No indeed, this technique is used to attract an exciting new lover/partner or to get a marriage proposal from a serious relationship. It can be used by both men and women. It is never used for married people to stimulate romance; there are other techniques for that; this book discusses them all. If married couples use the Peach Blossom technique, a third party or "outsider" may show up.

Remember this is a method that is used to attract a new romantic partner to your life, and it not designed to bring harmony to those relationships in trouble. There are other techniques better suited for that such as activating your +70 (Yen Nien) and good stars. It is best used for:

- Single people looking for new love interests
- A woman waiting for a marriage proposal
- Singles looking to increase 'attractiveness" or the power to attract

For more information on how to use the Peach Blossom method, refer to *Feng Shui That Rocks the House* by the author.

Pearl String Formations

Pearl Strings are also known as *Continuous Bead* formations. They are special wealth-producing Flying Star charts of that system. These incredible formations are said to bring great wealth and pearls, rare and expensive treasures, to the occupants of a house or building. Pearl Strings are based on the facing direction of a structure and always fall in the Northwest and Southeast directions. However, they will only involve a specific 15-degree increment in those directions.

There are actually two types of Pearl String Formations—one that attracts money luck and one that fosters luck with people. Both are auspicious, but if you want to increase affluence, the Pearl String for wealth is the preferred facing. Both Pearl String charts must be supported by a mountain in the front and water in the back. Notice the two charts on the next page. The numbers will run in a sequence (like a string of pearls) in every single palace/sector. For example, 123, 456, 789 and so forth. The numbers that 'run' towards the *facing star* is lucky for money, and the ones that 'run' towards the *mountain star* are lucky for people.

If these formations are not activated properly, for instance the water and the mountain are switched, misfortune can ensue. Pearl String Formations are effective for twenty years and attract wealth only in the current Period. After its time has passed, the Feng Shui must be adjusted. For example, all Period 7 Pearl Strings have expired and soon the Period 8 Pearl Strings will expire.

These special charts occur four times in Period 7 *(Southeast 2, Southeast 3, Northwest 2, and Northwest 3)*, and only twice in Period 8 *(Southeast 1 and Northwest 1)*. They do not occur at all in the Period 9 charts. Below is a Period 7, NW 2, and a Period 8, SE 1.

	SE	
7 6 5	5 7 6	1 3 2
9 2 1	6 8 7	3 5 4
2 4 3	7 9 8	8 1 9

(E, NE, N on left; S, SW, W on right; NW at bottom arrow)

	NW	
2 9 1	1 8 9	5 3 4
6 4 5	9 7 8	3 1 2
4 2 3	8 6 7	7 5 6

(W, SW, S on left; N, NE, E on right; SE at bottom arrow)

Parent String Gua Formations

Parent Strings are also referred to as *Three Combinations,* and they are the third, wealth-producing Xuan Kong Flying Star chart. These charts represent the Cosmic Trinity—heaven-earth-man or father-mother-son energies. Because of this, some Feng Shui texts hold that this prosperous chi will permeate endlessly and transcend all periods. This is actually an over-exaggeration. These charts are lucky only in their period, which last at most twenty years. For example, the luck of the Parent String charts for Period 8 will expire in Period 9, beginning February 4, 2024.

In all nine palaces, one of these combinations will show up—in no particular order—as 1, 4, 7, or 2, 5, 8, or 3, 6, 9. In other words, it doesn't matter whether the number is the mountain, facing, or time star. The three combinations must be grouped as described above and must occur in every palace to be a Parent String chart.

The Parent String also has an *up the mountain, down the river* flow of energy. Thus, these wealth-producing charts are activated like a Pearl String—mountain in front, water in back. They are said to bring *three* times the good fortune when extracted correctly. These rare charts deliver outstanding health, ample fame, good reputation, great fortunes, and harmony to the lucky recipients. These charts are very rare and do not occur at all in Period 7. However, in Period 8 there are four occurrences (*Southwest 2, Southwest 3, Northeast 2* and *Northeast 3)*. They do not occur at all in the Period 9 charts.

Combination of Ten

The *Combination of Ten* is a special Flying Star chart that brings wealth, opportunities, prestige, and powerful connections. To the Chinese, the number ten represents completion; ten is also considered auspicious in the Xuan Kong Flying Star system. Combination of Ten charts offer the potential to double the fortune of a house, however, just like Pearl and Parent Strings, they must be activated specifically and correctly.

The Combination of Ten also offers two different types of charts—'money luck' and 'people luck'. Some say that these special charts override any negative aspects of a house. This statement, however, is simply not true. In fact, bad landforms and the wealth-depleting scenarios can totally negate the potential of these charts. These special charts occur four times in Period 7 (*South 2, South 3, North 2,* and *North 3)* and only twice in Period 8 (*Southwest 1* and *Northeast 1)*. They occur in Southeast 2/3 and Northwest 2/3 facing properties in Period 9.

Below are Period 8 charts facing SW 1 and Northeast 1. Notice how the time star and either the facing star or mountain star add to 10 in every palace/sector. When the time star + mountain star add to 10, this chart is lucky for people. When the time star + facing star add to 10, it's lucky for money.

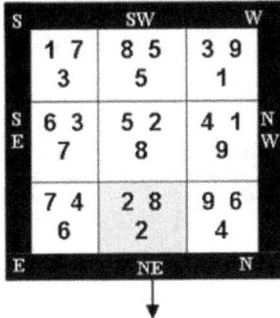

The Worst of San Yuan: *Disharmony, Divorce, Blood-related Accidents, Death. These formulas are for assessment purposes only and not for implementation.*

Robbery Mountain Sha
Indicates getting hurt by knives, strange diseases and disasters

This negative formation will rob vital energy from a house, though money loss is merely one aspect of the trouble you might encounter. The *Robbery Mountain Sha* technique does not use the door direction or the facing of your home. Rather, it is based on the back of the property, which is referred to as the sitting direction.

For example, if a home sits East (97.6°-112.5°) and there is a negative feature located in the Southwest (262.6°-277.5°), this forms a *Robbery Mountain Sha*. Negative features, such as high-tension electrical towers; a broken mountain (one that has been excavated, scarred, or marred); a quarry; a jagged cliff; lampposts; or a huge dead tree will activate the *Robbery Mountain* position. A jagged or broken mountain, however, is the most detrimental to the occupants. These attributes emit noxious and poisonous energies. When this unfortunate formation exists, family members could contract a strange disease, get hurt by knives, or encounter all sorts of disasters, including loss of wealth.

Figure 15: **This type of jagged mountains, if located in the Robbery Mountain position near your property, can cause hosts of negative events.**

Four Annual Afflictions: *Three Killings, Grand Duke Jupiter, Year Breaker, and 5 Yellow Star*

At its core, Feng Shui is about enhancing your luck and opportunities, so timing is an important factor, good and bad. Not all Feng Shui masters accept the validity of the 'sha' energy that we will discuss here. Sha means poisonous or killing energy. Keep in mind that it would be remise to ignore the effects of negative energy. Good Feng Shui can turn bad due to nothing more than the passage of time. The key is to be prepared. Keep the energy flow refreshed and up-to-date. This creates beautiful energy for the home and you will enjoy good fortune, secure wellness, and maintain a harmonious environment for you and your family.

There are four different types of energy that visit four sectors/directions of your property each year. They are inauspicious and these afflictions can cause negative events in your life. Depending on the type of affliction it is, and in which sector the affliction visits, these malevolent energies can cause bankruptcy, loss, illness, divorce, separations, business collapse, and in extreme cases, death.

This happened in 2008 when three of the four shas visited the South. Disturbing this area in that year could have had devastating results. Several of the afflictions/shas are based on planetary alignments and magnetic fields; these areas are taboo for deep ground digging or major renovations. The four negative energies are the Grand Duke Jupiter (*Tai Sui*), Year Breaker (*Sui Po*), Three Killings (*Sam Sart*), and the annual *5 Yellow Star*. Each year, beginning February 4th, they will migrate to a new area/direction.

The Three Killings Taboo

The *Three Killings* can be the most serious of the four negative energies. Disturbing the *Three Killings* has various levels of consequences. Some people have reported illnesses, accidents, marital problems, and money loss. Extreme bad luck is rare, but if unfavorable landforms are also present, it is possible.

Do not renovate landscape, hang new doors, remove big trees from the roots, or install a pool or pond in this direction or location if you can avoid it. If this is not a frequented part of your home or yard, there is no need to implement a cure or countermeasure. Basic gardening will have no affect on the *Three Killings* area of your yard because it does not displace enough dirt.

It is common for the Chinese to place three bronze Chi Lin dragons, a turtle, laughing Buddha or the God of War in the *Three Killings* location. All of these items should be made of metal; that is the real cure, not the *image* of the object. In ancient times, masters used the God of War (Guan Di) most often, as it was believed that the *Three Killings* was a gang of thieves that would rob and injure you. The powerful Guan Di could easily banish the three Bandits. However, the best cure is NOT to dig in the *Three Killing* area at all!

The *Three Killings* involves not only 45° of the afflicted direction but also 15° to the left and right for a total of 75°. For example, in 2020 (*Year of the Rat*), the *Three Killings* was located in the South. However, it also involved the last 15° of Southeast (known as SE 3) and the first 15° of Southwest (known as SW 1). These left and right 15° areas are called the 'assistant killers'.

Figure 16: It is taboo to engage in deep digging, construction, demolition or remodeling in the *Three Killings* position.

The 5 Yellow Star

The 5 star in the *Flying Stars* system is the worst possible energy—but rest assured, the 5 annual star will only visit one direction or sector of your house a year. If it takes up residence in the front of your home, you may experience difficulties with money, health, or relationships. By placing metal in this location, it can be countered or completely averted. However, *do not* place metal where the *5 Yellow Star* visit if you have an 8 facing star there; this will weaken the most powerful, benevolent energy. The 8 energy is more powerful than the 5 and is 'friends' with it (they are both earth energy). The 8 energy, especially if it is activated by real water, will protect you from the normal affects of the *5 Yellow Star*.

Here's a recap of the annual 'sha' energies; the most serious is the *Three Killings* and then the *5 Yellow Star*. It is taboo to engage in earth-moving activities such as prepping a swimming pool, pond, lake or removing a huge tree stump. Construction or remodeling where there is extensive demolition, shaking of the house or walls may also trigger negative events in your life.

Grand Duke Jupiter and Year Breaker

The *Grand Duke Jupiter* and the *Year Breaker* are intangible stars, and are a more esoteric aspect of Feng Shui. However, it is widely respected by the Chinese and some attention is devoted to these visiting energies. The Grand Duke Jupiter always corresponds to the ruling animal year, for example 2021 is the *Year of the Ox* (location is Northeast 1). Other names for the Grand Duke are the Grand General or the Commander of the Year. The *Year Breaker* is in the exact opposite location as the Grand Duke. While the *Grand Duke* and *Year Breaker* are not as serious as the 5 Yellow and the Three Killings, you will still want to avoid construction work or digging in these directions. For protection, you may bury some metal objects (brass, bronze, copper and so forth) near the construction site as an extra precaution. Some believe you should not face the Grand Duke Jupiter or Year Breaker directions for the year as it may 'offend' him. We don't advocate avoiding this if it has a great facing star.

The Annual Afflications and Renovation Taboos
Do not renovate or dig deep into the earth in these areas for the year!

The Year	Grand Duke	Year Breaker	Three Killings	The 5 Yellow
2020 *Year of the Rat*	North 2	South 2	South +SE 3 & SW 1	East
2021 *Year of the Ox*	Northeast 1	Southwest 1	East + NE 3 & SE 1	Southeast
2022 *Year of the Tiger*	Northeast 3	Southwest 3	North +NE 1 & NW 3	Center
2023 *Year of the Rabbit*	East 2	West 2	West +NW 1 & SW 3	Northwest
2024 *Year of the Dragon*	Southeast 1	Northwest 1	South +SE 3 & SW 1	West
2025 *Year of the Snake*	Southeast 3	Northwest 3	East + NE 3 & SE 1	Northeast
2026 *Year of the Horse*	South 2	North 2	North +NE 1 & NW 3	South

The Great Sun Formula

It is said that *"When the Sun arrives, all evil will subside"*. The Great Sun Position formula *(Tai Yang Dou San Pan)* is when the Sun will come to the facing and sitting position of your home which happens twice a year. First, find the facing direction of your home. You will need to take a compass direction as the chart deals with 15° increments. Once you have the degree, refer to if needed to the 24 Mountains/Directions chart to find the Feng Shui term such as Northwest 2, or Southwest 1 and so forth. You will have four set of dates to *begin* your construction that safeguards you against any negative result by disturbing the afflicted area. The dates are just start-date or widows of time. The work does not need to be completed.

✷ The Great Sun Formula ✷	
"When the SUN arrives, all evil will subside"	
Facing	**Dates to START** *(repairs, construction, remodeling or digging)*
North 1	Feb 4-18; April 6-18; August 8-23; Dec 7-22
North 2	Jan 21-Feb 4; March 18-April 5; July 28-Aug 8; Nov 22-Dec 6
North 3	Jan 6-21; March 6-21; June 6-21; Nov 7-22
Northeast 1	April-18-May 6; June 21-July 7; Oct 23-Nov 6; Dec 22-Jan 6
Northeast 2	Feb 4-18; June 6-21; Oct 8-23; Dec 7-22
Northeast 3	Jan 21-Feb 4; May 21-June 6; Sept 23-Oct 7; Nov 22-Dec 7
East 1	Jan 6-21; May 6-21; Oct 8-23; Nov 7-22
East 2	April 19-May 6; Sept 23-Oct 6; Oct 23-Nov 7; Dec 22-Jan 6
East 3	Feb 4-March 18; April 5-19 ; Oct 8-23; Dec 7-22
Southeast 1	Mar 18-April 5; July 23-Aug 8; Sept 23-Oct 8; Nov 22-Dec 6
Southeast 2	March 5-21; July 7-23; Sept 8-23; Nov 7-22
Southeast 3	Feb 18-Mar 6; June 21-July 7; Aug 23-Sept 8; Oct 23-Nov 7
South 1	Feb 4-18; June 6-21; August 8-23; Oct 8-23
South 2	Jan 21-Feb 4; May 21-June 6; July 28-Aug 8; Sept 23-Oct 6
South 3	Jan 6-21; May 6-21; July 7-28; Sept 8-23
Southwest 1	Dec 22-Jan 6; April 6-18; June 21-Jul 7; Sept 23-Oct 8
Southwest 2	April 6-19; June 6-21; Oct 8-23; Dec 7-22
Southwest 3	March 18-April 6; May 21-June 6; July 23-Aug 8; Nov 22-Dec 7
West 1	March 6-18; May 6-21; July 7-23; Nov 7-22
West 2	Feb 18-March 6; April 19-May 6; June 21– July 7; Oct 23– Nov 7
West 3	Feb 4-March 18; April 5-19; June 6-21; Oct 8-23
Northwest 1	March 18-April 5; May 21-June 6; Sept 23-Oct 8; Dec 21-Jan 6
Northwest 2	Jan 6-21; March 6-18; May 6-21; Sept 8-23
Northwest 3	Feb 18-March 6; April 6-18; Aug 23-Sept 8; Dec 22-Jan 6

CHAPTER FIVE
The Period 9 Charts and Activation

Your home is automatically a Period 9 house if you move in between Feb 4, 2024 to Feb 3, 2044. If you undertake major remodeling projects *during* those years, other Period homes become a Period 9 house.

Preparing for Period 9

We enter Period 9 on February 4, 2024; this is considered a capital change in Feng Shui energy around the world! In order to proceed and to locate your unique chart and to set things into motion, you'll need the facing direction. If you have not already discovered the facing direction, refer to the section of the book entitled *'How to Determine the Facing'* on page 49. Once you have the degree check the 24 Mountains chart on page 51. Your move-in date determines which Period your house falls into. Draw a floor plan of your home. Divide it up into nine cells and overlay the directions and Star  Chart. Place this information outside the floor plan so that you can sketch in possible bed locations, desks, water, and so forth as you read the recommendations. If you are unsure which directions go where, you will find them in the Natal Star Charts in the little black area outside the numbers. Only one chart applies to your home and its unique energy. The rest of the charts serve as great reference material assisting your friends, family, co-workers or if you move into another home. You'll be able to arrange everything perfectly—again!

It does take some time to fully master Flying Stars (not to mention all the other systems for that matter), so the charts have been fully evaluated for you. The recommendations and assessments have made use of the five elements, cosmic trinity, timeliness of the stars, annual stars, proper activation of mountain and facing stars, He Tu, Luo Shu, the two Ba Guas, Eight Mansions, Flying Stars, San Yuan and San He formulas. The recommendations for the charts include enhancements and cures needed to realize its full potential. This will ensure that the most positive energy is being fully extracted. The 'Watchful Eye' alerts include when the 5, 2 or 9 star visits certain areas and when the Three Killings comes to visit the *front* of the property as this is an important area. You will need to check the chart for other areas if construction is planned and use the *Great Sun Formula* if warranted. All the Star Charts have been turned to the facing direction, they look different when 'flown'.

Water

This chapter will give you recommendations to extract the best energy from your Period 9 home. Chapters Six and Seven will do so for Period 8 and 7 homes. This is where all

systems of Feng Shui are brought together for a comprehensive assessment and experience. Installing water in the recommended area will be one of the most important things you can do to set the energy in motion. Studies now show that water is actually alive and has a consciousness of sort.

Interesting Facts about the Period 9 Charts

Some unusual things happen regarding the Period 9 charts. There are no *Pearl String* or *Parent String* charts, no *Wang Shan Wang Shui* (Prosperous Facing and Sitting), and all charts will have double 9's either meeting in the front or back. There are two special *Combination of Ten* charts on the Southeast 2/3 and Northwest 2/3 facings. Also, all charts have the mountain and facing stars adding to 9! This happens in *every* palace of *every* chart except the front and back ones where the double 9's appear! While this brings some beautiful combinations of stars, it also delivers some really bad ones that will need to be cured.

Keep in mind that in Feng Shui *direction* rules and this includes the Flying Stars system! There is too much credence given to the location by some experts. For instance, if there are bad stars in a room, they will recommend you move out. This is simply not a practical approach, nor necessary. While it is excellent to make use of both location and direction, the more powerful results will come from the direction.

PERIOD 9

South 1 (157.6° to 172.5°) Facing Name: Bing
Chart: **Double Stars Meet at Facing** (*Shuang Xing Dao Xiang*)

Activating the OUTDOORS
Needs Water and Mountain in Front

South 1

This chart has the double 9's at the front of the property known as *Double Stars Meet at Facing*. South-facing structures support people of authority, who are charismatic and the family can accumulate lots of property. It can also bring descendants who will achieve high-ranking positions in politics. To fully capture the most benevolent energy and activate health, wealth and harmony, place big water and a 'mountain' in the front of the home. The water could be a large stone fountain, pond, or waterfall.

The *mountain* could be landscaping mounds seen on golf courses, boulders (no sharp or jagged edges), courtyard walls, tall and heavy planter pots, basalt pillars, stone/brick fireplaces or other tall and heavy items (earth materials) in the front or near the front entrance. Trees cannot represent a mountain. For those living in an apartment, high-rise building, townhome, condominium or a rented space and are not able to install a water feature outdoors, place one indoors in the recommended area. To activate the mountain in the recommended area, use a tall armoire, heavy bookcases or stone statues; any of these items will sufficiently activate the energy.

Backyard Swimming Pool
While the front requires water, you may place a swimming pool in the North or Northeast sector of the backyard to get a good result.

These Formations are Possible, Not Definite!
There is a potential *Eight Roads of Destruction* if there is a road or real water coming from/exiting the Southeast direction; they are notorious for bringing bankruptcy, disease, and divorce. This house also has a potential *Robbery Mountain Sha* formation if there is a jagged cliff, electrical tower, huge dead tree, or a broken mountain in the Southwest.

Figure 17: For a Period 9, South 1 chart, this water feature placed in the front would properly activate the 9 facing star that is needed. The stone base and sphere would activate the 9 mountain star.

Activating the INDOORS
Move your Stuff!

Excellent Doors
Always use and activate good doors; the best ones for this chart are facing to the *South, North, Northeast and East.* This applies to all exterior doors as well as an interior garage door used to enter the house. In modern homes, an interior garage door is often the main entry into the house, therefore it is extremely important! If one of these directions is also your +90, you will be very fortunate with wealth! If the house has a door angled to the Southeast, it activates a 5 facing star. *Cure:* If this door is used daily, cure it with metal next to or directly on the door. Brass, bronze, copper, pewter, and stainless steel are some high-vibrating metals to use, or large metal wind chimes. See Classical Feng Shui cures and enhancements on page 290.

Master Bedroom + Family
There are two ways to enhance health, harmony and prosperity in the bedroom and that is location and direction. The *direction* of the bed will give you the most powerful results. Locate the master bedroom in the *North, South* (second floor), *Northeast* or *Northwest* as they have good mountain stars. **Bed Directions:** Place the owner's/marital headboard/bed to the *North, Northeast* or *East, or South* direction (all Guas). These bed directions have a good mountain *and* facing star combination with excellent energy. Place all family members using the above directions.

For this house the *West* and *Southwest* (7, 2 and 2,7 combinations) have negative energy. If the master bedroom is already located in either sector, make sure that the *bed direction* is not also either *West* or *Southwest*. If so, reposition immediately; activating this direction indicates stomach illness, leukemia, miscarriages, women fighting, divorce, fire hazards, abortions, illicit affairs, money loss, and robberies.

Figure 18: The owner's/marital bed direction is one of the most important placements in the home.

Home Office + Study
Face your desk/body to the *South, North, Northeast or East* (all Guas). Choose one of the above facing directions coupled with your +80 to enhance health, +70 for relationships or +90 for wealth if possible. For example, the 4 Guas can face the South, it has great energy and it's their +80; the 7 Guas can face Northeast, it has prosperous energy and it's their +70. *For students, bloggers, writers, use the above directions to energize learning and success in exams. South has the most potent wealth energy!*

Stoves and Toilets
The best directions for the stove knobs, buttons or controls are *North, South and Northeast*. You will struggle with money, health and relationships if there is a stove or toilet located in your +90, +80 or +70 sector of the house. Select and use a toilet located in one of your negative sectors of the house (-90, -80, -70, or -60). *This section applies to the head/s of household or breadwinner.*

Family Room + Dining Room
In the dining room and family room, arrange your furniture so that you and family members can face *South, North, Northeast* or *East*. These directions have the best energy of the house. No one should face *Southeast* in any room!

Watchful Eye: *Annual Stars and Three Killings*
This chart has two negative areas to pay attention to; in certain years they become more dangerous. In 2024 the 5 annual visits the **West** (2 facing star) and in 2026 the 9 annual visits the **Southeast** (5 facing star). No water *(pools, fountains, etc)* or fire *(stoves, fire place/pits or grills)* should be placed in either area, *no matter the year*; it will activate the negative energy in these areas! The *Three Killings* visits the front of the house in 2024 and 2028 and it is taboo to engage in deep digging, remodeling or demolition. Use good dates from the *Great Sun Formula* if you must touch this area.

How to Implement the Recommendations
On the next page you will find an example of how you might implement the recommendations for a South 1-facing property. We will pretend that the homeowners are a married couple and own a farm-to-table upscale restaurant in Los Angeles, CA. Richard born 3-18-1982 is a 9 Life Gua (Dog Year) and Lydia was born 6-1-1985 and is also a 9 Life Gua (Ox Year).

The home has the prosperous energy but it needs a water feature to be fully captured. The front door and interior garage activate wealth energy with every use. The bed should be placed on the North wall/window. They should have a substantial headboard and blinds/drapes to close at night. The stove is excellent sitting on a 9 mountain star (South) with the controls facing North and an 8 facing star. They both have an office and can face South as it has the best wealth energy. While sitting in the living/family room, face South or North. There is a dead tree in the Southwest and it activates the *Robbery Mountain Sha* position and will need to be removed. A swimming pool may be located in the North or Northeast or cover both sectors.

Period 9, South 1
Richard and Lydia, 9 Life Guas

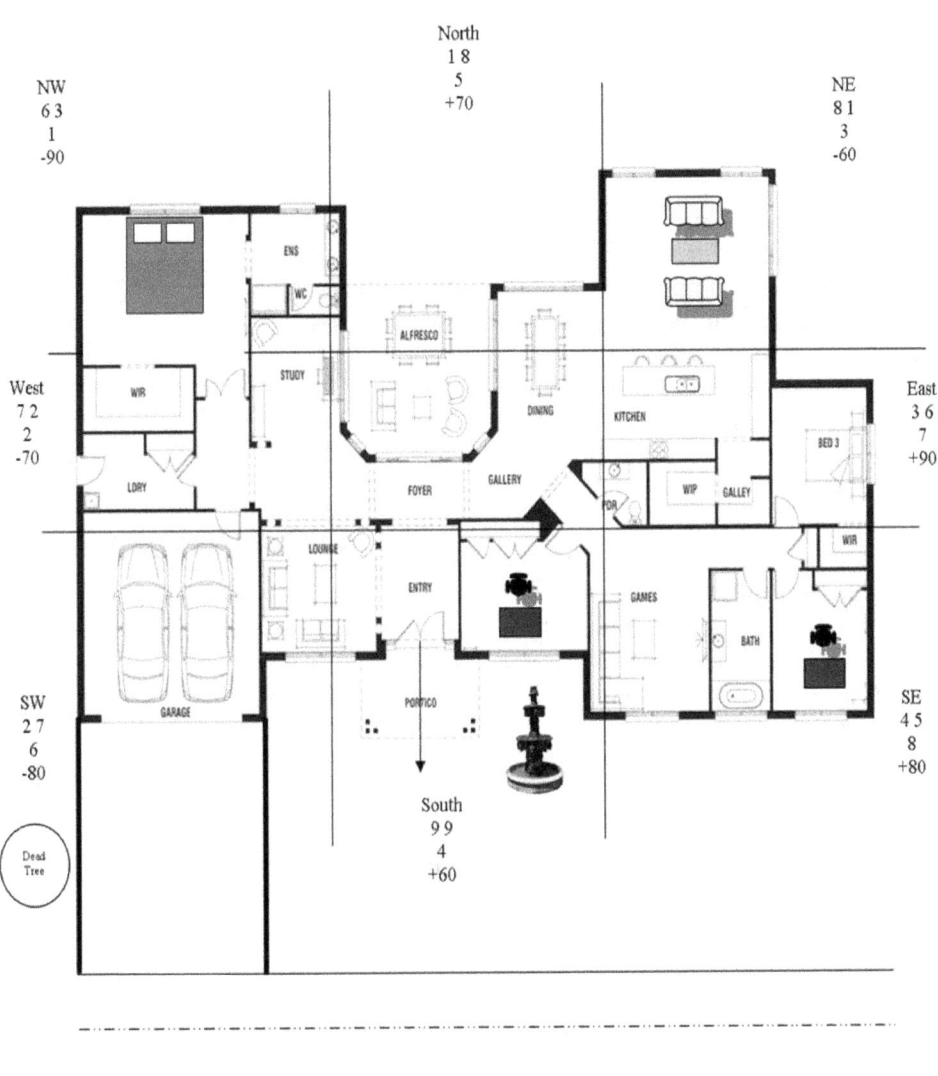

PERIOD 9

South 2 *(172.6° to 187.5°)* Facing name: **Wu** and the **Horse**

South 3 *(187.6° to 202.5°)* Facing name: **Ting/Ding**

Chart: **Double Stars Meet at Sitting** *(Shuang Xing Dao Zuo)*

Activating the OUTDOORS
Needs Mountain and Water at Back

The excellent energy of the double 9's are located at the back of the property known as *Double Stars Meet at Sitting* and can bring great health, relationships and money. It is important to activate this chart by installing a *mountain* and *water*. The 'mountain' can be higher ground, landscape mounds, boulders (no sharp or jagged edges) or any combination (the mountain should be 3 feet or higher). A water fountain, pond, swimming pool, or stream may be placed at the back. If you live in a home where you are not able to place an outdoor water feature, place one inside in the recommended area; consider a wall fountain. For those living in an apartment, high-rise building, townhome, condominium or a rented space and are not able to install a water feature outdoors, place one indoors in the recommended area. To activate the mountain in the recommended area, use a tall armoire, heavy bookcases or stone statues; these will sufficiently activate the energy.

	NW	N	NE	
	4 5 1	9 9 5	2 7 3	
W	3 6 2	5 4 9	7 2 7	E
	8 1 6	1 8 4	6 3 8	
	SW	S	SE	

South 2 & 3

Backyard Swimming Pools
If a pool is desired it should be located in the North for the best results. It cannot touch or be located in the Northwest!

These Formations are Possible, Not Definite!
For homes that face **South 2**, there is a possible *Eight Killing Forces* if there is a mountain located in the Northwest direction. If there is a road coming from the East, it could activate the *Peach Blossom Sha*. These homes also may have a *Robbery Mountain Sha* formation if there is a jagged cliff, electrical tower, huge dead tree, lamppost, or a broken mountain in the Southeast. For homes that face to **South 3,** there is a possible *Eight Roads of Destruction* if there is a road or water coming from/exiting the Southwest direction, it is common for them to bring bankruptcy, disease, and divorce.

Figure 19: For this Period 9, South 2 & 3 house, a water feature located at the back of the property would activate the 9 mountain as well as the 9 facing star!

Activating the INDOORS
Move your Stuff!

Excellent Doors
Always use and activate good doors; the best ones for this chart are facing to the *South, North, West* and *Southwest*. This applies to all exterior doors as well as an interior garage door used to enter the house. In modern homes, an interior garage door is often the main entry into the house, therefore it is extremely important! If one of these directions is also your +90, you will be very lucky for wealth.

Master Bedroom + Family
There are two ways to activate great energy in the bedroom and that is location and direction; the *direction* of the bed will give you the most powerful results. Locate the master bedroom in the *South* (second floor), *North, Southwest* or *Southeast* as these sectors have good mountain stars. **Bed Directions**: Place the owner's/marital headboard/bed to the *South, Southeast, North, West* or *Southwest* (all Guas). These bed directions have a good mountain *and* facing star combination with excellent energy. Place all other family members using the above directions.

Take special caution regarding the East and Northeast (2, 7 combos), do not use if at all possible. If the master bedroom is already located there, make sure that the bed direction is not also East or Northeast. If so, reposition immediately; activating this direction indicates stomach illness, leukemia, miscarriages, women fighting, divorce, and fires.

Family Room + Dining Room
In the dining room and family room, arrange your furniture so that you and family members can face *South, North, Southwest* or *West*. These directions have the best energy of the house. No one should face *Northwest* in any room!

Home Office + Study
While sitting at your desk, face *South, North, West or Southwest*. Choose one of these facing directions coupled with your +80 to enhance health, +70 for relationships or +90 for wealth if possible. For example, if you are a 7 Gua, choose the *Southwest* direction as it is your +80 and supports health and money.

Figure 20: For this Period 9, South 2 & 3 house, while sitting at the dining room table, face South, North, Southwest or West to activate great energy.

Stoves and Toilets
The best directions for the stove knobs, buttons or controls are *South, North or Southwest*. If there is a stove or toilet located in your +90, +80 or +70 sector of the house, health and money-loss are at a high risk. This also makes it difficult to conceive children. Select and use a toilet located in one of your negative sectors of the house (-90, -80, -70, or -60). *This section applies to the head/s of household or breadwinner.*

Watchful Eye: *Annual Stars and Three Killings*
This chart has two negative areas to pay attention and in certain years they become more dangerous. They are in 2025 when the 9 annual star visits the **East** (2 facing star) and in 2026 when the annual 2 visits the **Northwest** (5 facing star). No water *(pools, fountains, etc)* or fire *(stoves, fire place/pits or grills)* should be placed in either area, *no matter the year*; it will activate the negative energy in these areas! The *Three Killings* visits the front of the house in 2024 and 2028 and it is taboo to engage in deep digging, remodeling or demolition. Use good dates from the *Great Sun Formula* if you must touch this area.

PERIOD 9

Southwest 1 *(202.6° to 217.5°)* Facing name: **Wei** and the **Goat**
Chart: **Double Stars Meet at Facing** *(Shuang Xing Dao Xiang)*

Activating the OUTDOORS
Install Water and Mountain in Front

This property has the most auspicious stars of Period 9 at the front known as *Double Stars Meet at Facing*. The energy is extremely lucky for all categories of Feng Shui, prosperity, health and harmony! The Southwest-facing properties are also known for turning bad fortunes into lucrative opportunities and may also denote the birth of an intelligent, wealthy and prosperous person. To fully capture this great energy, you will need to place a water feature and a mountain in the front garden.

The 'mountain' can be higher ground, courtyard walls, landscape mounds, boulders (no sharp or jagged edges) or any combination (the mountain should be 3 feet or higher. The water feature could be a fountain, stream or Koi pond. For those living in an apartment, high-rise building, townhome, condominium or a rented space and are not able to install a water feature outdoors, place one indoors in the recommended area. To activate the mountain in the recommended area, use a tall armoire, heavy bookcases or stone statues; these will sufficiently activate the energy.

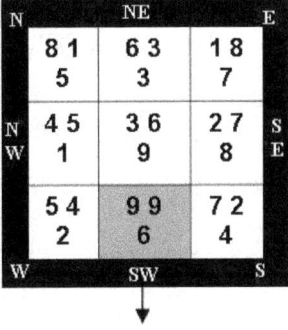

Southwest 1

Backyard Swimming Pools
If a swimming pool is desired in the backyard, it should be located in the East (right-hand corner) or North (left-hand corner) but cannot touch between 352.6° to 7.5° or it may activate affairs. Water in the Northeast may cause lawsuits and water located in the Northwest can activate disasters.

These Formations are Possible, Not Definite!
These homes also may have a *Robbery Mountain Sha* formation if there is a jagged cliff, electrical tower, huge dead tree, lamppost, or a broken mountain in the *Southeast* and a *Peach Blossom Sha* if there is water located in the *North*.

Figure 21: For this Period 9, SW 1 house, water is needed in the front of the property. It also needs a mountain. The water feature here is both a mountain (heavy, earthen pots) and water.

Activating the INDOORS
Move your Stuff!

Excellent Doors
Always use and activate good doors; the best ones for this chart are facing to the *Southwest, North, West* and *East*. This applies to all exterior doors as well as an interior garage door used to enter the house. In modern homes, an interior garage door is often the main entry into the house, therefore it is extremely important! *Cures:* If the interior garage door is facing either **Northwest** or **Southeast**, they will need to be cured. Cure the Northwest-facing door with metal. Such as a brass kick plate, metal art on or near the door, metal bells on the door handle or a metal statue near the door. The Southeast door should be painted red. Place a red rug as well. If there is an angled front door to the **South** (2 facing star), you will need to cure it with metal if used. See page 290 to learn more about metal cures used in Classical Feng Shui.

Master Bedroom + Family
There are two ways to activate great energy in the bedroom and that is location and direction; the *direction* of the bed will give you the most powerful results. Locate the master bedroom in the *Southwest, North, Northeast, or East* as these sectors have good mountain stars. **Bed Directions:** Place the owner's/marital headboard/bed to the *Southwest, North, Northeast or East (all Guas)*. These bed directions have a good

mountain *and* facing star combination with excellent energy. Use the above directions when placing the bed for other family members.

Family Room + Dining Room
In the dining room and family room, arrange your furniture so that you and family members can face *Southwest, North, or East*. These directions have the best energy of the house. No one should face *Northwest* in any room!

Home Office + Study
For the best energy, face to the *Southwest, North, or East* (all Guas). Choose one of these facing directions coupled with your +80 to enhance health, +70 for relationships or +90 for wealth if possible. For example if you are an 8 Gua, face to the Southwest; this is your wealth direction and it has prosperous energy. If you are a 1 Gua, you could face to the East, this is your +80 and it has wealth energy. For students, use the above directions to energize learning and success in exams.

Stoves and Toilets
The stove knobs, buttons or controls should face to the *Southwest, North, or East*. You will struggle with money, health and relationships if there is a stove or toilet located in your +90, +80 or +70 sector of the house. Select a toilet located in one of your negative sectors of the house (-90, -80, -70, or -60). This house *cannot* have a stove located in the *West* (angled) or *Southeast* of the kitchen (5 & 2 mountain stars); it can bring serious health and money issues. *This section applies to the head/s of household or breadwinner.*

Watchful Eye: *Annual Stars*
This chart has two negative areas to pay attention to regarding money and health; in certain years they become more serious. They are the **South** (2 facing star) in 2026, 2029, 2031 and the **Northwest** (5 facing star) in 2026, 2028, 2032. There should be no water *(pools, fountains, etc)* or fire *(stoves, fire place/pits or grills)* should be placed in this area, *no matter the year*, it gets activated!

Figure 22: The knobs/controls for this house should face to the Southwest, North or East.

How to Implement the Recommendations

Tom is a 4 Life Gua (7-26-1960) and Rose is a 3 Life Gua (11-7-1961) have a home-based business and they both work from home. The home needs water in the front to activate the prosperous energy. The master bed should be placed on the SW wall. In the offices, one can face Southwest and the other East, both directions have wealth energy. The stove is only half good; it sits on a good 4 star but activates a 7 facing star. While not detrimental, it does not activate good luck.

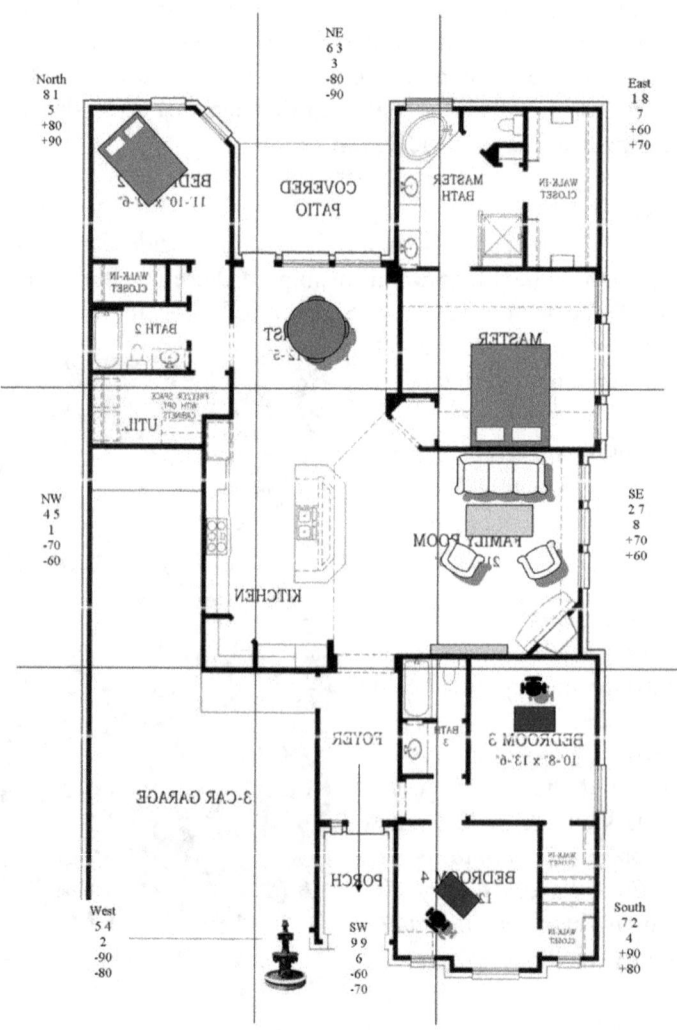

PERIOD 9
Southwest 2 *(217.6° to 232.5°)* Facing name: **Kun**
Southwest 3 *(232.6° to 247.5°)* Facing name: **Shen** and the **Monkey**
Chart: **Double Stars Meet at Sitting** *(Shuang Xing Dao Zuo)*

Activating the OUTDOORS
Install a Mountain and Water at Back

This property has the current prosperity and benevolent energy located at the back of the site known as *Double Stars Meet at Sitting*. The Southwest-facing properties are known for turning bad fortunes into lucrative opportunities and may also denote the birth of an intelligent, wealthy and prosperous person. To activate this chart properly, you will need both water and a mountain at the back. The 'mountain' could be a solid wall or fence comprised of stucco, brick, or stone; even smartly designed, tiered landscaping or a series of stacked terraces would work brilliantly. While designing this important feature, incorporate a large water feature in proportion to the size of your home and garden in the back. If you live in an apartment, high-rise, townhome, condo or a rented space and are not able to install an outdoor water feature, place one inside at the back of your space (east). Also, large heavy bookcases or armories can represent your mountain; it should be place on the back wall as well.

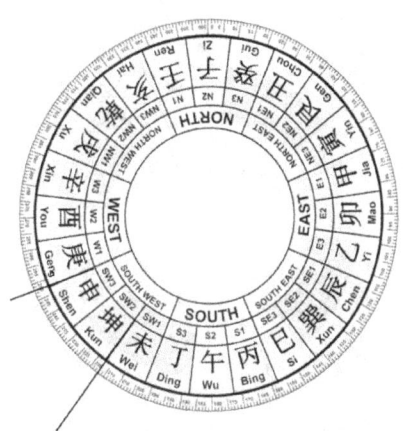

SW 2 & 3

Backyard Swimming Pools
If a swimming pool is desired, it should be located in the Northeast (center) of the backyard. Water in the North may cause illness and water located in the Southeast can activate disasters.

These Formations are Possible, Not Definite!
The **Southwest 2** homes have a possible *Eight Roads of Destruction* if there is a road/water coming from/exiting certain areas of the South and West directions; they are noted for bringing disease, bankruptcy and divorce. These homes also may have a *Robbery Mountain Sha* formation if there is a jagged cliff, electrical tower, huge dead tree, lamppost, or a broken mountain in the South; they indicate everyone in household getting an unusual disease, hurt by knives and disasters.

Figure 23: This Southwest 2 & 3 chart needs both water and a mountain at the back. A water feature with rocks, boulders and brick would activate both. The fire pit also will activate the 9 facing star.

The **Southwest 3** facing properties may have an *Eight Killing* formation if there is a mountain located in the East. A *Peach Blossom Sha* is activated with a road coming from the West. These homes also may have a *Robbery Mountain Sha* formation if there is a jagged cliff, electrical tower, huge dead tree, lamppost, or a broken mountain in the Southwest.

Activating the INDOORS
Move your Stuff!

Excellent Doors
Always use and activate good doors; the best ones for this chart are facing to the *Northeast, South, and West.* This applies to all exterior doors as well as an interior garage door used to enter the house. In modern homes, an interior garage door is often the main entry into the house, therefore it is extremely important! *Cures:* If the interior garage door is facing either **Northwest** or **Southeast**, they will need to be cured. Cure the Southeast-facing door with metal. Such as a brass kick plate, metal art on or near the door, metal bells on the door handle or a metal statue near the door. The Northwest door should be painted red. Place a red rug as well. See page 290 to learn more about cures used in Classical Feng Shui.

Master Bedroom + Family
There are two ways to activate great energy in the bedroom and that is location and direction. The *direction* of the bed will give you the most powerful results. Locate the master bedroom in the *Northeast, South, Southwest or West* sectors of the house as these sectors have good mountain stars. **Bed Directions:** Place the owner's/marital on the *Northeast, South, Southwest* or *West* wall of the bedroom. Place all other family members using the above directions.

Family Room + Dining Room
In the dining room and family room, arrange your furniture so that you and family members can face *Northeast, East, South, or West*. These directions have the best energy of the house. No one should face *Southeast* in any room.

Home Office + Study
For the best energy face *Northeast, East, South, or West*. Choose one of these facing directions coupled with your +80 to enhance health, +70 for relationships or +90 for wealth if possible. For example, if you are a 3 Gua, face to the South it's your +90 and has prosperous energy. For students, writers, and blogger use the East direction to energize learning and success in exams and publishing.

Figure 24: Keep in mind the good facing directions while arranging the living or sitting room. For this Southwest 2 & 3 chart, face *Northeast, East, South* or *West.*

Figure 25: Ideally, a toilet should not be located in your good directions/locations (+90, +80, +70, or +60). Likewise, they should not be located on good facing stars such as a 9, 8, or 1. Guest baths or powder rooms too close to the front door are not auspicious.

Stoves and Toilets
The best directions for the stove knobs, buttons or controls are *Northeast, East, South, or West*. If there is a stove or toilet located in your +90, +80 or +70 sector of the house, health and money-loss are at a high risk. Select a toilet located in one of your negative sectors of the house (-90, -80, -70, or -60). This house *cannot* have a stove located in the *East* (angled) or *Northwest* of the kitchen (5 & 2 mountain stars); it can bring serious health and money issues. *This section applies to the head/s of household or breadwinner.*

Watchful Eye: *Annual Stars*
This chart has two negative areas to pay attention to regarding money and health; in certain years they become more serious. They are the **North** (2 facing star) in 2027, 2032 and the **Southeast** (5 facing star) in 2024 and 2026. No water *(pools, fountains, etc)* or fire *(stoves, fire place/pits or grills)* should be placed in this area, *no matter the year*, it gets activated!

PERIOD 9
West 1 (247.6° to 262.5°) Facing name: **Geng**
Chart: **Double Stars Meet at Facing** *(Shuang Xing Dao Xiang)*

Activating the OUTDOORS
Need a Mountain and Water in Front

This property has the current prosperity and benevolent energy with the double 9's located in the front of the site known as *Double Stars Meet at Facing*. These West-facing properties produce well-educated, intelligent, polite and charming people who can become very wealthy through good business management, or getting involved in politics. To fully capture the most benevolent energy and activate health, wealth and harmony, place water and a 'mountain' in the front of the home. The water could be a large stone fountain, pond, or waterfall. The *mountain* could be landscaping mounds seen on golf courses, boulders (no sharp or jagged edges), courtyard walls, tall and heavy planter pots, basalt pillars, stone/brick fireplaces or other tall and heavy items (earth materials) in the front or near the front entrance. Trees cannot represent a mountain. If you live in an apartment, high-rise, townhome, condo or a rented space and are not able to install an outdoor water feature, place one inside on the recommended area. Also, large heavy bookcases or armories can represent your mountain; it should be place on the West wall.

NE	E	SE
1 8 3	5 4 7	6 3 8
3 6 5	7 2 9	2 7 4
8 1 1	9 9 2	4 5 6
NW	W	SW

West 1

Backyard Swimming Pools
If a swimming pool is desired, it should be located in the Northeast (left-hand corner). Water in the East (center) is good for writers, teachers and those with a public persona otherwise it may cause affairs and bad romance.

These Formations are Possible, Not Definite!
The house does have a possible *Eight Roads of Destruction* formation if there is a road/driveway coming from and exiting the Southwest direction; noted for bankruptcy, disease or divorce. These homes also may have a *Robbery Mountain Sha* formation if there is a jagged cliff, electrical tower, huge dead tree, lamppost, or a broken mountain in the South; they indicate everyone in household getting an unusual disease, hurt by knives and disasters.

Figure 26: This chart needs water and a mountain in the front to activate the double 9's. A water feature such as this would activate both. The tall modern sculpture activates the 9 mountain while the real, moving water activates the 9 facing star.

Activating the INDOORS
Move your Stuff!

Excellent Doors
Always use and activate good doors; the best ones for this chart are facing to the *West, Northwest, North, and Northeast*. This applies to all exterior doors as well as an interior garage door used to enter the house. In modern homes, an interior garage door is often the main entry into the house, therefore it is extremely important. If there is an angled front door to the Southwest, you will need to cure it with metal. With daily use, it will activate a 5 facing star. See page 290 to learn more about cures used in Classical Feng Shui.

Master Bedroom + Family
There are two ways to activate great energy in the bedroom and that is location and direction; the *direction* of the bed will give you the most powerful results. Locate the master bedroom in the *West, Northwest, Northeast and Southeast* as these sectors have good mountain stars. **Bed Directions:** Place the owner's/marital headboard/bed on the *West, Northwest* or *Northeast* wall in the bedroom (all Guas). These bed directions have a good mountain *and* facing star combination with excellent energy. Place all other family members using the same directions as above for the best results.

Family Room + Dining Room
In the dining room and family room, arrange your furniture so that you and family members can face *West, Northwest, North, and Northeast*. These directions have the best energy of the house. No one should face *Southwest* in any room!

Home Office + Study
To enhance great energy, face your desk/body to the *West, Northwest, North, and Northeast (*all Guas). Choose one of these facing directions coupled with your +80 to enhance health, +70 for relationships or +90 for wealth if possible. For example, if you are a 2 Gua, choose the *West* direction; it has wealth energy and it's your +80. Or if you are 6 Gua, choose to face the *Northeast*—it has benevolent/wealth energy and it's your health direction. For students, use the above directions to energize learning and success in exams.

Stoves and Toilets
The stove knobs, buttons or controls can face to the *West, Northwest, and Northeast.* These directions have good facing stars. You will struggle with money, health and relationships if there is a stove or toilet located in your +90, +80 or +70 sector of the house. Select a toilet located in one of your negative sectors of the house (-90, -80, -70, or -60). *This section applies to the head/s of household or breadwinner.*

Watchful Eye: *Annual Stars and Three Killings*
This chart has one negative area to pay attention to regarding money and health. In certain years it can be more serious. The Southwest (particularly if there is an angled front door) will have more negative energy 2024. No water *(pools, fountains, etc)* or fire *(stoves, fire place/pits or grills))* should be placed in either area, *no matter the year;* it will activate the negative energy in these areas! The *Three Killings* position comes to the front of this house in 2027. It is taboo to engage in deep digging, remodeling or demolition. Use good dates from the *Great Sun Formula* if you must touch this area.

Period 9 West 1 on implementing recommendations regardless of the Life Guas. This home has the prosperous energy at the front door and the interior garage door entrance. The stove is excellent as it sits on a 9 mountain star and the knobs activate the 4 facing star. The beds are best placed on the West, North, NE or SE. The fireplace is excellent activating the 9 facing star. It needs water in the front.

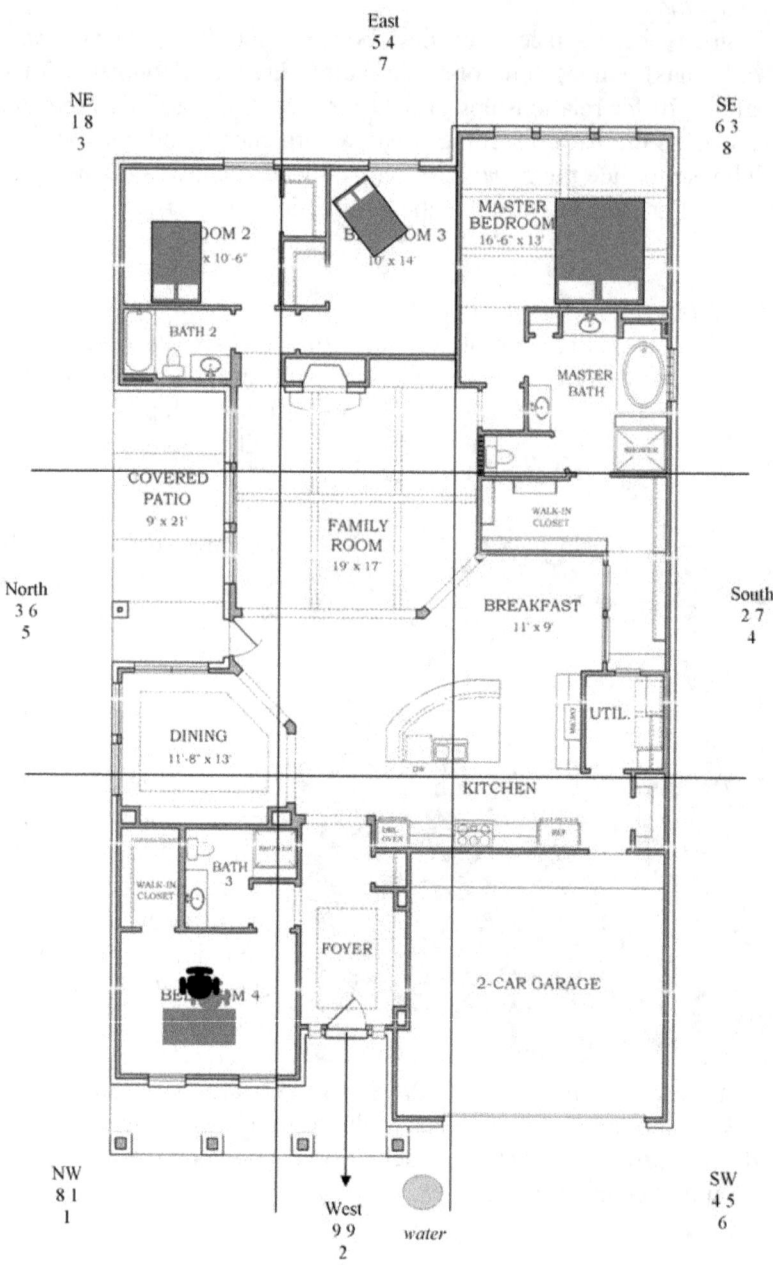

PERIOD 9

West 2 (262.6° to 277.5°) Facing name: **You** and the **Rooster**
West 3 (277.6° to 292.5°) Facing name: **Xin/Sin**
Chart: **Double Stars Meet at Sitting** *(Shuang Xing Dao Zuo)*

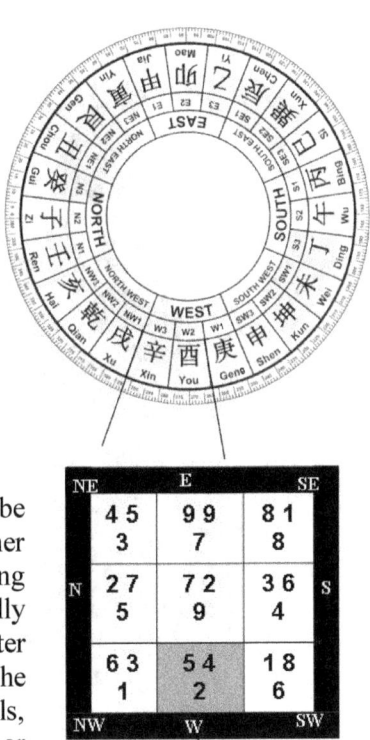

West 2 & 3

Activating the OUTDOORS
Install a Mountain and Water at Back

This property has the current prosperity and the most benevolent energy (9's) at the back known as the *Double Stars Meet at Sitting*. The West-facing homes produce dynamic individuals who will be successful and able to accumulate great wealth rather quickly. It also supports powerful politicians, outstanding academic achievements and super athletes. To fully capture this great energy, you will need to place a water feature and a mountain in the back garden. The 'mountain' can be higher ground, courtyard walls, landscape mounds, boulders (no sharp or jagged edges) or any combination (the mountain should be 3 feet or higher. Install a beautiful water feature such as a fountain, stream or Koi pond in the front as well. For those living in an apartment, high-rise building, townhome, condominium or a rented space and are not able to install a water feature outdoors, place one indoors in the recommended area. To activate the mountain in the recommended area, use a tall armoire, heavy bookcases or stone statues; these will sufficiently activate the energy.

Backyard Swimming Pools
If a swimming pool is desired, it should be located in the East but can also be located in the Southeast. Often, pool designs touch two sectors. Water in the Northeast (left-hand corner) of the backyard can activate disasters.

These Formations are Possible, Not Definite!
The **West 2** homes also have a possible *Eight Killing Forces* if there is mountain chi coming from the Southeast. A *Peach Blossom Sha* is activated with a road coming from the South. These homes also may have a *Robbery Mountain Sha* formation if there is a jagged cliff, electrical tower, huge dead tree, lamppost, or a broken mountain in the South. The **West 3** facing homes have a possible *Eight Roads of Destruction* formation if there is a road/driveway coming from and exiting the Northwest direction; these indicate money-loss. This direction also has a possible *Robbery Mountain Sha* in the Southwest.

Figure 27: If you are unable to place an outdoor fountain, you can install a wall fountain. This would activate the facing star as well as the mountain star if it were granite, slate, marble or other natural stone.

Activating the INDOORS
Move your Stuff!

Excellent Doors
Always use and activate good doors; the best ones for this chart are facing to the *East, Southeast, South* and *Southwest*. This applies to all exterior doors as well as an interior garage door used to enter the house. In modern homes, an interior garage door is often the main entry into the house, therefore it is extremely important! If there is an angled back door to the *Northeast*, you will need to cure it with metal. With daily use, it will activate a 5 facing star. See page 290 for cures used in Classical Feng Shui.

Master Bedroom + Family
There are two ways to health, harmony and prosperity in the bedroom and that is location and direction; the *direction* of the bed will give you the most powerful results. Locate the master bedroom in the *East, Southeast, Southwest or Northwest;* these sectors have good mountain stars. **Bed Directions:** Place the owner's/marital headboard/bed to the *East, Southeast, South, Southwest, or Northwest (all Guas)*. These bed directions have a good mountain *and* facing star combination with excellent energy. Use the above directions to place beds for all family members.

Family Room + Dining Room
In the dining room and family room, arrange your furniture so that you and family members can face *East, Southeast, South and Southwest*. These directions have the best energy of the house. No one should face *Northeast* in any room of the house.

Home Office + Study
Face your desk/body to the *East, Southeast, South and Southwest;* these directions have excellent energy and facing stars. Choose one of these facing directions coupled with your +80 to enhance health, +70 for relationships or +90 for wealth if possible. For example, if you are a 6 Gua, face to the Southwest; this is your +70 and would activate romance and wealth energy. If you are an 8 Gua, choose the Southwest, this is your +90 and it has wealth energy. For students, use the above directions to support learning and success in exams.

Stoves and Toilets
The best directions for the stove knobs, buttons, or controls are *East, Southeast, or Southwest*. You will struggle with money, health and relationships if there is a stove or toilet located in your +90, +80 or +70 sector of the house. The stove should not sit on either the North or West within the kitchen, it will cause money and health issues. Select a toilet located in one of your negative sectors of the house (-90, -80, -70, or -60). This section applies to the head/s of household or breadwinner.

Watchful Eye: *Three Killing Position*
The *Three Killings* position comes to the front of this house in 2027 and it is taboo to engage in deep digging, remodeling or demolition. Use good dates from the *Great Sun Formula* if you must touch this area.

PERIOD 9
Northwest 1 (292.6° to 307.5°)
Facing name: **Xu** and the **Dog**
Chart: **Double Stars Meet at Sitting** *(Shuang Xing Dao Zuo)*

Activating the OUTDOORS
Needs Mountain and Water at Back

This property has the current prosperity and the most benevolent energy (9's) at the back known as the *Double Stars Meet at Sitting*. When the landforms are good, the Northwest-facing properties can make people very rich indeed. To fully capture the fabulous potential of this chart, you will need a mountain and water at the back. The 'mountain' can be higher ground, landscape mounds, boulders (no sharp or jagged edges) or any combination (the mountain should be 3 feet or higher). Even smartly designed, tiered landscaping or a series of stacked terraces would work effectively. Place water at the back by installing a swimming pool, waterfall/pond, Koi pond, lake or spa. For those living in an apartment, high-rise building, townhome, condominium or a rented space and are not able to install a water feature outdoors, place one indoors in the recommended area. To activate the mountain in the recommended area, use a tall armoire, heavy bookcases or stone statues; these will sufficiently activate the energy.

Backyard Swimming Pools
If a swimming pool is desired, it should be located in the Southeast but can also be in the East (left-hand corner) of the backyard. However, the water should not be between 82.5° to 97.5° as it may activate affairs. Water in the South (right-hand corner) can activate disasters.

These Formations are Possible, Not Definite!
These homes may have a *Robbery Mountain Sha* formation if there is a jagged cliff, electrical tower, huge dead tree, lamppost, or a broken mountain in the *Southwest*; they indicate everyone in household getting an unusual disease, hurt by knives and disasters. You could also activate a *Peach Blossom Sha* if there is water or road in the *East*.

Flying Stars Feng Shui for Period 9 | 117

Figure 28: This Northwest 1 chart requires water and mountain at the back of the property. The pool pictured here would activate the facing star and a mountain such as boulders or even the pool house would activate the mountain star.

Activating the INDOORS
Move your Stuff!

Excellent Doors
Always use and activate good doors; the best ones for this chart are facing to the *North, Northeast, East and Southeast.* This applies to all exterior doors as well as an interior garage door used to enter the house. In modern homes, an interior garage door is often the main entry into the house, therefore it is extremely important! A South-facing door, in this chart has a 5 facing star; this would be an angled back door. Cure: If this is your only door to backyard, you will need to cure it with lots of metal next to or directly on the door. Brass, bronze, copper, pewter, and stainless steel are some high-vibrating metals to use, or large metal wind chimes.

Master Bedroom + Family
There are two ways to activate great energy in the bedroom and that is location and direction; the *direction* of the bed will give you the most powerful results. Locate the master bedroom in the *East, Southeast or West* as these rooms have good mountain stars.
Bed Directions: Place the owner's/marital headboard/bed to the *Southeast, East, West or North (all Guas).* These bed directions have a good mountain *and* facing star combination with excellent energy. Use the above directions to place beds for the family.

Family Room + Dining Room
In the dining room and family room, arrange your furniture so that you and family members can face *North, Northeast, East and Southeast*. These directions have the best energy of the house. No one should face *South* in any room of the house.

Home Office + Study
Place your desk/face to the *North, Northeast, East and Southeast* (all Guas). These directions have great facing stars with benevolent energy. Choose one of these facing directions coupled with your +80 to enhance health, +70 for relationships or +90 for wealth if possible. *For students, use the above directions to energize learning and success in exams.*

Stoves and Toilets
The best directions for the stove knobs, buttons, or controls are the *Northeast, East and Southeast*. If there is a stove or toilet located in your +90, +80 or +70 sector of the house, disharmony and money-loss are at a high risk. Select a toilet located in one of your negative sectors of the house (-90, -80, -70, or -60). *This section applies to the head/s of household or breadwinner.*

Watchful Eye: *Annual Stars*
This chart has two negative areas to pay attention to regarding health; in certain years they become more dangerous. They are the **South** (*5 facing star*) and the **Northwest** (*2 facing star*). The South becomes more serious in 2026, 2031 while the Northwest in 2026, 2032. No water *(pools, fountains, etc)* or fire *(stoves, fire place/pits or grills)* should be placed in either area, *no matter the year*; it will activate the negative energy in these areas!

How to Implement the Recommendations
On the next page you will find an example of how you might implement the recommendations for a Period 9 NW 1 house. The home has a 2 facing star at the front door and interior garage door and it will need to be cured with metal. The prosperous energy is at the back (SE) and will need water to counterbalance the sickness energy of the house. The stove sits on a 2 mountain star and also activates illness and disease if used daily. The kitchen should be remodeled so that the stove sits on West and faces the East. It could also sit NW and face SE. The master bed is best placed on the SE wall. Since it has windows the headboard should be at least 6 feet tall and of solid wood. While sitting in the office, face SE or East for the best money luck. The couple is a 1 Life Gua and 3 Life Gua.

Flying Stars Feng Shui for Period 9 | 119

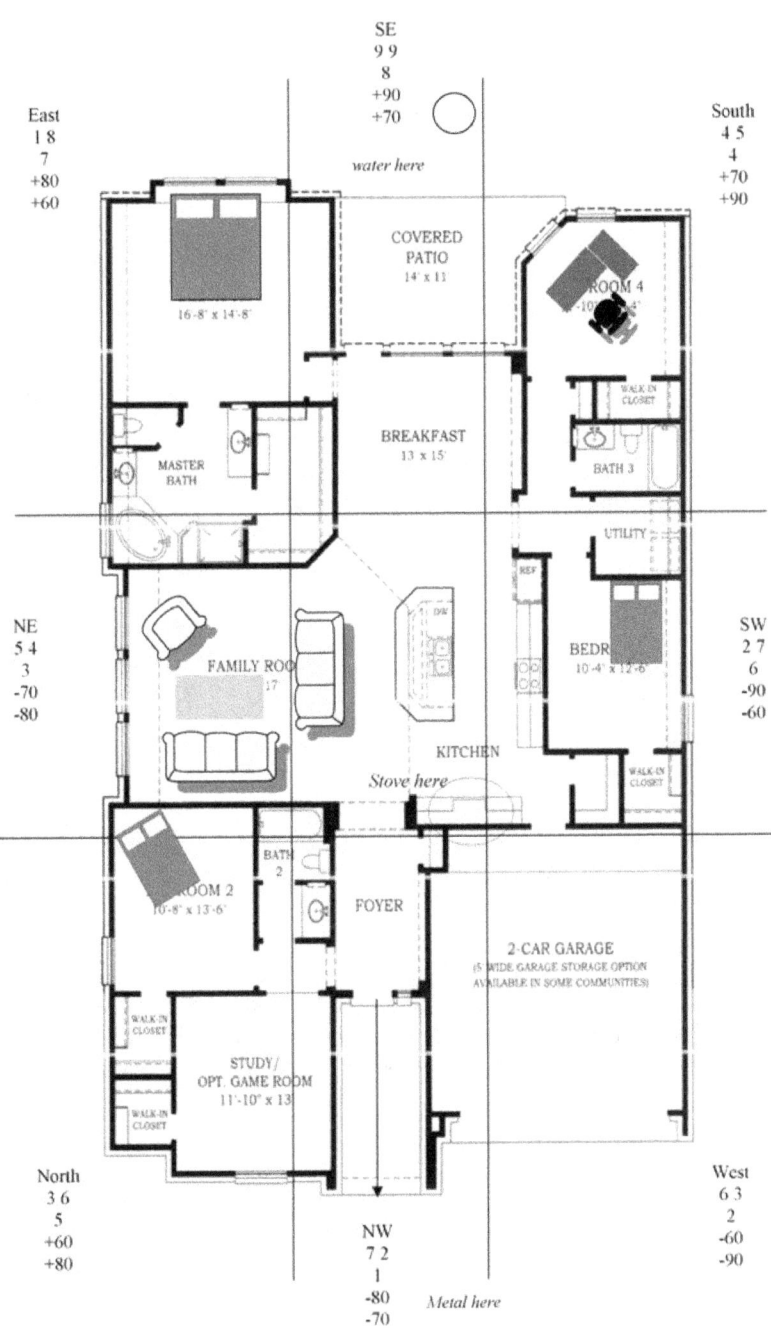

PERIOD 9

Northwest 2 *(307.6° to 322.5°)* Facing name: **Chien/Qian**
Northwest 3 *(322.6° to 337.5°)* Facing name: **Hai** and the **Pig**
Chart: **Double Stars Meet at Facing** *(Shuang Xing Dao Xiang)*

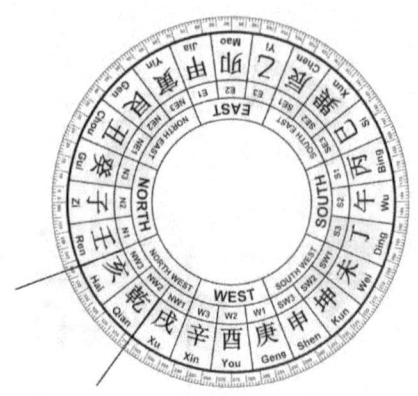

Activating the OUTDOORS
Needs Water and Mountain in Front

This is a very auspicious chart known as *Double Stars Meet at Facing*. When the landforms are good, the Northwest-facing properties can make people very rich indeed. To activate this chart properly, you will need both water and a mountain in the front. The water could be a large stone fountain, pond, or waterfall. The *mountain* could be landscaping mounds seen on golf courses, boulders (no sharp or jagged edges), courtyard walls, tall and heavy planter pots, basalt pillars, stone/brick fireplaces or other tall and heavy items (earth materials) in the front or near the front entrance. Trees cannot represent a mountain. For those living in an apartment, high-rise building, townhome, condominium or a rented space and are not able to install a water feature outdoors, place one indoors in the recommended area. To activate the mountain in the recommended area, use a tall armoire, heavy bookcases or stone statues; these will sufficiently activate the energy.

Backyard Swimming Pools
If a swimming pool is desired, the only location is the South (right-hand corner) and this is not ideal but does not harm the household. If placed in the Southeast (center), sickness will ensue and in the East (left-hand corner) it may activate lawsuits and lots of family disharmony.

These Formations are Possible, Not Definite!
For homes that face **Northwest 2,** there is a possible *Eight Roads of Destruction* if you have a road coming from/exiting from either the West or North directions. These homes also may have a *Robbery Mountain Sha* formation if there a jagged cliff, electrical tower, huge dead tree, lamppost, or a broken mountain in the North. For the **Northwest 3** facing homes if a mountain is located in the South you could have an *Eight Killing Forces*. A possible *Robbery Mountain Sha* in the West. A *Peach Blossom Sha* if water is in the North.

Activating the INDOORS
Move your Stuff!

Excellent Doors
Always use and activate good doors; the best ones for this chart are facing *Northwest, South, Southwest and West*. This applies to all exterior doors as well as an interior garage door used to enter the house. In modern homes, an interior garage door is often the main entry into the house, therefore it is extremely important.

Figure 29: Placing a tall, stone fountain in the front of this Period 9, NW 2 & 3 home would activate the 9 facing star as well as the 9 mountain star.

Master Bedroom + Family
There are two ways to activate great energy in the bedroom and that is location and direction. The *direction* of the bed will give you the most powerful results. Locate the master bedroom in the *Northwest (second floor), East, North or West* as these rooms all have good mountain stars. **Bed Directions:** Place the marital/owner's bed to the *Northwest, East, South or West* (all Guas). These bed directions have a good mountain *and* facing star combination with excellent energy. *Use the above directions when placing the bed for other family members.*

Family Room + Dining Room
In the dining room and family room, arrange your furniture so that you and family members can face *Northwest, South, Southwest and West*. These directions have the best energy of the house. No one should face *North*.

Home Office + Study
Face the *Northwest, South, Southwest and West* while sitting at your desk (all Guas). Choose one of these facing directions coupled with your +80 to enhance health, +70 for relationships or +90 for wealth if possible. For example if you are a 4 Gua, face the South as this is your health direction and has benevolent energy. *For students, use the above directions to energize learning and success in exams.*

Stoves and Toilets
The best directions for the stove knobs, buttons or controls are the *Northwest, Southwest and West.* as these are good facing stars. You will struggle with money, health and relationships if there is a stove or toilet located in your +90, +80 or +70 sector of the house. Choose a toilet in your negative sectors of the house (-90, -80, -70, or -60). *This section applies to the head/s of household or breadwinner.*

Watchful Eye: *Annual Stars*
This chart has two negative areas to pay attention that can harm money, health and harmony and in certain years they become more dangerous. They are the **North** (5 facing star) and the **Southeast** (2 facing star). The North becomes more serious in of 2027 and 2032; the Southeast in 2024 and 2026. If there are doors facing these directions, they will need to be cure with metal. No water *(pools, fountains, etc)* or fire *(stoves, fire place/pits or grills)* should be placed in either area, *no matter the year;* it will activate the negative energy in these areas!

PERIOD 9

North 1 (337.6° to 352.5°) Facing name: **Ren**
Chart: **Double Stars Meet at Sitting** *(Shuang Xing Dao Zuo)*

Activating the OUTDOORS
Install Water and Mountain at Back

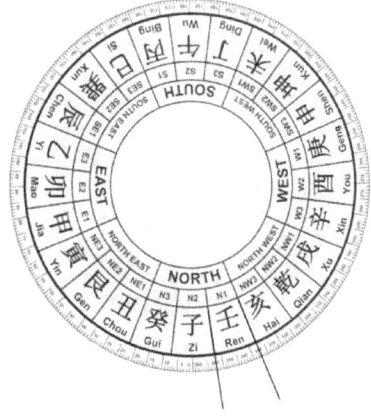

This property has the two 9 stars at the back known as *Double Stars Meet at Sitting.* The North-facing properties indicate success, charismatic people, and wealth luck. In order for this chart to support health and money, it's very important to install a water feature and a 'mountain' in the back garden. The 'mountain' can be higher ground, landscape mounds, boulders (no sharp or jagged edges) or any combination (the mountain should be 3 feet or higher). Even smartly designed, tiered landscaping or a series of stacked terraces would work brilliantly. Place water at the back by installing a swimming pool, waterfall/pond, Koi pond, lake or spa. For those living in an apartment, high-rise building, townhome, condominium or a rented space and are not able to install a water feature outdoors, place one indoors in the recommended area. To activate the mountain in the recommended area, use a tall armoire, heavy bookcases or stone statues; these will sufficiently activate the energy.

Backyard Swimming Pools
If a swimming pool is desired, it should be located in the South but can touch the Southeast as well if you there are teachers, writers or those who have a public persona other water in the Southeast may cause affairs. Water in the Southwest (right-hand corner) will activate sickness, disease and constant aliments.

These Formations are Possible, Not Definite!
There is a possible *Eight Roads of Destruction* with this facing if there is a road coming from/exiting the Northwest direction; they are famous for bringing money-loss and disasters. These homes also may have a *Robbery Mountain Sha* formation if there is a jagged cliff, electrical tower, huge dead tree, lamppost, or a broken mountain in the West; they indicate everyone in household getting an unusual disease, hurt by knives and disasters.

Figure 30: This chart needs a mountain and water at the back of the property. Installing a brick wall with mini-waterfalls as shown in this photo would activate both.

Activating the INDOORS
Move your Stuff!

Excellent Doors
Always use and activate good doors; the best ones for this chart are facing to the *North, Northeast, Southeast, South, and Northwest*. This applies to all exterior doors as well as an interior garage door used to enter the house. In modern homes, an interior garage door is often the main entry into the house, therefore it is extremely important!

Master Bedroom + Family
There are two ways to activate great energy in the bedroom and that is location and direction; the *direction* of the bed will give you the most powerful results. Locate the master bedroom in the *South, Northwest North or Northeast* sectors of the house as they are good mountain stars. **Bed Directions:** Place your headboard/bed to the *North, South, Northwest, East or Northeast*. These bed directions have a good mountain *and* facing star combination with excellent energy. Take special care regarding the West; do not use if at all possible. If the master bedroom is already located there, make sure that the bed direction is not also West. If so, reposition immediately; activating this direction activates all types of sickness and disease. Use the above directions when placing the bed for other family members.

Family Room + Dining Room
In the dining room and family room, arrange your furniture so that you and family members can face *North, Northeast, Southeast, South, and Northwest*. These directions have the best energy of the house.

Home Office + Study
Place your desk/face to *North, Northeast, Southeast, South, and Northwest* (all Guas). Choose one of these facing directions coupled with your +80 to enhance health, +70 for relationships or +90 for wealth if possible. For example, if you are a 6 Gua, face to the Northeast, it has wealth energy; furthermore it indicates being protected by 'the doctor from heaven' and 'unexpected wealth from the heavens'. For students, use the above directions to energize learning and success in exams.

Stoves and Toilets
The best directions for the stove knobs, buttons or controls are, *Northeast, Southeast, and South;* they have good facing stars. You will struggle with money, health and relationships if there is a stove or toilet located in your +90, +80 or +70 sector of the house. Select a toilet located in one of your negative sectors of the house (-90, -80, -70, or -60). *This section applies to the head/s of household or breadwinner.*

Watchful Eye: Annual and Three Killings
This chart has one negative area to pay attention to regarding health; in certain years they become more dangerous. It is the *Southwest* (2 facing star) and becomes worse in 2024. Cure this with high quality metal. No water *(pools, fountains, etc)* or fire *(stoves, fire place/pits or grills)* should be placed in this area, *no matter the year;* it will activate the negative energy there! Also the Three Killings visits the North in 2026, 2028. It is taboo to engage in demolition, construction or deep digging.

How to Implement the Recommendations
On the next page you will find an example of how you might implement the recommendations for a Period 9, North 1 home. The prosperous energy is at the back and will need water. The front door and interior garage door have good energy. The stove is excellent as it sits on the 8 mountain star and activate the 9 facing star. The master bed should be placed on either the North or South wall. Face South while sitting in the home office. Arrange the living room furniture so that you mainly sit either North or South. The fireplace is good and activates romance, travel and studies. Keeping things simple, these recommendations are good no matter the Life Gua. There can be no water or fire in the Southwest as it will activate disease and sickness in the household.

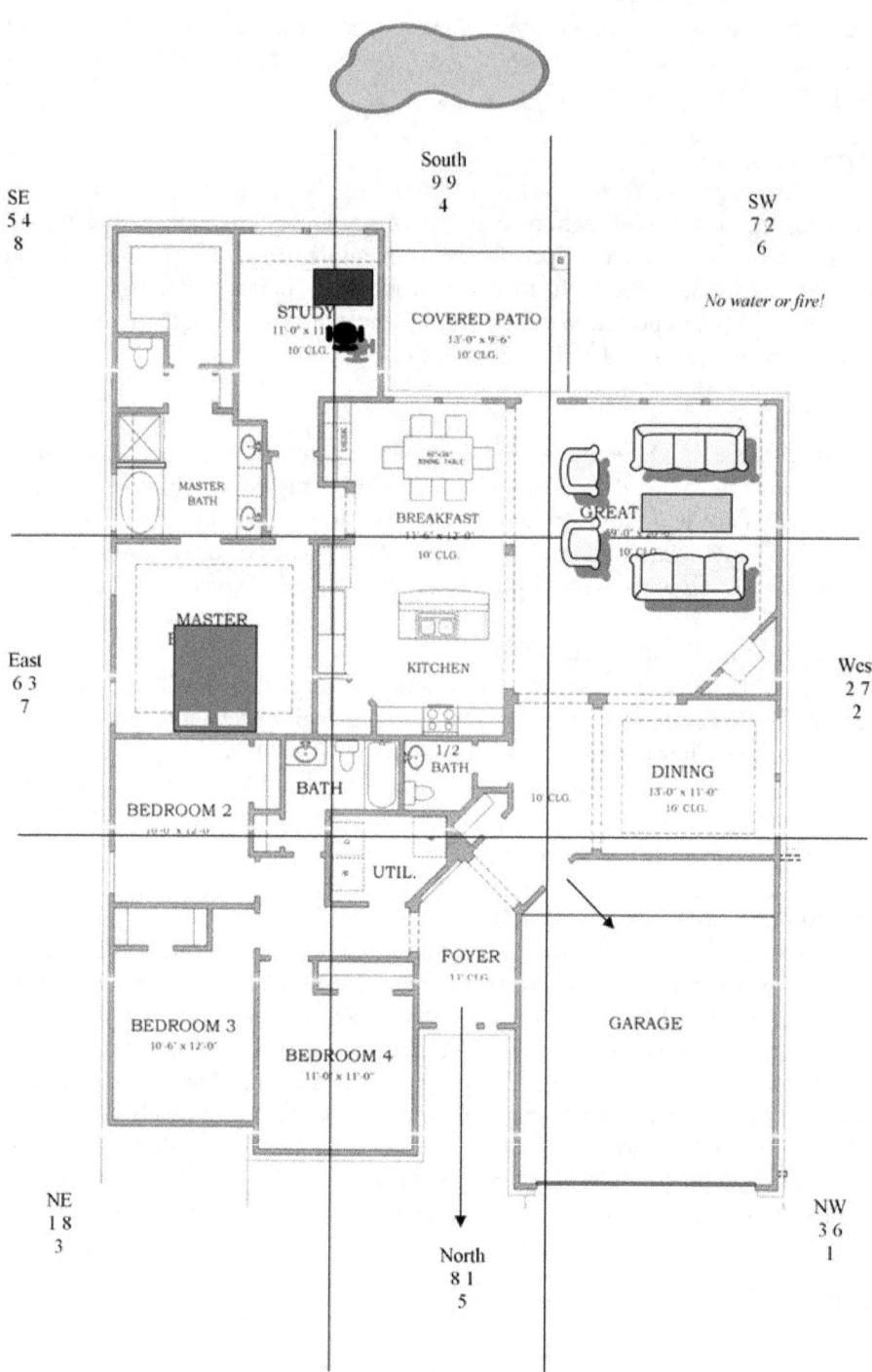

PERIOD 9

North 2 (352.6° to 7.5°) Facing name: **Tzi/Zi** and the **Rat**
North 3 (7.6° to 22.5) Facing name: **Kwei/Gui**
Chart: **Double Stars Meet at Facing** (*Shuang Xing Dao Xiang*)

Activating the OUTDOORS
Needs Mountain and Water in Front

This chart has the two 9's in the front known as *Double Stars Meet at Facing*. The North-facing properties indicate success, charismatic people, and wealth luck. It also brings the occupants success in business and business relationships that will take them all over the world. To fully capture the most benevolent energy and activate health, wealth and harmony, place big water and a 'mountain' in the front of the home. For those living in an apartment, high-rise building, townhome, condominium or a rented space and are not able to install a water feature outdoors, place one indoors in the recommended area. To activate the mountain in the recommended area, use a tall armoire, heavy bookcases or stone statues; these will sufficiently activate the energy.

North 2 & 3

Backyard Swimming Pools
If a swimming pool is desired, it can be located anywhere in the backyard, although the South and Southwest sectors are the best (center and right-hand corner). Many pool designs touch two sectors.

These Formations are Possible, Not Definite!
The **North 2** properties may have a *Robbery Mountain Sha* formation if there a jagged cliff, electrical tower, huge dead tree, lamppost, or a broken mountain in the West. A *Peach Blossom Sha* is activated by real water or a road coming from the West. For homes that face **North 3**, there is a possible *Eight Roads of Destruction* if you have a road/driveway coming from and exiting the Northeast direction. These homes also may have a *Robbery Mountain Sha* formation if there is a jagged cliff, electrical tower, huge dead tree, lamppost, or a broken mountain in the Northeast.

Activating the INTERIOR Environment
Move your Stuff!

Excellent Doors
Always use and activate good doors; the best ones for this chart are facing to the *North, Southeast, South, Southwest, and Northwest*. This applies to all exterior doors as well as an interior garage door used to enter the house. In modern homes, an interior garage door is often the main entry into the house, therefore it is extremely important! An angled front door towards the *Northeast* (2 facing star) can cause sickness; cure with high quality metal.

Master Bedroom + Family
There are two ways to activate great energy in the bedroom and that is location and direction; the *direction* of the bed will give you the most powerful results. Locate the master bedroom in the *North, South, Southwest and West* as all of these areas have good mountain stars. **Bed Directions:** Place the marital/owner's bed towards the *North, Southwest, South, Southwest or West*. These bed directions have a good mountain *and* facing star combination with excellent energy. Use the above directions when placing the bed for other family members.

Figure 31: Install a tall fountain in the front of this house to fully capture the energy of this chart. If it's tall and made from stone, concrete or granite it will also activate the 'mountain' star.

Family Room + Dining Room
In the dining room and family room, arrange your furniture so that you and family members can face *North, Southeast, South, Southwest, and Northwest.*. These directions have the best energy of the house.

Home Office + Study
While sitting at your desk, face *North, Southeast, South, Southwest, and Northwest*. Choose one of these facing directions coupled with your +80 to enhance health, +70 for relationships or +90 for wealth if possible. For example, if you are a 4 Gua, face the South, it has wealth energy and it's your +80; this arrangement indicates recognition at work or a promotion and good health. *For students, use the above directions to energize learning and success in exams.*

Stoves and Toilets
The best directions for the stove knobs, buttons or controls are the *North, South, Southwest, and Northwest.* You will struggle with money, health and relationships if there is a stove or toilet located in your +90, +80 or +70 sector of the house. Select a toilet located in one of your negative sectors of the house (-90, -80, -70, or -60). *This section applies to the head/s of household or breadwinner.*

Watchful Eye: *Annual Stars and Three Killings*
This chart has one negative area to pay attention to regarding health; in certain years they become more dangerous. It is the *Northeast* (2 facing star) and becomes worse in 2025. Cure this with high quality metal. No water *(pools, fountains, etc)* or fire *(stoves, fire place/pits or grills)* should be placed in this area, *no matter the year;* it will activate the negative energy there! Also the Three Killings visits the North in 2026 and it is taboo to engage in demolition, construction or deep digging.

The Three Killings positions changes locations every year. It is taboo to engage in construction, demolition or deep digging such as a swimming pool. For this home, it visits the front of the front (North) in 2026.

PERIOD 9

Northeast 1 *(22.6° to 37.5°)*
Facing name: **Chou** and the **Ox**
Chart: **Double Stars Meet at Sitting** *(Shuang Xing Dao Zuo)*

Activating the OUTDOORS
Install Water and Mountain at Back

This property has the two 9 stars at the back known as *Double Stars Meet at Sitting*. These properties can enjoy prosperity and nobility. In order for this chart to support health, relationships and money, it's very important to install a water feature and a 'mountain' in the back garden. The 'mountain' can be higher ground, landscape mounds, boulders (no sharp or jagged edges) or any combination (the mountain should be 3 feet or higher). Even smartly designed, tiered landscaping or a series of stacked terraces would work brilliantly. Place water at the back by installing a swimming pool, waterfall/pond, Koi pond, lake or spa.

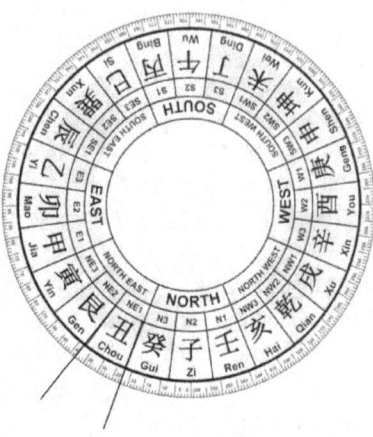

Northeast 1

For those living in an apartment, high-rise building, townhome, condominium or a rented space and are not able to install a water feature outdoors, place one indoors in the recommended area. To activate the mountain in the recommended area, use a tall armoire, heavy bookcases or stone statues; these will sufficiently activate the energy.

Backyard Swimming Pools
If a swimming pool is desired, it should be located in the Southwest. If a bit of the pool design touches the South, it will not harm the occupants. Water in the West (right-hand corner) can activate disasters.

These Formations are Possible, Not Definite!
These sites may also have a *Robbery Mountain Sha* formation if there is a jagged cliff, electrical tower, huge dead tree, lamppost, or a broken mountain in the North; they indicate that everyone in household getting an unusual disease, hurt by knives and disasters. A *Peach Blossom Sha* is activated with a road coming from the South famous for causing affairs and sexual misconduct.

Figure 32: This Period 9, Northeast 1 chart needs a mountain and water at the back of the property. The water feature pictured here would fulfill both criteria.

Activating the INDOORS
Move your Stuff!

Excellent Doors
Always use and activate good doors; the best ones for this chart are facing to the *Southwest, North, Northeast, or East*. This applies to all exterior doors as well as an interior garage door used to enter the house. In modern homes, an interior garage door is often the main entry into the house, therefore it is extremely important!

Master Bedroom + Family
There are two ways to activate great energy in the bedroom and that is location and direction. The *direction* of the bed will give you the most powerful results. Locate the master bedroom in the *East, Southwest or North* sectors of the house as these areas all have good mountain stars. **Bed Directions:** Place the marital/owner's bed to the *Southwest, North, Northeast or East*. These bed directions have a good mountain *and* facing star combination with excellent energy. Use the above directions when placing the bed for other family members.

Family Room + Dining Room
In the dining room and family room, arrange your furniture so that you and family members can face *Southwest, North, Northeast, or East*. No one should face to the *West* in any room of the house.

Home Office + Study
While sitting at your desk, face *Southwest, North, Northeast, or East*. Choose one of these facing directions coupled with your +80 to enhance health, +70 for relationships or +90 for wealth if possible. For example if you are an 8 Gua face the *Southwest*, it has strong wealth energy. For students, use the above directions to energize learning and success in exams.

Stoves and Toilets
The stove knobs, buttons or controls should face *Southwest, North, or East*. If there is a stove or toilet located in your +90, +80 or +70 sector of the house, health and money-loss are at a high risk. Select a toilet located in one of your negative sectors of the house (-90, -80, -70, or -60). *This section applies to the head/s of household or breadwinner.*

Watchful Eye: *Annual Stars*
This chart has one negative area to pay attention regarding money and health. It is the *West* (5 facing star) and can be worse in 2024. No water *(pools, fountains, etc)* or fire *(stoves, fire place/pits or grills)* should be placed in this area, *no matter the area*, it gets activated!

Figure 33: Arrange the family room so that people will face Southwest, North, Northeast or East while watching TV, reading or working on their phones or laptops.

Period 9, NE 1 6 Life Gua. The house needs water at the back. Water should not be located in the West, it will attract disasters. The stove is good suppressing the 7 mountain star and activating the 4 facing star. The master bed should be placed on the SW wall. Desks can face SW or East. The front door has good energy. Arrange the living room so that the family can face NE, SW, East, NW or North.

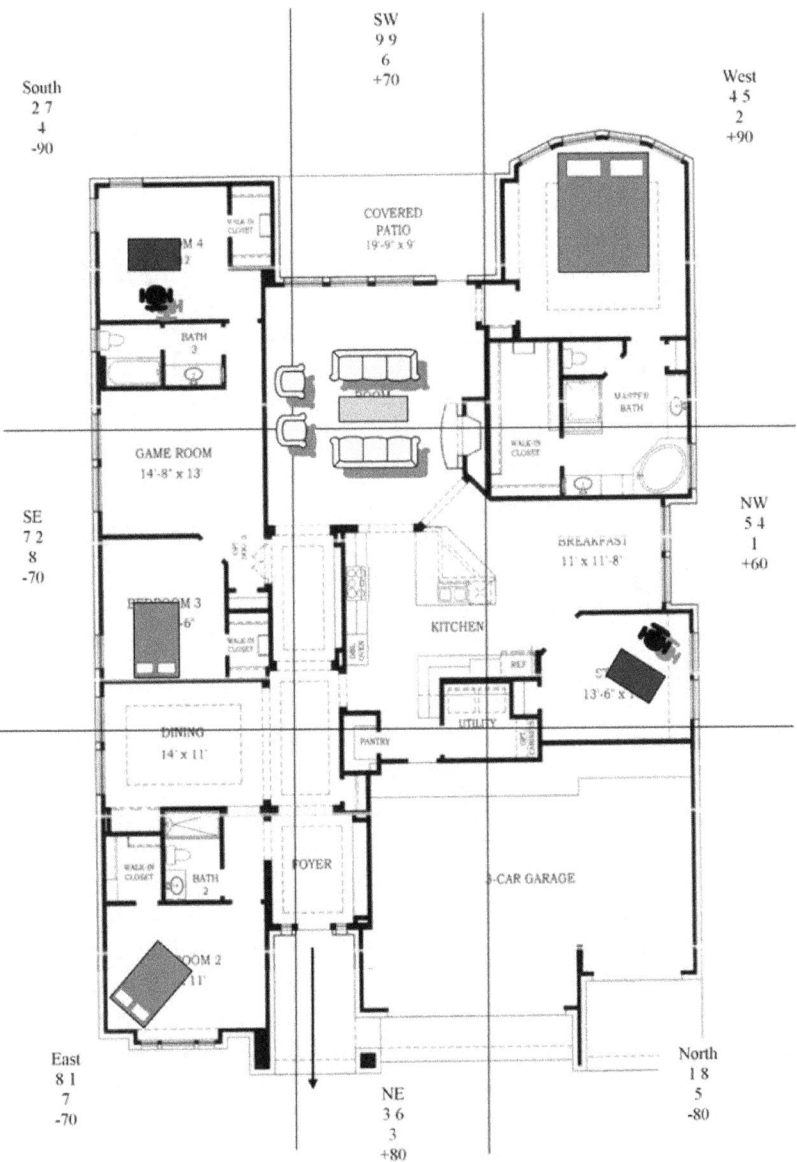

PERIOD 9

Northeast 2 *(37.6° to 52.5°)* Facing name: **Gen/Ken**
Northeast 3 *(52.6° to 67.5°)* Facing name: **Yin** and the **Tiger**
Chart: **Double Stars Meet at Facing** *(Shuang Xing Dao Xiang)*

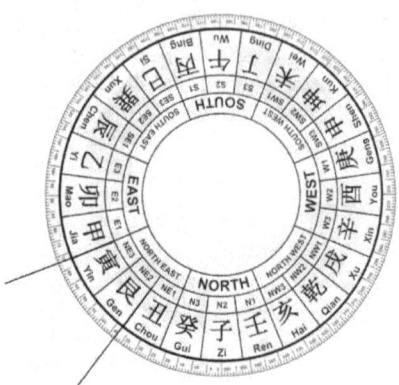

Activating the OUTDOORS
Install a Mountain and Water in Front

This chart has the two 9's in the front known as *Double Stars Meet at Facing*. The Northeast-facing properties indicate prosperity and nobility. To activate this chart properly, you will need both water and a mountain in the front. The water could be a large stone fountain, pond, or waterfall. The 'mountain' can be higher ground, landscape mounds, boulders (no sharp or jagged edges) or any combination (the mountain should be 3 feet or higher). For those living in an apartment, high-rise building, townhome, condominium or a rented space and are not able to install a water feature outdoors, place one indoors in the recommended area. To activate the mountain in the recommended area, use a tall armoire, heavy bookcases or stone statues; these will sufficiently activate the energy.

Backyard Swimming Pools
If a swimming pool is desired, it can be located anywhere in the backyard. However, the South or West corners will bring the best luck. In the South, the water cannot be between 176.6° to 187.5° or it may activate affairs.

These Formations are Possible, Not Definite!
For homes facing **Northeast 2** there is a possible *Eight Roads of Destruction* if you have a road/driveway coming from and exiting the North and East directions. These properties may also have a *Robbery Mountain Sha* formation if there is a jagged cliff, electrical tower, huge dead tree, lamppost, or a broken mountain in the East; they indicate everyone in household getting an unusual disease, hurt by knives and disasters. For the **Northeast 3** facing properties there is a possible *Eight Killing Forces* if there is a real mountain in front of the property on the left-hand side (Northeast). A *Peach Blossom Sha* is activated with a road coming from the South famous for causing affairs and sexual misconduct. There is also a possible *Robbery Mountain Sha* in the North.

Figure 34: Installing a water feature using front courtyard walls would active both the 9 mountain star as well as the 9 facing star.

Activating the INDOORS
Move your Stuff!

Excellent Doors
Always use and activate good doors; the best ones for this chart are facing to the *Northeast, South, Southwest and West*. This applies to all exterior doors as well as an interior garage door used to enter the house. In modern homes, an interior garage door is often the main entry into the house, therefore it is extremely important! If there is an angled front door to the *East*, it will need to be cured with high-quality metal.

Master Bedroom + Family
There are two ways to activate great energy in the bedroom and that is location and direction. The *direction* of the bed will give you the most powerful results. Locate the master bedroom in the *Northeast, South or West* as these areas have good mountain stars. **Bed Directions:** Place the marital/owner's bed to the *Northeast, South Southwest or West* (all Guas). These bed directions have a good mountain *and* facing star combination with excellent energy. Use the above directions when placing the bed for other family members.

Family Room + Dining Room
In the dining room and family room, arrange your furniture so that you and family members can face *Northeast, South, Southwest and West*. These directions have the best energy of the house. No one should face *East* in any room of the house.

Home Office + Study
While sitting at your desk, face *Northeast, South, Southwest and West* (all Guas). Choose one of these facing directions coupled with your +80 to enhance health, +70 for relationships or +90 for wealth if possible. For example if you are a 7 Gua face the *Northeast* with prosperous energy. It is also your +90 money direction. For students, use the above directions to energize learning and success in exams.

Stoves and Toilets
The best directions for the stove knobs, buttons or controls are *Northeast, South,* and *West*. You will struggle with money, health and relationships if there is a stove or toilet located in your +90, +80 or +70 sector of the house. Select a toilet located in one of your negative sectors of the house (-90, -80, -70, or -60). *This section applies to the head/s of household or breadwinner.*

Watchful Eye: *Annual Stars*
This chart has one negative area to pay attention regarding money and health. It is the **East** (5 facing star) and gets worse in 2025, 2029. Cure this area with high quality metal. No water *(pools, fountains, etc)* or fire *(stoves, fire place/pits or grills)* should be placed in this area, *no matter the year*, it gets activated!

PERIOD 9

East 1 *(67.6° to 82.5°)* Facing name: **Jia**
Chart: **Double Stars Meet at Sitting** *(Shuang Xing Dao Zuo)*

Activating the OUTDOORS
Install Water and Mountain at Back

This property has the two 9 stars at the back known as *Double Stars Meet at Sitting*. These properties can produce residents with high academic achievements or great success in the educational field. To fully extract the best energy you will need to install a water feature and a 'mountain' in the back garden. The 'mountain' can be higher ground, landscape mounds, boulders (no sharp or jagged edges) or any combination (the mountain should be 3 feet or higher). Even smartly designed, tiered landscaping or a series of stacked terraces would work brilliantly. Place water at the back by installing a swimming pool, waterfall/pond, Koi pond, lake or hot tub/spa. For those living in an apartment, high-rise building, townhome, condominium or a rented space and are not able to install a water feature outdoors, place one indoors in the recommended area. To activate the mountain in the recommended area, use a tall armoire, heavy bookcases or stone statues; these will sufficiently activate the energy.

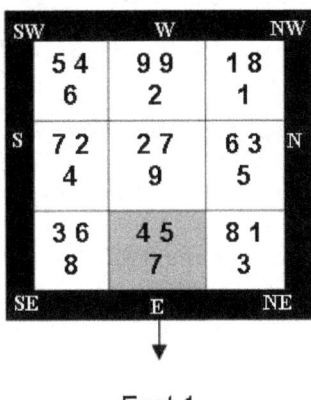

East 1

Backyard Swimming Pools
If a swimming pool is desired, it should be located in the West (center) but the Northwest is also excellent. Often pool designs touch two sectors.

These Formations are Possible, Not Definite!
There is a possible *Eight Roads of Destruction* formation if you have a road/driveway coming from and exiting the Northeast direction; they are notorious for bringing illness, bankruptcy, and divorce. There is also a possible *Robbery Mountain Sha* formation if there a jagged cliff, electrical tower, huge dead tree, lamppost, or a broken mountain in the South; they indicate everyone in household getting an unusual disease, hurt by knives and disasters.

Figure 35: This Period 9, East 1 chart requires water and a mountain at the back of the property. While a pool would activate the water, a 'mountain' is needed. Trees *cannot* represent a mountain.

Activating the INDOORS
Move your Stuff!

Excellent Doors
Always use and activate good doors; the best ones for this chart are facing to the *West, Northwest, Northeast, and Southeast.* This applies to all exterior doors as well as an interior garage door used to enter the house. In modern homes, an interior garage door is often the main entry into the house, therefore it is extremely important! Unfortunately, if the front door faces *East* it has the evil 5 facing star and its energy can attract all types of disasters. If this is a well-used door, you will need to cure it with lots of metal next to or directly on the door. Brass, bronze, copper, pewter, and stainless steel are some high-vibrating metals to use, or large metal wind chimes.

Master Bedroom + Family
There are two ways to activate great energy in the bedroom and that is location and direction; the *direction* of the bed will give you the most powerful results. Locate the master bedroom in the *West, Northwest, North, or Northeast* as these areas have good mountain stars with great energy. **Bed Directions:** Place the marital/owner's headboard/bed to the *West, Northwest, North, Northeast or Southeast* (all Guas). These

bed directions have a good mountain *and* facing star combination with superior energy. Use the above directions when placing the bed for other family members.

Family Room + Dining Room
In the dining room and family room, arrange your furniture so that you and family members can face *West, Northwest, Northeast, and Southeast*. These directions have the best energy of the house. No one should face *East* in any room of the house.

Home Office + Study
While sitting at your desk, face to the *West, Northwest, Northeast, or Southeast* (all Guas) these directions have good facing stars that will support many opportunities. Choose one of these facing directions coupled with your +80 to enhance health, +70 for relationships or +90 for wealth if possible. For example, if you are a 1 Gua, choose the *Southeast* it has good energy and it's your +90. *For students, use the above directions to energize learning and success in exams.*

Stoves and Toilets
The best directions for the stove knobs, buttons or controls to face are to the *West, Northwest, Northeast, and Southeast*. You will struggle with money, health and relationships if there is a stove or toilet located in your +90, +80 or +70 sector of the house. Select a toilet located in one of your negative sectors of the house (-90, -80, -70, or -60). *This section applies to the head/s of household or breadwinner.*

Watchful Eye: *Annual Stars and Three Killings*
This chart has two negative areas to pay attention to regarding health; in certain years they become more dangerous. They are the **East** (5 facing) and the **South** (2 facing). The *East* becomes more serious in 2025, 2029, 2032 and the *South* in 2026, 2031. Cure with high quality metal. No water *(pools, fountains, etc)* or fire *(stoves, fire place/pits or grills)* should be placed in either area, *no matter the year*; it will activate the negative energy in these areas!

Also the Three Killings visits the East in 2025 and 2029. It is taboo to engage in demolition, construction or deep digging. If you must touch this area, use the Great Sun Formula to protect against bad luck.

How to Implement the Recommendations
On the next page you will find an example of how you might implement the recommendations for a Period 9, East 1 home for any Life Gua. The stove is good as it burns up the 7 mountain star, but it would be better as a stove top with right-handed knobs activating the 9 facing star. Water is needed at the back. The front door with a 5 facing star should be cured with metal and not used more than 1% of the time. The angled Northeast-facing interior garage door is excellent with the 1 facing star and should be used 99% of the time.

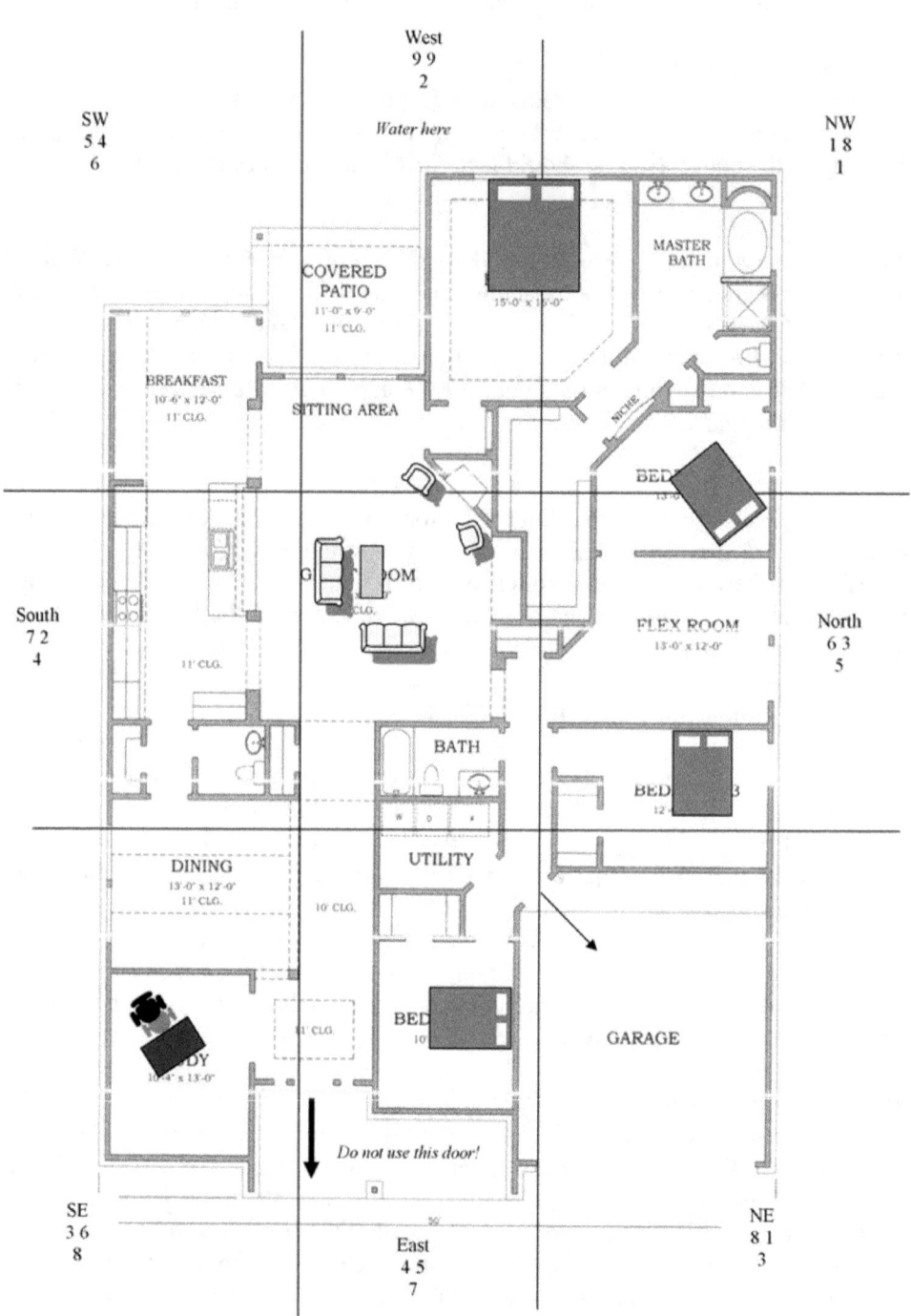

PERIOD 9

East 2 *(82.6° to 97.5°)* Facing name: **Mao** and the **Rabbit**
East 3 *(97.6° to 112.5°)* Facing name: **Yi**
Chart: **Double Stars Meet at Facing** *(Shuang Xing Dao Xiang)*

Activating the OUTDOORS
Install Mountain and Water in Front

This chart has the two 9's in the front known as *Double Stars Meet at Facing*. The East-facing properties can produce righteous, charismatic, loyal, faithful professionals such as doctors, lawyers, and philosophers who are both wealthy and noble. To activate this chart properly, you will need both water and a mountain in the front. The water could be a large stone fountain, pond, or waterfall. The 'mountain' can be higher ground, landscape mounds, boulders (no sharp or jagged edges) or any combination (the mountain should be 3 feet or higher). For those living in an apartment, high-rise building, townhome, condominium or a rented space and are not able to install a water feature outdoors, place one indoors in the recommended area. To activate the mountain in the recommended area, use a tall armoire, heavy bookcases or stone statues; these will sufficiently activate the energy.

East 2 & 3

Backyard Swimming Pools
If a swimming pool is desired, it should be located in the Southwest for the best results. Water in the West (center) can activate all types of disasters.

These Formations are Possible, Not Definite!
For homes facing **East 2** there is a possible *Eight Killings* formation if there is a mountain from the Southwest direction noted for activating blood-related accidents. A *Peach Blossom Sha* is activated with a road coming from the North famous for causing affairs and sexual misconduct. For homes that face to **East 3,** there is a possible *Eight Roads of Destruction* if there is a road/driveway coming from and exiting from the Southeast direction. There is also a possible *Robbery Mountain Sha* formation if there a jagged cliff, electrical tower, huge dead tree, lamppost, or a broken mountain in the Northeast for *both* East 2 and East 3 homes.

Figure 36: This chart needs a mountain and water at the front. A stone, tall fountain featured in this photo would active both 9's.

Activating the INDOORS
Move your Stuff!

Excellent Doors
Always use and activate good doors; the best ones for this chart are facing *East, Southeast, Southwest, Northeast and Northwest*. This applies to all exterior doors as well as an interior garage door used to enter the house. In modern homes, an interior garage door is often the main entry into the house, therefore it is extremely important! If you have a North-facing front or interior garage door or West-facing backdoor, you will need to cure it with high quality metal such as brass, bronze, copper, pewter, and stainless steel. See page 290 for ideas on metal cures.

Master Bedroom + Family:
There are two ways to activate great energy in the bedroom and that is location and direction; the *direction* of the bed will give you the most powerful results. Locate the bedrooms in the *East, Southeast, South, or Southwest* as these areas have good mountain stars. **Bed Directions:** Place the marital/owner's bed to the *East (upstairs), Southeast, South, Southwest or Northwest*. These directions have a good facing *and* mountain star combination that will enhance health, prosperity and harmony in the house. Use the above directions when placing the bed for other family members.

Family Room + Dining Room
In the dining room and family room, arrange your furniture so that you and family members can face *East, Southeast, Southwest, Northeast or Northwest*. These directions have the best energy of the house. No one should face *West* (5 facing star).

Home Office + Study
While sitting at your desk, face *East, Southeast, Southwest, Northeast* or *Northwest*. These directions have great facing stars/energy and support all Guas. Choose one of these facing directions coupled with your +80 to enhance health, +70 for relationships or +90 for wealth if possible. For example, if you are a 4 Gua, Southeast is your +60 and it has wonderful wealth energy. For students, use the above directions to energize learning and success in exams.

Stoves and Toilets
The best directions for the stove knobs, buttons or controls are *East, Southeast, Northeast or Southwest* these directions activate great facing stars. You will struggle with money, health and relationships if there is a stove or toilet located in your +90, +80 or +70 sector of the house. Select a toilet located in one of your negative sectors of the house (-90, -80, -70, or -60). *This section applies to the head/s of household or breadwinner.*

Watchful Eye: *Annual Stars and Three Killings*
This chart has two negative areas to pay attention to regarding health; in certain years they become more dangerous. They are the **North** (2 facing) and the **West** (5 facing). The *North* becomes more serious in 2027, 2032 and the *West* in 2024, 2027. No water *(pools, fountains, etc)* or fire *(stoves, fire place/pits or grills)* should be placed in either area, *no matter the year*; it will activate the negative energy! The Three Killings visits the East in 2029 as does the 5 Yellow Star. Use the Great Sun Formula if you must touch this area. Use metal to cure the 5 for that year; see metal cure ideas on page 290.

PERIOD 9

Southeast 1 *(112.6° to 127.5°)* Facing name: **Chen** and the **Dragon**
Chart: **Double Stars Meet at Facing** *(Shuang Xing Dao Xiang)*

Activating the OUTDOORS
Install Mountain and Water in Front

This chart has the two 9's in the front known as *Double Stars Meet at Facing*. These Southeast-facing properties can produce great talent in all sports, including martial arts. The children of this house may also excel in sciences, especially those requiring technical expertise. To activate this chart properly, you will need both water and a mountain in the front. The water could be a large stone fountain, pond, or waterfall. The 'mountain' can be higher ground, landscape mounds, boulders (no sharp or jagged edges) or any combination (the mountain should be 3 feet or higher). For those living in an apartment, high-rise building, townhome, condominium or a rented space and are not able to install a water feature outdoors, place one indoors in the recommended area. To activate the mountain in the recommended area, use a tall armoire, heavy bookcases or stone statues; these will sufficiently activate the energy.

Southeast 1

Backyard Swimming Pools
If a swimming pool is desired, it should be located in West (left-hand corner). While not ideal it will not harm the occupants. Water in the West should not be between 262.6° to 277.5° as it may cause affairs.

These Formations are Possible, Not Definite!
An *Eight Killings* formation is possible if there is a mountain bringing energy to the house from the North direction. A *Peach Blossom Sha* is activated with a road coming from the West famous for causing affairs and sexual misconduct. There is also a possible *Robbery Mountain Sha* formation if there a jagged cliff, electrical tower, huge dead tree, lamppost, or a broken mountain in the Northeast; they indicate everyone in household getting an unusual disease, hurt by knives and disasters.

Flying Stars Feng Shui for Period 9 | 145

Figure 37: This Period 9, Southeast 1 chart needs a mountain and water in the front. A tall stone fountain would activate the double 9's beautifully.

Activating the INDOORS

Excellent Doors
Always use and activate great doors; for this chart they are facing to the *South, Southeast, West and East*. This applies to all exterior doors as well as an interior garage door used to enter the house. In modern homes, an interior garage door is often the main entry into the house, therefore it is extremely important! If you have a door that faces either *Northeast* or *Southwest*, you will need to cure it with high quality metal such as brass, bronze, copper, pewter, and stainless steel. See page 290 for ideas for metal cures.

Master Bedroom + Family
There are two ways to activate great energy in the bedroom and that is location and direction; the *direction* of the bed will give you the most powerful results. Locate the master bedroom in the *North, East or Southeast* (second floor) as these areas have good mountain stars. **Bed Directions:** Place the marital/owner's headboard/bed to the *Southeast, West, North* or *East*. These bed directions have a good mountain *and* facing star combination with excellent energy. Use the above directions when placing the bed for other family members.

Family Room + Dining Room
In the dining room and family room, arrange your furniture so that you and family members can face *South, Southeast, West and East.* These directions have the best energy of the house. No one should face *Northeast* in any room.

Home Office + Study
While sitting at your desk, face to the *South, Southeast, West and East.* Choose one of these facing directions coupled with your +80 to enhance health, +70 for relationships or +90 for wealth if possible. For students, bloggers and writers use the *South* as it indicates publishing luck, learning and success in exams.

Stoves and Toilets
The best directions for the stove knobs, buttons or controls are *South, Southeast, and East.* If there is a stove or toilet located in your +90, +80 or +70 sector of the house, health and money-loss are at a high risk. Select a toilet located in one of your negative sectors of the house (-90, -80, -70, or -60). *This section applies to the head/s of household or breadwinner.*

Watchful Eye: *Annual Stars*
This chart has two negative areas to pay attention to regarding health; in certain years they become more dangerous. They are the **Northeast** (5 facing star) and the **Southwest** (2 facing star). The *Northeast* becomes more serious in 2025, 2030 and the *Southwest* 2024, 2028. No water *(pools, fountains, etc)* or fire *(stoves, fire place/pits or grills))* should be placed in either area, *no matter the year*; it will activate the negative energy in these areas!

How to Implement the Recommendations

Here's an example of how to implement the recommendations for a Period 9, SE 1 house. The front door is excellent but the interior garage door should be re-configured and angled to face East. The stove knobs activate the 2 facing star; replace with a stove-top with right-handed knobs to activate the SE and 9 facing star.

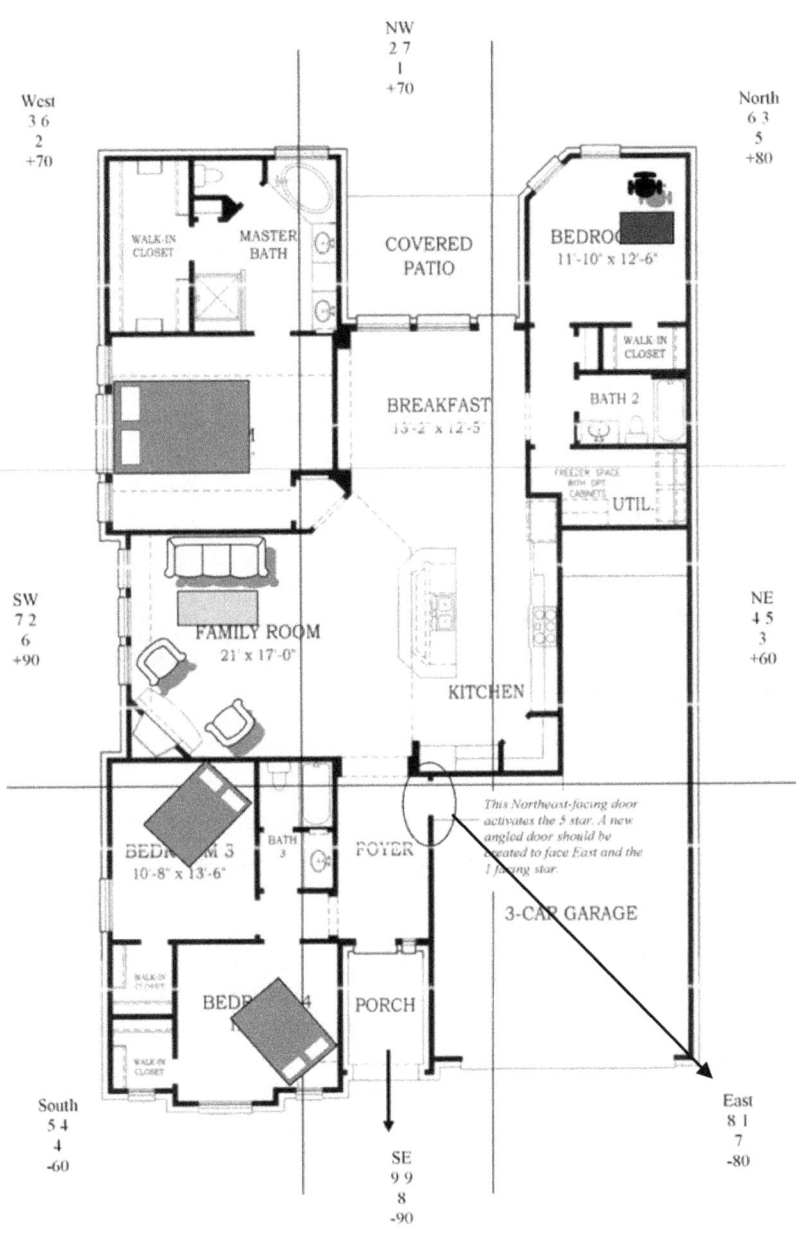

PERIOD 9

Southeast 2 *(127.6° to 142.5°)* Facing name: **Xun**
Southeast 3 *(142.6° to 157.5°)* Facing name: **Su/Si** and the **Snake**
Chart: **Double Stars Meet at Sitting** *(Shuang Xing Dao Zuo)* and **Combination of Ten**

Activating the OUTDOORS
Install Water and Mountain at Back

This property has the two 9 stars at the back known as *Double Stars Meet at Sitting*. This chart can produce those who have high morals, nobility, trustworthiness and the Southeast-facing is suited for philosophers, performers, singer, and artists. To fully extract the best energy you will need to install a water feature and a 'mountain' in the back garden. The 'mountain' can be higher ground, landscape mounds, boulders (no sharp or jagged edges) or any combination (the mountain should be 3 feet or higher). Even smartly designed, tiered landscaping or a series of stacked terraces would work beautifully. Place water at the back by installing a swimming pool, waterfall/pond, Koi pond, lake or spa. For those living in an apartment, high-rise building, townhome, condominium or a rented space and are not able to install a water feature outdoors, place one indoors in the recommended area. To activate the mountain in the recommended area, use a tall armoire, heavy bookcases or stone statues; these will sufficiently activate the energy.

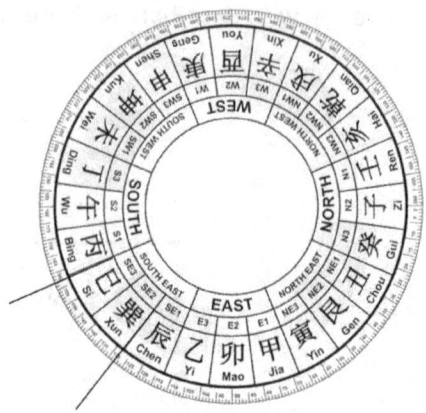

SE 2 & 3

Backyard Swimming Pools
If a swimming pool is desired, it should be located in the Northwest (center) but can also be in the West (left-hand corner). Pool designs often touch two sectors.

These Formations are Possible, Not Definite!
There is a possible *Eight Roads of Destruction* if the house faces **Southeast 2** and a road/driveway comes from/exits the South or East. An *Eight Killings* formation is possible for homes facing **Southeast 3** if there is a mountain bringing energy to the house from the West direction. A *Peach Blossom Sha* is activated with a road coming from the South. There is also a possible *Robbery Mountain Sha* formation if there a jagged cliff, electrical tower, huge dead tree, lamppost, or a broken mountain in the East.

Flying Stars Feng Shui for Period 9 | 149

Figure 38: This Period 9, Southeast 2 & 3 chart needs water and a mountain at the back. The tall stone walls seen in this photo could represent the mountain while the narrow pool will activate the 9 facing star.

Activating the INSIDE
Move your Stuff!

Excellent Doors
Always use and activate good doors; the best ones for this chart are facing to the *Northwest, North, East or West* directions. This applies to all exterior doors as well as an interior garage door used to enter the house. In modern homes, an interior garage door is often the main entry into the house, therefore it is extremely important!

Master Bedroom + Family
There are two ways to activate great energy in the bedroom and that is location and direction; the *direction* of the bed will give you the most powerful results. Locate the master/owner's bedroom in the *West, Northwest or South* as these have good mountain stars. **Bed Directions:** Place the owner's bed on the *Northwest, East, South, and West*. These bed directions have a good mountain *and* facing star combination with excellent energy. Use the above directions when placing the bed for other family members.

Family Room + Dining Room
In the dining room and family room, arrange your furniture so that you and family members can face *Northwest, North, East or West*. These directions have the best energy of the house. No one should face *Southwest* in any room of the house.

Home Office + Study
While sitting at your desk, face to the *Northwest, North, East or West*. Choose one of these facing directions coupled with your +80 to enhance health, +70 for relationships or +90 for wealth if possible. For example if you are an 8 Gua, face to the *Northwest*—this arrangement indicates that the *Tien Yi* (heavenly doctor) protects you and brings you 'unexpected wealth from the heavens'. The best direction to face for wealth is the Northwest (9 facing star).

Stoves and Toilets
The best directions for the stove knobs, buttons or controls are *Northwest, North, or West.* You will struggle with money, health and relationships if there is a stove or toilet located in your +90, +80 or +70 sector of the house. Select a toilet located in one of your negative sectors of the house (-90, -80, -70, or -60). *This section applies to the head/s of household or breadwinner.*

Watchful Eye: *Annual Stars*
This chart has two negative areas to pay attention to. They are the **Southwest** (5 facing star) and the **Northeast** (2 facing star). *The Southwest* becomes more serious in 2024, 2028 and the Northeast in 2025, 2030. No water *(pools, fountains, etc)* or fire *(stoves, fire place/pits or grills)* should be placed in either area, *no matter the year*; it will activate the negative energy in these areas!

CHAPTER SIX
The Period 8 Charts and Activation

The Period 8 homes are still very lucky and will continue to be so during Period 9 (2024-2044) and even into Period 1 (2044-2064). However, activate the *9 facing star* and the *9 mountain star* to usher in this prosperous energy now, no need to wait until Period 9!

Your home is a Period 8 home if you moved in between Feb 4, 2004 to Feb 3, 2024. In order to proceed and to locate your unique Flying Star Chart and to set things into motion, you'll need the facing direction. If you have not already discovered the facing direction, refer to the section of the book entitled *'How to Determine the Facing'* on page 49. Once you have the degree check the 24 Mountains chart on page 51. Draw a floor plan of your home. Divide it up into nine cells and overlay the directions and Star Chart. Place this information outside the floor plan so that you can sketch in possible bed locations, desks, water, and so forth as you read the recommendations. If you are unsure which directions go where, you will find them in the Natal Star Charts in the little black area outside the numbers. Only one chart applies to your home and its unique energy. The rest of the charts serve as great reference material assisting your friends, family, co-workers or if you move into another home. You'll be able to arrange everything perfectly—again!

It does take some time to fully master Flying Stars (not to mention all the other systems for that matter), so the charts have been fully evaluated for you. The recommendations and assessments have made use of the five elements, cosmic trinity, timeliness of the stars, annual stars, proper activation of mountain and facing stars, He Tu, Luo Shu, the two Ba Guas, Eight Mansions, Flying Stars, San Yuan and San He formulas. The recommendations for the charts include enhancements and cures needed to realize its full potential. This will ensure that the most positive energy is being fully extracted.

Every home has areas where there is negative energy. The *Watchful Eye* is to alert you to pay attention to these areas as in certain years, they can be worse. No fire or water should be located there, no matter the year, as they will be activated. Cure these areas as recommended so that they become neutral. You will also need to be aware of when the *Three Killings* visits the front of your property. It is taboo to engage in deep digging, remodeling or demolition. Use good dates from the *Great Sun Formula* if you must touch this area. These dates will protect you from inauspicious events occurring.

The *Period 9 Perks* in this chapter will capture the energy for the new Period. They always involve water and mountain. The 'mountain' can be higher ground, landscape mounds, courtyard walls, boulders, or any combination. Even smartly designed, tiered landscaping or a series of stacked stone terraces are good representatives for mountains. The water could be a swimming pool, pond, waterfall, huge fountain, or lake.

PERIOD 8

South 1 (157.6° to 172.5°) Facing Name: Bing
Chart: **Double Stars Meet at Back** *(Shuang Xing Dao Zuo)*

Activating the OUTDOORS
Install Water and Mountain in the North

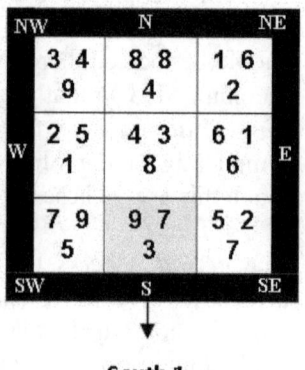

South 1

This chart has the double 8's at the rear of the site known as *Double Stars Meet at the Sitting*. South-facing structures support people of authority, who are charismatic and the family can accumulate lots of property. It can also bring descendants who will achieve high-ranking positions in politics. To fully capture the most benevolent energy and activate health, wealth and harmony, place big water and solid backing in the back of the property (North). The 'mountain' can be higher ground, landscape mounds, boulders (no sharp or jagged edges) or any combination (the mountain should be 3 feet or higher). Even smartly designed, tiered landscaping or a series of stacked terraces would work brilliantly. The water could be a pool, pond, waterfall, huge fountain, or lake.

For those living in an apartment, high-rise building, townhome, condominium or a rented space and are not able to install a water feature outdoors, place one indoors in the recommended area. To activate the mountain in the recommended area, use a tall armoire, heavy bookcases or stone statues; these will sufficiently activate the energy.

Period 9 Perks! Install a mountain in the *South*. The 'mountain' can be higher ground, landscape mounds, courtyard walls, boulders or any combination. Place water in the *Southwest* area of the front yard such as a fountain.

These Formations are Possible, Not Definite!
There is a potential *Eight Roads of Destruction* if there is a road or real water coming from/exiting the Southeast direction; they are notorious for bringing bankruptcy, disease, and divorce. This house also has a potential *Robbery Mountain Sha* formation if there is a jagged cliff, electrical tower, huge dead tree, lamppost, or a broken mountain in the Southwest that indicates being hurt by knives, unusual diseases and disasters.

Activating the INDOORS
Move your Stuff!

Excellent Doors
Always use and activate doors with excellent facing stars; for this chart they are the *North, Northeast, East, Northwest* and *Southwest*. This applies to all exterior doors as

well as an interior garage door used to enter the house. If the front door faces South, it will need to be cured with a small fountain or birdbath (still water and no more than 1-2 gallons) or paint the door red. You may do both, however, this still should not become the most-used door in the house.

A West-facing door, in this chart (likely a side door), is seriously negative. If this is a well-used door, you will need to cure it with lots of metal next to or directly on the door. However, these doors can never be fully cured, only *weakened* as the movement/use of it will always keep it activated. For the best luck, use another door.

Master Bedroom + Family
There are two ways to enhance health, harmony and prosperity in the bedroom and that is location and direction; the *direction* of the bed will give you the most powerful results. Locate the master bedroom in the *North*, *South* (second floor), *Northeast* or *East* as they have good mountain stars. **Bed Directions:** Place marital/owner's headboard/bed to the *North*, *Northeast* or *East* direction; these bed directions have a good mountain *and* facing star combination with excellent energy.

If there are any bedrooms located in either the West or Southeast, take special care. These sectors of the house have very negative energy. In the event the marital/owner's bedroom is already situated there; make sure the bed is not placed to either direction. As an extra measure, place high quality metal in the room and keep the colors soft and neutral. Use the recommended directions when placing the bed for other family members.

Home Office + Study
Place your desk/body to the *North, Northeast, East, Northwest* or *Southwest;* these directions have great facing stars. For students, writers, teachers or bloggers face to the East or Northwest as it has the strongest 'scholarly' energy and indicate success in examinations, accelerating intelligence and accomplishments in literary pursuits.

Stoves, Grills and Fireplaces
The best direction for the stove knobs, buttons or controls is the *North, East* or *Southwest*; this applies to outdoor kitchens/grills as well. Fireplaces, either inside or outdoors, can face to *the North, East or Southwest;* this house should not have a two-way fireplace in any room.

Watchful Eye: Annual Stars and Three Killings
This chart has two negative areas to pay attention to that can harm your money, health and household harmony. They are the **West** (2, 5) and the **Southeast** (5, 2). The Southeast becomes more serious in 2021 and the West in 2020. Cure with high quality metal such as brass, bronze, stainless steel, pewter or copper. No water *(pools, fountains, etc)* or fire *(stoves, fire place/pits or grills)* should be placed in either area, *no matter the year*, it will activate them! The *Three Killings* visits the front of the house in 2024 and 2028. It is taboo to engage in deep digging, remodeling or demolition. Use good dates from the *Great Sun Formula* if you must touch this area.

PERIOD 8

South 2 *(172.6° to 187.5°)* Facing name: **Wu** and the **Horse**
South 3 *(187.6° to 202.5°)* Facing name: **Ting**
Chart: **Double Stars Meet at Front** (*Shuang Xing Dao Xiang*)

Activating the OUTDOORS
Needs Mountain and Water in the Front

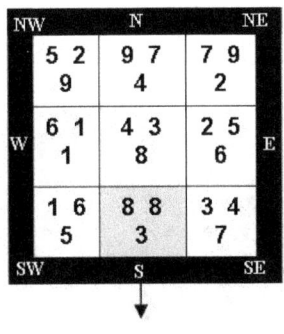

South 2 & 3

The excellent energy of the double 8's are located in the front of the property known as *Double Stars Meet at the Facing* and can bring great health, relationships and money. It is important to activate this chart by installing a *mountain* and *water*. The 'mountain' can be higher ground, courtyard walls, landscape mounds, boulders (no sharp or jagged edges) or any combination (the mountain should be 3 feet or higher). A water fountain, pond or stream may be placed in the front. If you live in a home where you are not able to place an outdoor water feature, place one inside in the recommended area; consider a wall fountain. For those living in an apartment, high-rise building, townhome, condominium or a rented space and are not able to install a water feature outdoors, place one indoors in the recommended area. To activate the mountain in the recommended area, use a tall armoire, heavy bookcases or stone statues; these will sufficiently activate the energy.

Period 9 Perks! Install a mountain in the *North*. The 'mountain' can be higher ground, landscape mounds, raised brick/stone decking, boulders or any combination. Place water in the *Northeast* area of the back yard such as a pool, pond or fountain.

These Formations are Possible, Not Definite!
For homes that face **South 2**, there is a possible *Eight Killing Forces* if there is a mountain located in the Northwest direction. If there is a road coming from the East, it could activate the *Peach Blossom Sha*. These homes also may have a *Robbery Mountain Sha* formation if there is a jagged cliff, electrical tower, huge dead tree, lamppost, or a broken mountain in the Southeast. For homes that face to **South 3,** there is a possible *Eight Roads of Destruction* if there is a road or water coming from/exiting the Southwest direction, it is common for them to bring bankruptcy, disease, and divorce.

Activating the INDOORS
Move your Stuff!

Excellent Doors
Always use and activate doors with excellent facing stars; for this chart they face *South, Southeast, West, Northeast* and *Southwest*. This applies to all exterior doors as well as an interior garage door used to enter the house. If the back door faces North, it will need to be cured with a small fountain or birdbath (still water and no more than 1-2 gallons) or paint the door red. You may do both, as back doors are frequently used.

An East-facing door (likely an interior garage door or a side 'front' door) in this chart is seriously negative. If this is a well-used door, you will need to cure it with lots of metal next to or directly on the door. Use brass, bronze, stainless steel, pewter or copper.

Master Bedroom + Family
There are two ways to enhance health, harmony and prosperity in the bedroom and that is location and direction; the *direction* of the bed will give you the most powerful results. Locate the master bedroom in the *South* (second floor), *North, West, or*

Southwest as these sectors have good mountain stars. **Bed Directions**: Place the marital/owner's headboard/bed to the *South, Southeast, West or Southwest;* these bed directions have a good mountain *and* facing star combination with excellent energy. If there are any bedrooms located in either the East or Northwest, take special care. These sectors of the house have very negative energy. In the event the marital/owner's bedroom is already situated there; make sure the bed is not placed to either direction. As an extra measure, place high quality metal in the room and keep the colors soft and neutral. Use the recommended directions when placing the bed for other family members.

Home Office + Study
Place your desk/body to the *South, Southeast, West, Northeast or Southwest*; these directions have excellent facing stars. For students, writers, teachers or bloggers face to the West or Southeast as they have the strongest 'scholarly' energy and indicate success in examinations, accelerating intelligence and accomplishments in literary pursuits.

Stoves, Grills and Fireplaces
The best directions for the stove knobs, buttons or controls are *South, West* or *Northeast*; this applies to outdoor kitchens/grills as well. Fireplaces, either inside or outdoors, can face to *the South, West or Northeast*; this house should not have a two-way fireplace in any room.

Watchful Eye: Annual Stars and Three Killings
This chart has two negative areas to pay attention to. They are the **East** (2, 5) and the **Northwest** (5, 2); these sectors have very negative energy. The East becomes worse in 2020 and 2023 while the Northwest in 2023. Cure with high quality metal such as brass, bronze, stainless steel, pewter or copper. <u>No water</u> *(pools, fountains, etc)* or <u>fire</u> *(stoves, fire place/pits or grills)* should be placed in either area, *no matter the year,* it will activate them! The *Three Killings* visits the front of the house in 2024 and 2028. It is taboo to engage in deep digging, remodeling or demolition. Use good dates from the *Great Sun Formula* if you must touch this area.

PERIOD 8

Southwest 1 *(202.6° to 217.5°)* Facing name: **Wei** and the Goat
Very Special Chart: **Combination of Ten** *(He Shih Chu)* **and Prosperous Sitting Prosperous Facing** *(Wang Shan Wang Shui)*

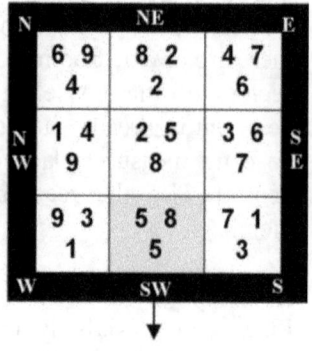

Southwest 1

Activating the OUTDOORS
Needs Water in front, Solid Wall or Mountain at the back

This property is one of the most auspicious charts of Period 8 with two special aspects known as a *Combination of Ten* and *Prosperous Sitting, Prosperous Facing.* The energy is extremely lucky for all categories of Feng Shui—prosperity, health and harmony; it is a very special chart! The Southwest-facing properties are also known for turning bad fortunes into lucrative opportunities and may also denote in the birth of an intelligent, wealthy and prosperous person. Having a significant backing is the key to fully realizing the chart's potential.

Obviously, if you have a hill or mountain at the back of your house, this is extremely auspicious! If not, you can create a "mountain" at the back with a very high, solid fence, dense landscaping, high ground and so forth. If you have water at the back of the house, there could be serious illness in the house especially for the woman/mother of the house. Also, you would have lost the opportunity to correctly extract the health and people luck available with this chart. It is important that this home have a beautiful water feature such as a stream, Koi pond, waterfall, or fountain at the front of the property, place it as center of your garden as possible however do not directly align of block the front door.

For those living in an apartment, high-rise building, townhome, condominium or a rented space and are not able to install a water feature outdoors, place one indoors in the recommended area. To activate the mountain in the recommended area, use a tall armoire, heavy bookcases or stone statues; these will sufficiently activate the energy.

Period 9 Perks! Install a mountain in the *West* of the front yard. The 'mountain' can be higher ground, landscape mounds, boulders or any combination. Place water in the *North* area of the back yard such as a fountain, pond or pool. The water should not be between 352.6° to 7.5° in the North as it may activate affairs.

These Formations are Possible, Not Definite!
These homes also may have a *Robbery Mountain Sha* formation if there is a jagged cliff, electrical tower, huge dead tree, lamppost, or a broken mountain in the *Southeast* and a *Peach Blossom Sha* if there is water located in the *North*.

Activating the INDOORS
Move your Stuff!

Excellent Doors
Always use and activate doors with excellent facing stars; for this chart they face *Southwest, North, South, Southeast,* or *Northwest*. While a Southwest-facing **front door** has the most excellent energy, a Northeast-facing **back door** does not. It will need to be cured with lots of high-quality metal. No water or fire can be located in the NE. An interior garage door rates very high because in modern homes this is often the main entry into the house, therefore it is extremely important!

Master Bedroom + Family
There are two ways to enhance health, harmony and prosperity in the bedroom and that is location and direction; the *direction* of the bed will give you the most powerful results. Locate the master bedroom in the *North, Northwest, West* or *Northeast* as these sectors have good mountain stars. **Bed Directions:** Place the marital/owner's headboard/bed to the *North or Northwest* direction; these bed directions have a good mountain *and* facing star combination with excellent energy. *Use the above directions when placing the bed for other family members.* Note: Sleeping to either the Southwest of Northeast will cause lots of illness and money-loss.

Home Office + Study

Place your desk/body to the *North, Southeast, South, Northwest* or *Southwest*; these directions have great facing stars and energy. For students, writers, teachers or bloggers face to the Northwest as it has the strongest 'scholarly' energy and indicate success in examinations, accelerating intelligence and accomplishments in literary pursuits.

Stoves, Grills and Fireplaces

The best direction for the stove knobs, buttons or controls is the *North, South, Southwest* or *Northwest*; this applies to outdoor kitchens/grills as well. This house cannot have a kitchen or fireplace in the **center** of the home (2, 5 combination); it can bring serious health issues such as heart attacks and high blood pressure. Fireplaces, either inside or outdoors, can face to *the North, South, Southwest* or *Northwest*; this house can also have a two-way fireplace on the North-South axis; these directions activate opportunities, prosperity and money luck.

Watchful Eye: *Annual Stars*

This chart has one negative area to pay attention to that can harm your money, health and household harmony; in certain years it becomes more dangerous. The **Northeast** *(2 facing star)* will become double trouble in 2021. Cure with high quality metal such as brass, bronze, stainless steel, pewter or copper. <u>No water</u> *(pools, fountains, etc)* or <u>fire</u> *(stoves, fire place/pits or grills)* should be placed in this area, *no matter the year,* it gets activated!

PERIOD 8

Southwest 2 *(217.6° to 232.5°)* Facing name: **Kun**
Southwest 3 *(232.6° to 247.5°)* Facing name: **Shen** and the **Monkey**
Very Special Chart: **Parent String** *(Fu Mo San Poon Gua)*

Activating the OUTDOORS
Need a Mountain in Front, Water at the Back

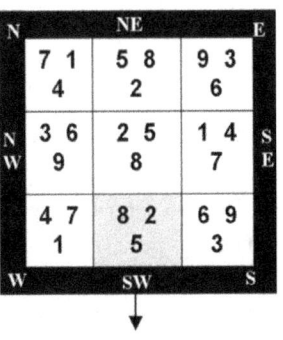

Southwest 2 & 3

This property (Southwest 2 and 3) has a very special chart called a *Parent String* formation and it is alleged to bring triple good luck to the occupants! Parent Strings are also noted for creating fast fortunes, wealth, powerful families, and turning bad deals into opportunities. These charts must be activated using a special technique; there must be a mountain in front and water at the back. The 'mountain' can be higher ground, courtyard walls, landscape mounds, boulders (no sharp or jagged edges) or any combination (the mountain should be 3 feet or higher). Install a gorgeous water feature at the back of your house with a waterfall, large fountain, pond or swimming pool. Keep it in the center of the garden. For those living in an apartment, high-rise building, townhome, condominium or a rented space and are not able to install a water feature outdoors, place one indoors in the recommended area. To activate the mountain in the recommended area, use a tall armoire, heavy bookcases or stone statues; these will sufficiently activate the energy.

Period 9 Perks! Install a mountain in the *East*. The 'mountain' can be higher ground, landscape mounds, elevated brick decking, boulders or any combination. Place water in the *South* area of the front yard such as a fountain.

These Formations are Possible, Not Definite!
The **Southwest 2** homes have a possible *Eight Roads of Destruction* if there is a road/water coming from/exiting certain areas of the South and West directions. These homes also may have a *Robbery Mountain Sha* formation if there is a jagged cliff, electrical tower, huge dead tree, lamppost, or a broken mountain in the South. The **Southwest 3** facing properties may have an *Eight Killing* formation if there is a mountain located in the East. A *Peach Blossom Sha* is activated with a road coming from the West. These homes also may have a *Robbery Mountain Sha* formation if there is a jagged cliff, electrical tower, huge dead tree, lamppost, or a broken mountain in the Southwest.

Activating the INDOORS
Move your Stuff!

Excellent Doors
Always use and activate doors with excellent facing stars; for this chart they are the *Northeast, Northwest, North, Southeast* and *South*. This applies to all exterior doors as well as an interior garage door used to enter the house. A Southwest-facing **front door** is seriously negative and can cause disease and sickness. If this is a well-used door, you will need to cure it with lots of metal next to or directly on the door. However, these doors can never be fully cured, only *weakened* as the movement/use of it will always keep it activated. For the best luck, use another door.

Master Bedroom + Family
There are two ways to enhance health, harmony and prosperity in the bedroom and that is location and direction; the *direction* of the bed will give you the most powerful results. Locate the master bedroom in the *South, Southeast, Southwest, West* or *East* sectors of the house as these sectors have good mountain stars. **Bed Directions:** Place the marital/owner's headboard/bed to the *Northwest, North, Southeast* or *South*; these bed directions have a good mountain *and* facing star combination with excellent energy. Use the above directions when placing the bed for other family members.

Home Office + Study
Place your desk/body to the *Northeast, Northwest, North, Southeast* or *South* as these directions have good facing stars with wealth and harmonious energy. For students, writers, teachers or bloggers face to the Southeast as it has the strongest 'scholarly' energy and indicate success in examinations, accelerating intelligence and accomplishments in literary pursuits.

Stoves, Grills and Fireplaces
The best direction for the stove knobs, buttons or controls is *Northeast, South, Southeast* or *North;* this applies to outdoor kitchens/grills as well. This house cannot have a kitchen or fireplace in the center of the home (2, 5 combination); it can bring serious health issues such as heart attacks and high blood pressure. Fireplaces, either inside or outdoors, can face to the *Northeast, South, Southeast* or *North*; this house can also have a two-way fireplace on the North-South axis; this activates prosperity.

Watchful Eye: *Annual Stars*
This chart has one negative area to pay attention to that can harm your money, health and household harmony; in certain years it becomes more dangerous. It is the Southwest *(2 facing star),* and it can bring real trouble in 2022. Cure with high quality metal such as brass, bronze, stainless steel, pewter or copper. No water *(pools, fountains, etc)* or fire *(stoves, fire place/pits or grills)* should be placed in this area, *no matter the year*, it gets activated!

PERIOD 8
West 1 (247.6° to 262.5°) Facing name: **Geng**
Chart: **Double Stars Meet at Sitting** *(Shuang Xing Dao Zuo)*

Activating the OUTDOORS
Need a Mountain and Water at the Back

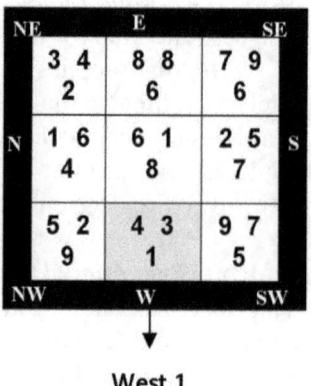

West 1

This property has the current prosperity and benevolent energy located at the back of the site known as *Double Stars Meet at Sitting.* These West-facing properties produce well-educated, intelligent, polite and charming people who can become very wealthy through good business management, or getting involved in politics. To fully activate this chart properly, you will need both water and a mountain at the back. The 'mountain' could be a solid wall or fence comprised of stucco, brick, or stone; even smartly designed, tiered landscaping or a series of stacked terraces would work brilliantly. While designing this important feature, incorporate a large water feature in proportion to the size of your home and garden in the back. If you live in an apartment, high-rise, townhome, condo or a rented space and are not able to install an outdoor water feature, place one inside at the back of your space (east). Also, large heavy bookcases or armories can represent your mountain; it should be place on the back wall as well.

Period 9 Perks! Install a mountain in the *Southwest* front yard. The 'mountain' can be higher ground, landscape mounds, courtyard walls, boulders or any combination. Place water in the *Southeast* area of the backyard such as a pond, pool or fountain.

These Formations are Possible, Not Definite!
The house does have a possible *Eight Roads of Destruction* formation if there is a road/driveway coming from and exiting the Southwest direction; noted for bankruptcy, disease or divorce. These homes also may have a *Robbery Mountain Sha* formation if there is a jagged cliff, electrical tower, huge dead tree, lamppost, or a broken mountain in the South; they indicate everyone in household getting an unusual disease, hurt by knives and disasters.

Activating the INDOORS
Move your Stuff!

Excellent Doors
Always use and activate doors with excellent facing stars; for this chart they face *North, Northeast, East* and *Southeast*. If there is a West-facing front door, it will need to be cured with either metal or fire, or both. Paint the door red (fire) and place metal wind

chimes near the door. A South-facing 'front door' (likely a side door/entrance), in this chart, is seriously negative. If this is a well-used door, cure with high quality metal such as brass, bronze, stainless steel, pewter or copper, either directly on the door or near it. See page 290 for metal cure ideas.

Master Bedroom + Family
There are two ways to enhance health, harmony and prosperity in the bedroom and that is location and direction; the *direction* of the bed will give you the most powerful results. Locate the master bedroom in the *North, East, West* or *Southwest* as these sectors have good mountain stars. **Bed Directions:** Place your headboard/bed to the *East* or *North* and *Northeast* is acceptable; these bed directions have a good mountain *and* facing star combination with excellent energy. If there are any bedrooms located in either the South or Northwest, take special care. These sectors of the house have very negative energy. In the event the marital/owner's bedroom is already situated there; make sure the bed is not placed to either direction. As an extra measure, place high quality metal in the room and keep the colors soft and neutral. Use the recommended directions when placing the bed for other family members.

Home Office + Study
Place your desk/body to the *North, Southeast, Northeast* or *East;* these directions have good facing stars with very auspicious energy. For students, writers, teachers or bloggers face to the Northeast or North as they have the strongest 'scholarly' energy and indicate success in examinations, accelerating intelligence and accomplishments in literary pursuits.

Stoves, Grills and Fireplaces
The best direction for the stove knobs, buttons or controls is *East*, *Southeast* and the *Northeast;* this applies to outdoor kitchens/grills as well. Fireplaces, either inside or outdoors, can face to the *East*, *Southeast* and the *Northeast*; this house should not have a two-way fireplace in any room.

Watchful Eye: Annual Stars and Three Killings
This chart has two negative areas to pay attention to that can harm your money, health and household harmony. They are the **South** (2, 5) and the **Northwest** (5, 2). The South becomes worse in 2020 and 2022 while the Northwest in 2023. Cure with high quality metal such as brass, bronze, stainless steel, pewter or copper. No water *(pools, fountains, etc)* or fire *(stoves, fire place/pits or grills))* should be placed in either area, *no matter the year,* it will activate them!

The *Three Killings* position comes to the front of this house in 2023 and 2027. It is taboo to engage in deep digging, remodeling or demolition. Use good dates from the *Great Sun Formula* if you must touch this area.

PERIOD 8

West 2 (262.6° to 277.5°) Facing name: **You** and the **Rooster**
West 3 (277.6° to 292.5°) Facing name: **Xin**
Chart: **Double Stars Meet at Facing** *(Shuang Xing Dao Xiang)*

Activating the OUTDOORS
Needs Mountain and Water in Front

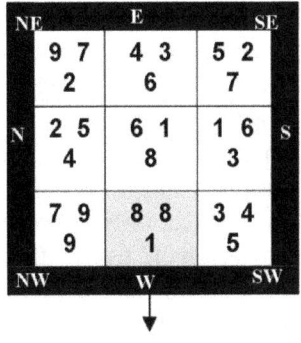

West 2 & 3

This property has the current prosperity and the most benevolent energy (8's) in the front known as the *Double Stars Meet at Facing*. The West-facing homes produce dynamic individuals who will be successful and able to accumulate great wealth rather quickly. It also supports powerful politicians, outstanding academic achievements and super athletes. To fully capture this great energy, you will need to place a water feature and a mountain in the front garden. The 'mountain' can be higher ground, courtyard walls, landscape mounds, boulders (no sharp or jagged edges) or any combination (the mountain should be 3 feet or higher). Install a beautiful water feature such as a fountain, stream or Koi pond in the front as well. For those living in an apartment, high-rise building, townhome, condominium or a rented space and are not able to install a water feature outdoors, place one indoors in the recommended area. To activate the mountain in the recommended area, use a tall armoire, heavy bookcases or stone statues; these will sufficiently activate the energy.

Period 9 Perks! Install a mountain in the *Northeast* corner of the backyard. The 'mountain' can be higher ground, landscape mounds, boulders or any combination. Place water in the *Northwest* area of the front yard such as a fountain.

These Formations are Possible, Not Definite!
The **West 2** homes also have a possible *Eight Killing Forces* if there is mountain chi coming from the Southeast. A *Peach Blossom Sha* is activated with a road coming from the South. These homes also may have a *Robbery Mountain Sha* formation if there is a jagged cliff, electrical tower, huge dead tree, lamppost, or a broken mountain in the South. The **West 3** facing homes have a possible *Eight Roads of Destruction* formation if there is a road/driveway coming from and exiting the Northwest direction; these indicate money-loss. This direction also has a possible *Robbery Mountain Sha* in the Southwest.

Activating the INDOORS
Move your Stuff!

Excellent Doors
Always use and activate doors with excellent facing stars; for this chart they are *West, Southwest, Northwest* and *South*. This applies to all exterior doors as well as an interior garage door. A North-facing 'front door' (likely a side door/entrance) in this chart, is seriously negative. Cure it with high-quality metal. However, these doors can never be fully cured, only *weakened* as the movement/use of it will always keep it activated. For the best luck, use another door. An East-facing back door needs a metal or fire cure; you may do both as back doors are used often. Paint the door red (fire) and place metal wind chimes near the door. A fire pit is a great fire cure as well.

Master Bedroom + Family
There are two ways to health, harmony and prosperity in the bedroom and that is location and direction; the *direction* of the bed will give you the most powerful results. Locate the master bedroom in the *West* (second floor), *South, East* or the *Northeast*, these sectors have good mountain stars. **Bed Directions:** Place the marital/owner's headboard/bed to the *West, Southwest* or *South*; these bed directions have a good mountain *and* facing star combination with excellent energy. If there are any bedrooms located in either the North or Southeast, take special care. These sectors of the house

have very negative energy. In the event the marital/owner's bedroom is already situated there; make sure the bed is not placed to either direction. As an extra measure, place high quality metal in the room and keep the colors soft and neutral. Use the recommended directions when placing the bed for other family members.

Home Office + Study
Place your desk/body to the *West, Southwest, Northwest* or *South* as these directions have good facing stars with auspicious energy. For students, writers, teachers or bloggers face to the Southwest or South as they have the strongest 'scholarly' energy and indicate success in examinations, accelerating intelligence and accomplishments in literary pursuits.

Stoves, Grills and Fireplaces
The best direction for the stove knobs, buttons or controls is *West, Southwest* or *Northwest*; this applies to outdoor kitchens/grills as well. Fireplaces, either inside or outdoors, can face to the *West, Southwest* or *Northwest*; this house should not have a two-way fireplace in any room.

Watchful Eye: Annual Stars and Three Killing
This chart has two negative areas to pay attention to that can harm your money, health and household harmony. They are the **North** (2, 5) and the **Southeast** (5, 2); these sectors have very negative energy. The North is worse in 2021 and 2023 while the Southeast in 2021. No water *(pools, fountains, etc)* or fire *(stoves, fire place/pits or grills)* should be placed in either area, *no matter the year*, it will activate them!

The *Three Killings* position comes to the front of this house in 2023 and 2027. It is taboo to engage in deep digging, remodeling or demolition. Use good dates from the *Great Sun Formula* if you must touch this area.

PERIOD 8
Northwest 1 (292.6° to 307.5°) Facing name: **Xu** and the **Dog**
Very Special Chart: **Pearl String** *(Lin Cu San Poon Gua)*

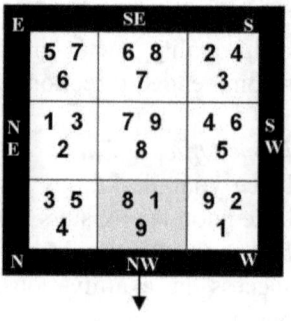

Northwest 1

Activating the OUTDOORS
Needs Mountain in Front and Water at Back

This property has the very desirable **Pearl String** formation, which is also referred to by some masters as the *Continuous Bead Formation*. This facing is famous for turning almost everything to an advantage; this is especially true involving business. It's also said that, when activated properly, this chart can bring the recipients triple good luck/opportunities. To fully capture the fabulous potential of this chart, you will need a mountain in front and water at the back. The 'mountain' can be higher ground, courtyard walls, landscape mounds, boulders (no sharp or jagged edges) or any combination (the mountain should be 3 feet or higher). Keep these features as center of the garden as possible, but do not block the front door. Place water at the back by installing a pool, waterfall/pond, Koi pond, lake or spa.

If you're unable to activate this chart via the exterior, then place water on the back wall using a wall fountain or large fish tank, then add two heavy objects (preferably stone, granite or marble) on both sides of the front door, either interior or exterior.

Period 9 Perks! Install a mountain in the *West* area of the front yard. The 'mountain' can be higher ground, landscape mounds, courtyard walls, boulders or any combination. *Note:* The 9 facing star is trapped in the middle and cannot be activated with water. However, if you activate the 8 facing star as recommended, you will enhance prosperity for this home.

These Formations are Possible, Not Definite!
These homes may have a *Robbery Mountain Sha* formation if there is a jagged cliff, electrical tower, huge dead tree, lamppost, or a broken mountain in the *Southwest*; they indicate everyone in household getting an unusual disease, hurt by knives and disasters. You could also activate a *Peach Blossom Sha* if there is water or road in the *East*.

Activating the INDOORS
Move your Stuff!

Excellent Doors
Always use and activate doors with excellent facing stars; for this chart they are the *Northwest, South, Southwest* and *Southeast;* this applies to all exterior doors as well as

an interior garage door used to enter the house. A North-facing front door (which will be angled) is seriously negative. If this is a well-used door, you will need to cure it with lots of metal next to or directly on the door. However, these doors can never be fully cured, only *weakened* as the movement/use of it will always keep it activated. For the best luck, use another door.

Master Bedroom + Family
There are two ways to enhance health, harmony and prosperity in the bedroom and that is location and direction; the *direction* of the bed will give you the most powerful results. Locate the master bedroom in the *Southeast, West, Northeast, Southwest* or *Northwest* (second floor) as these rooms have good mountain stars. **Bed Directions:** Place the marital/owner's headboard/bed to the *Northwest, Southwest* or *Southeast;* these directions have excellent mountain and facing star combinations. Use the above directions when placing the bed for other family members.

Home Office + Study
Place your desk/body to the *Northwest, South, Southwest* or *Southeast;* these directions have great facing stars with wealth and benevolent energy. For students, writers, teachers or bloggers face to the South as it has the strongest 'scholarly' energy and indicate success in examinations, accelerating intelligence and accomplishments in literary pursuits.

Stoves, Grills and Fireplaces
The best direction for the stove knobs, buttons or controls is the *Northwest, South* or *Southeast*; this applies to outdoor kitchens/grills as well. Fireplaces, either inside or outdoors, can face to the *Northwest, South* or *Southeast*; this house can also have a two-way fireplace on the Northwest-Southeast axis; this activates wealth and prosperity.

Watchful Eye: *Annual Stars*

This chart has two negative areas to pay attention to that can harm your money, health and household harmony. They are the **North** (*5 facing star*) and the **West** (*2 facing star*). The North becomes worse in 2021 and 2023 while the West in 2020. Cure with high quality metal such as brass, bronze, stainless steel, pewter or copper. No water *(pools, fountains, etc)* or fire *(stoves, fire place/pits or grills)* should be placed in either area, *no matter the year*, it will activate them!

PERIOD 8

Northwest 2 *(307.6° to 322.5°)* Facing name: **Chien**
Northwest 3 *(322.6° to 337.5°)* Facing name: **Hai** and the **Pig**
Special Chart: **Prosperous Sitting** and **Facing** *(Wang Shan Wang Shui)*

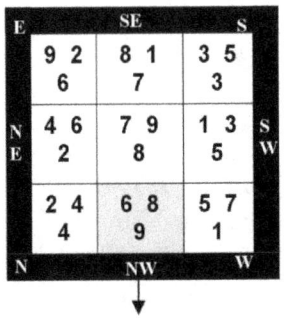

Northwest 2 & 3

Activating the OUTDOORS
Needs Water in Front, Mountain in Back

This is a very lucky chart known *as Prosperous Sitting and Facing*; also known as *'lucky for people, lucky for money'*. To fully extract the extraordinary potential of this chart, place a water feature in the front and make sure there is significant, solid backing emulating the energy of a mountain at the back. A tall, solid fence comprised of brick, wood, stucco, stone or any combination thereof is excellent. Beautiful retaining walls or tiered landscaping would work perfectly as well. If there is a natural mountain, hill or mound at the back of your site, you are very blessed. In the event that you live in an apartment, high-rise, townhome, condo or a rented space and are not able to place an outdoor water feature, install one inside near the front door. Place tall heavy bookcases or an armoire on the back wall (Southeast). If you have a back patio, then place heavy stone, marble or granite statues or planters there to represent your 'mountain'.

Period 9 Perks! Install a mountain in the *East* corner of the backyard. The 'mountain' can be higher ground, landscape mounds, elevated brick decking, boulders or any combination. *Note:* The 9 facing star is trapped in the middle and cannot be activated with water. However, if you activate the 8 facing star as recommended, you will enhance prosperity for this home.

These Formations are Possible, Not Definite!
For homes that face **Northwest 2,** there is a possible *Eight Roads of Destruction* if you have a road coming from/exiting from either the West or North directions; they are famous for bringing disharmony, bankruptcy, and divorce. These homes also may have a *Robbery Mountain Sha* formation if there a jagged cliff, electrical tower, huge dead tree, lamppost, or a broken mountain in the North.

For the **Northwest 3** facing homes if a mountain is located in the South you could have an *Eight Killing Forces*. These homes also may have a *Robbery Mountain Sha* formation if there is a jagged cliff, electrical tower, huge dead tree, lamppost, or a broken mountain in the West. A *Peach Blossom Sha* is activated with a road coming/exiting from the North.

Activating the INDOORS
Move your Stuff!

Excellent Doors
Always use and activate doors with excellent facing stars; for this chart they are the *Northwest, Northeast, Southeast,* and *North*. This applies to all exterior doors as well as an interior garage door used to enter the house. An interior garage door rates very high because in modern homes this is often the main entry into the house, therefore it is extremely important!

Master Bedroom + Family
There are two ways to enhance health, harmony and prosperity in the bedroom and that is location and direction; the *direction* of the bed will give you the most powerful results. Locate the master bedroom in the *East, Southeast, Southwest, Northeast* or *Northwest* (second floor) as these rooms all have good mountain stars. **Bed Directions:** Place the marital/owner's headboard/bed to the *Northwest, Northeast* or *Southeast;* these bed directions have a good mountain *and* facing star combination with excellent energy. *Use the above directions when placing the bed for other family members.*

Home Office + Study
Place your desk/body to the *Northwest, Northeast, Southeast* or *North;* these directions have great facing stars. For students, writers, teachers or bloggers face to the North as it has the strongest 'scholarly' energy and indicate success in examinations, accelerating intelligence and accomplishments in literary pursuits.

Stoves, Grills and Fireplaces
The best direction for the stove knobs, buttons or controls is *Northwest, North* or *Southeast;* this applies to outdoor kitchens/grills as well. Fireplaces, either inside or outdoors, can face to the *Northwest, North* or *Southeast*; this house can also have a two-way fireplace on the Northwest-Southeast axis (placed in any room); this activates wealth and prosperity.

Watchful Eye: *Annual Stars*
This chart has two negative areas to pay attention to that can harm your money, health and household harmony. They are the **South** (*5 facing star*) and the **East** (*2 facing star*). The South becomes worse in 2020 and 2022 while the East in 2020, 2023 and 2025. No water *(pools, fountains, etc)* or fire *(stoves, fire place/pits or grills)* should be placed in either area, *no matter the year,* it will activate them!

PERIOD 8

North 1 (337.6° to 352.5°) Facing name: **Ren**
Chart: **Double Stars Meet at the Facing** *(Shuang Xing Dao Xiang)*

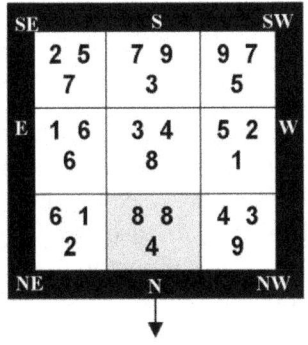

North 1

Activating the OUTDOORS
Needs Water and Mountain in Front

This property has the two 8 stars in the front known as *Double Stars Meet at the Facing*. The North-facing properties indicate success, charismatic people, and wealth luck. In order for this chart to support health and money, it's very important to install a water feature and a 'mountain' in the front garden. You can fulfill the criteria for both if you install a tall, heavy concert or marble fountain near (but not blocking) the front door. If you wish to construct two separate features, another way to activate the 'mountain' is with higher ground, courtyard walls, landscape mounds, boulders (no sharp or jagged edges) or any combination (the mountain should be 3 feet or higher). The water feature may be a stream, Koi pond, waterfall (flowing towards the house, not away from it), or a fountain.

If you are unable to place these features exterior to your site, install a water fountain near the front door inside. Place two heavy statues or stone planters on either side of the front door (inside or out).

Period 9 Perks! Install a mountain in the *Southwest* corner of the backyard. The 'mountain' can be higher ground, landscape mounds, elevated brick decking, boulders or any combination. Install a water feature in the South (9 facing star) such as a pool, pond or fountain.

These Formations are Possible, Not Definite!
There is a possible *Eight Roads of Destruction* with this facing if there is a road coming from/exiting the Northwest direction; they are famous for bringing money-loss and disasters. These homes also may have a *Robbery Mountain Sha* formation if there is a jagged cliff, electrical tower, huge dead tree, lamppost, or a broken mountain in the West; they indicate everyone in household getting an unusual disease, hurt by knives and disasters.

Activating the INDOORS
Move your Stuff!

Excellent Doors
Always use and activate doors with excellent facing stars; for this chart they are the *North, East, Northeast* and *South*. This applies to all exterior doors as well as an interior garage door used to enter the house. A West-facing front door is seriously negative and can cause disease and sickness. If this is a well-used door, you will need to cure it with lots of metal next to or directly on the door. Use brass, bronze, stainless steel, pewter or copper.

Master Bedroom + Family
There are two ways to enhance health, harmony and prosperity in the bedroom and that is location and direction; the *direction* of the bed will give you the most powerful results. Locate the master bedroom in the *East, Southwest, North* (second floor) or *Northeast* sectors of the house as they are good mountain stars. **Bed Directions:** Place the marital/owner's headboard/bed to the *North, East* or *Northeast*; these bed directions have a good mountain *and* facing star combination with excellent energy.

If there are any bedrooms located in either the West or Southeast, take special care. These sectors of the house have very negative energy. In the event the marital/owner's bedroom is already situated there; make sure the bed is not placed to either direction. As an extra measure, place high quality metal in the room and keep the colors soft and neutral. Use the recommended directions when placing the bed for other family members.

Home Office + Study
Place your desk/face to the *North, East, Northeast* or *South;* these directions have great facing stars with excellent energy. For students, writers, teachers or bloggers face to the Northeast as it has the strongest 'scholarly' energy and indicate success in examinations, accelerating intelligence and accomplishments in literary pursuits.

Stoves, Grills and Fireplaces
The best direction for the stove knobs, buttons or controls is *North, Northeast* or *South;* this applies to outdoor kitchens/grills as well. Fireplaces, either inside or outdoors, can face to *North, Northeast* and *South*; this house can also have a two-way fireplace on the North-South axis; this activates prosperity, promotions and business opportunities.

Watchful Eye: *Annual Stars and Three Killings*
This chart has two negative areas to pay attention to that can harm your money, health and household harmony. They are the **Southeast** (2, 5) and the **West** (5, 2). The Southeast becomes worse in 2021 2024, and 2026 while the West in 2020 and 2024. No water *(pools, fountains, etc)* or fire *(stoves, fire place/pits or grills)* should be placed in either area, *no matter the year,* it will activate them! Also the Three Killings visits the North in 2022 and 2026. It is taboo to engage in demolition, construction or deep digging.

PERIOD 8
North 2 (352.6° to 7.5°) Facing name: **Tzi** and the **Rat**
North 3 (7.6° to 22.5) Facing name: **Kwei**
Chart: **Double Stars Meet at Sitting** *(Shuang Xing Dao Zuo)*

Activating the OUTDOORS
Needs Mountain and Water at the Back

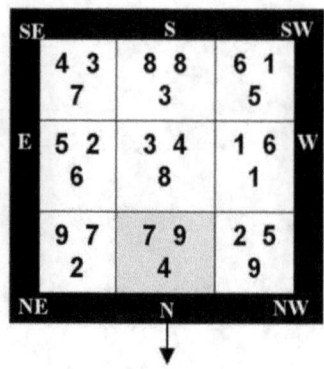

North 2 & 3

This chart has the two 8's at the back known as *Double Stars Meet at Sitting.* There are two important features are needed to fully realize the powerful, positive energy of this chart and that is it needs both a mountain and water. Install a pool with a rock waterfall and both elements are fully represented at the rear of the site. Make sure the house has substantial backing with high ground, terraced landscaping against a solid fence/wall. Keep the water as center as possible. If there is a natural hill or mountain already at the back, this is extremely auspicious. If you are unable to activate this chart on the exterior level, then install a water fountain near the back door. Place two stone planters or statues outside if you have a balcony or patio. If not, place them near the back door inside your living space. The North-facing charts can bring the occupants success in business and business relationships that will take them all over the world.

Period 9 Perks! Install a mountain in the *Northeast* of the front yard. The 'mountain' can be higher ground, landscape mounds, courtyard walls, boulders or any combination. Place water in the *North* area of the front yard such as a fountain. *Note:* this is the only Period 8 chart that has the 9 facing star in the front—very auspicious!

These Formations are Possible, Not Definite!
The **North 2** properties may have a *Robbery Mountain Sha* formation if there a jagged cliff, electrical tower, huge dead tree, lamppost, or a broken mountain in the West. A *Peach Blossom Sha* is activated by real water or a road coming from the West. For homes that face **North 3**, there is a possible *Eight Roads of Destruction* if you have a road/driveway coming from and exiting the Northeast direction. These homes also may have a *Robbery Mountain Sha* formation if there is a jagged cliff, electrical tower, huge dead tree, lamppost, or a broken mountain in the Northeast.

Activating the INDOORS
Move your Stuff!

Excellent Doors
Always use and activate doors with excellent facing stars; for this chart they are the *South, North, Southwest,* and *West*: this applies to all exterior doors as well as an interior garage door used to enter the house. A Northwest-facing front door (which will be angled) is seriously negative. Cure with high quality metal such as brass, bronze, stainless steel, pewter or copper. See page 290 for ideas regarding metal cures.

Master Bedroom + Family
There are two ways to enhance health, harmony and prosperity in the bedroom and that is location and direction; the *direction* of the bed will give you the most powerful results. Locate the master bedroom in the *South, Southwest, Southeast, West* or *Northeast* as all of these areas have good mountain stars with auspicious energy. **Bed Directions:** Place the marital/owner's headboard/bed to the *South, Southwest or West;* these bed directions have a good mountain *and* facing star combinations with excellent energy.

If there are any bedrooms located in either the East or Northwest, take special care. These sectors of the house have very negative energy. In the event the marital/owner's bedroom is already situated there; make sure the bed is not placed to either direction. As an extra measure, place high quality metal in the room and keep the colors soft and neutral. Use the recommended directions for other family members.

Home Office + Study
Place your desk/body to the *South, North, Southwest or West;* these directions have great facing stars with prosperous energy. For students, writers, teachers or bloggers face to the Southwest or West as they have the strongest 'scholarly' energy and indicate success in examinations, accelerating intelligence and accomplishments in literary pursuits.

Stoves, Grills and Fireplaces
The best direction for the stove knobs, buttons or controls is *South, North,* or *Southwest*; this applies to outdoor kitchens/grills as well. Fireplaces, either inside or outdoors, can face to the *South, North,* or *Southwest*; this house can also have a two-way fireplace on the North-South axis; this activates prosperity and romance.

Watchful Eye: Annual Stars and Three Killings
This chart has two negative areas to pay attention to that can harm your money, health and household harmony. They are the **Northwest** (2, 5) and the **East** (5, 2). The Northwest becomes worse in 2023 and 2026 while the East in 2020, 2023 and 2025. No water *(pools, fountains, etc)* or fire *(stoves, fire place/pits or grills)* should be placed in either area, *no matter the year,* it will activate them!

Also the Three Killings visits the North in 2022 and 2026. It is taboo to engage in demolition, construction or deep digging. Use the Great Sun Formula if you must touch this area.

The Three Killings positions changes locations every year. It is taboo to engage in construction, demolition or deep digging such as a swimming pool. For this Period 8 North 2 & 3 home, it visits the front (North) in 2022 and 2026.

PERIOD 8

Northeast 1 *(22.6° to 37.5°)* Facing name: **Chou** and the **Ox**

Very Special Chart: **Combination of Ten** *(He Shih Chu)* **and Prosperous Sitting and Facing** *(Wang Shan Wang Shui)*

Activating the OUTDOORS
Needs Water in Front, Mountain at Back

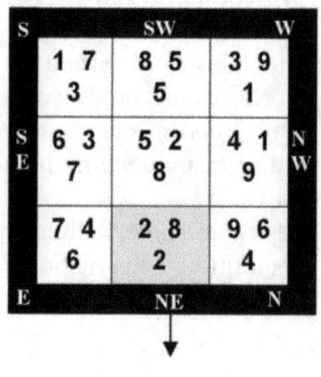

Northeast 1

This is one of the most auspicious charts of Period 8 boasting two very special aspects; it's a *Combination of Ten and Prosperous Sitting and Facing*. This chart can bring great prosperity and nobility to the occupants; they're very lucky for both *people* and *money*! To fully activate the enormous promise of this chart, you will need substantial backing such as a solid fence comprised of stucco, brick, rock or wood—or any combination of these elements. Installing tiered or terraced garden beds in front of the solid fence will magnify the effect. Place a beautiful water feature in the front such as a stream, Koi pond, water fountain or waterfall (it should flow towards the home).

For those living in an apartment, high-rise building, townhome, condominium or a rented space and are not able to install a water feature outdoors, place one indoors in the recommended area. To activate the mountain in the recommended area, use a tall armoire, heavy bookcases or stone statues; these will sufficiently activate the energy.

Period 9 Perks! Install a mountain in the *North* of the front yard. The 'mountain' can be higher ground, landscape mounds, courtyard walls, boulders or any combination. Place water in the *West* area of the backyard such as a pond, pool or fountain.

These Formations are Possible, Not Definite!
These sites may also have a *Robbery Mountain Sha* formation if there is a jagged cliff, electrical tower, huge dead tree, lamppost, or a broken mountain in the North; they indicate that everyone in household getting an unusual disease, hurt by knives and disasters. A *Peach Blossom Sha* is activated with a road coming from the South famous for causing affairs and sexual misconduct.

Activating the INDOORS
Move your Stuff!

Excellent Doors
Always use and activate doors with excellent facing stars; for this chart they are to the *Northeast, Northwest, West, North* and *East*. This applies to all exterior doors as well as an interior garage door used to enter the house. A Southwest-facing back door is seriously negative. Cure with high quality metal such as brass, bronze, stainless steel, pewter or copper.

Master Bedroom + Family
There are two ways to enhance health, harmony and prosperity in the bedroom and that is location and direction; the *direction* of the bed will give you the most powerful results. Locate the master bedroom in the *South, Southwest, North* or *Southeast* as these areas all have good mountain stars with auspicious energy. **Bed Directions:** Place the marital/owner's headboard/bed to the *Northwest* or *North* and the *West* is acceptable; these bed directions have a good mountain *and* facing star combination with excellent energy. *Use the above directions when placing the bed for other family members. Note:* Sleeping to either the Northeast or Southwest will cause illness and money loss.

Home Office + Study

Place your desk, face to the *Northeast, Northwest, East or West;* these directions have great facing stars with prosperous and auspicious energy! For students, writers, teachers or bloggers, face to the East or Northwest as they have the strongest 'scholarly' energy and indicate success in examinations, accelerating intelligence and accomplishments in literary pursuits.

Stoves, Grills and Fireplaces

To enhance health, harmony, and prosperity the stove knobs, buttons or controls should face *Northeast, East, Northwest* or *West;* this applies to outdoor kitchens/grills as well. This house *cannot* have a kitchen or fireplace in the **center** of the home (5, 2 combination); it can bring serious health issues such as heart attacks and high blood pressure. Fireplaces, either inside or outdoors, can face to the *Northeast, East, Northwest* or *West;* this house can also have a two-way fireplace on the East/West axis; this activates prosperity and romance.

Watchful Eye: Annual Stars

This chart has one negative area to pay attention to. It is the **Southwest** (5 facing star) and it becomes worse in 2022 and 2024. Cure with high quality metal such as brass, bronze, stainless steel, pewter or copper. No water *(pools, fountains, etc)* or fire *(stoves, fire place/pits or grills)* should be placed in this area, *no matter the area*, it gets activated!

PERIOD 8

Northeast 2 *(37.6° to 52.5°)* Facing name: **Gen**
Northeast 3 *(52.6° to 67.5°)* Facing name: **Yin** and the **Tiger**
Very Special Chart: **Parent String (***(Fu Mu San Poon Gua)*

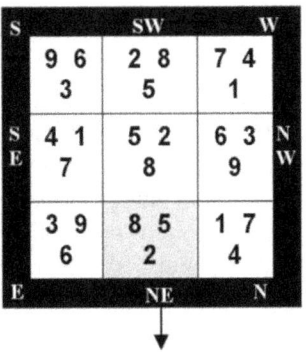

Northeast 2 & 3

Activating the OUTDOORS
Need Mountain in Front, Water at the Back

This property boasts one of the very special charts known as a *Parent String*. Properties that face the Northeast can produce open-minded and kind-hearted people, intelligent children, and the householders can amass fortunes. However, these special charts must be energized in special and specific ways with a mountain in the front and water at the back. The 'mountain' can be higher ground, courtyard walls, landscape mounds, boulders (no sharp or jagged edges) or any combination (the mountain should be 3 feet or higher). Keep the mountain as centered in the garden as possible without blocking the front door. Install a beautiful water feature such as a pool, waterfall, Koi pond or small lake in the center of the back garden. For those living in an apartment, high-rise building, townhome, condominium or a rented space and are not able to install a water feature outdoors, place one indoors in the recommended area. To activate the mountain in the recommended area, use a tall armoire, heavy bookcases or stone statues; these will sufficiently activate the energy.

Period 9 Perks! Install a mountain in the *South* corner of the backyard. The 'mountain' can be higher ground, landscape mounds, elevated brick/stone decking, boulders or any combination. Place water in the *East* area of the front yard such as a fountain.

These Formations are Possible, Not Definite!
For homes facing **Northeast 2** there is a possible *Eight Roads of Destruction* if you have a road/driveway coming from and exiting the North and East directions. These properties may also have a *Robbery Mountain Sha* formation if there is a jagged cliff, electrical tower, huge dead tree, lamppost, or a broken mountain in the East. For the **Northeast 3** facing properties there is a possible *Eight Killing Forces* if there is a mountain in front of the property on the left-hand side (Northeast). A *Peach Blossom Sha* is activated with a road coming from the South. There is also a possible *Robbery Mountain Sha* formation if there a jagged cliff, electrical tower, huge dead tree, lamppost, or a broken mountain in the North.

Activating the INDOORS
Move your Stuff!

Excellent Doors
Always use and activate doors with excellent facing stars; for this chart they are the *West, Southwest, Southeast, South,* and *East*. This applies to all exterior doors as well as an interior garage door used to enter the house. In modern homes, an interior garage door is often the main entry into the house, therefore it is extremely important. Unfortunately, the Northeast-facing front door is seriously negative. Cure with high quality metal such as brass, bronze, stainless steel, pewter or copper.

Master Bedroom + Family
There are two ways to enhance health, harmony and prosperity in the bedroom and that is location and direction; the *direction* of the bed will give you the most powerful results. Locate the master bedroom in the *South, North, Northwest,* or *Northeast* (second floor) as these areas have good mountain stars with great energy. **Bed Directions:** Place the marital/owner's headboard/bed to the *South* or *Southeast;* these bed directions have a good mountain *and* facing star combination with excellent energy. Use the above directions when placing the bed for other family members.

Home Office + Study
Place your desk/face to the *Southwest* or *West, Southeast, South* or *East* as these directions have good facing stars with romance, health or prosperity energy. For students, writers, teachers or bloggers, face to the West or Southeast as they have the strongest 'scholarly' energy and indicate success in examinations, accelerating intelligence and accomplishments in literary pursuits.

Stoves, Grills and Fireplaces
The best direction for the stove knobs, buttons or controls is *Southeast, Southwest, West* or *East*; this applies to outdoor kitchens/grills as well. This house *cannot* have a kitchen or fireplace in the center of the home (5, 2 combination); it can bring serious health issues such as heart attacks and high blood pressure. Fireplaces, either inside or outdoors, can face to the *Southeast, Southwest, West* or *East*; this house can also have a two-way fireplace on the East/West axis; this activates prosperity and romance.

Watchful Eye: *Annual Stars*
This chart has one negative area to pay attention to that can harm your money, health and household harmony. It is the **Northeast** (5 facing star) and it becomes worse in 2021 and 2025. No water *(pools, fountains, etc)* or fire *(stoves, fire place/pits or grills)* should be placed in this area, *no matter the year,* it gets activated!

PERIOD 8

East 1 *(67.6° to 82.5°)* Facing name: **Jia**
Chart: **Double Stars Meet at Facing** *(Shuang Xing Dao Xiang)*

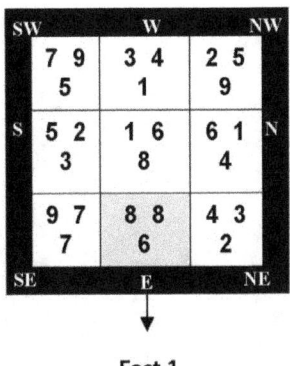

East 1

Activating the OUTDOORS
Need Water and Mountain at Front

These properties are referred to as the *Double Stars Meet at Facing,* and they have the two 8's in the front. When this chart is fully energized, it can produce residents with high academic achievements or great successes in the educational field. To do this, you will need both a mountain and beautiful water feature in the front garden area. The 'mountain' can be higher ground, courtyard walls, landscape mounds, boulders (no sharp or jagged edges) or any combination (the mountain should be 3 feet or higher). Install a water feature such as a Koi pond, waterfall or stream in the front garden. You could place a large, tall, stone or marble fountain in the front yard and this would fulfill the criteria of the mountain *and* water. For those living in an apartment, high-rise building, townhome, condominium or a rented space and are not able to install a water feature outdoors, place one indoors in the recommended area. To activate the mountain in the recommended area, use a tall armoire, heavy bookcases or stone statues; these will sufficiently activate the energy.

Period 9 Perks! Install a mountain in the *Southeast* area of the front yard. The 'mountain' can be higher ground, landscape mounds, courtyard walls, boulders or any combination. Place water in the *Southwest* area of the backyard such as a fountain, pond or pool.

These Formations are Possible, Not Definite!
There is a possible *Eight Roads of Destruction* formation if you have a road/driveway coming from and exiting the Northeast direction; they are notorious for bringing illness, bankruptcy, and divorce. There is also a possible *Robbery Mountain Sha* formation if there a jagged cliff, electrical tower, huge dead tree, lamppost, or a broken mountain in the South; they indicate everyone in household getting an unusual disease, hurt by knives and disasters.

Activating the INDOORS
Move your Stuff!

Excellent Doors
Always use and activate doors with excellent facing stars; for this chart they are the *North, East, West,* and *Southwest*. This applies to all exterior doors as well as an interior garage door used to enter the house An interior garage door rates very high because in modern homes this is often the main entry into the house, therefore it is extremely important!

Master Bedroom + Family
There are two ways to enhance health, harmony and prosperity in the bedroom and that is location and direction; the *direction* of the bed will give you the most powerful results. Locate the master bedroom in the *North, East,* or *Southeast* as these areas have good mountain stars with great energy. **Bed Directions:** Place the marital/owner's headboard/bed to the North or East direction; these bed directions have a good mountain *and* facing star combination with excellent energy.

If there are any bedrooms located in either the South or Northwest, take special care. These sectors of the house have very negative energy. In the event the marital/owner's bedroom is already situated there; make sure the bed is not placed to either direction. As an extra measure, place high quality metal in the room and keep the colors soft and neutral. Use the recommended directions when placing the bed for other family members.

Home Office + Study
Place your desk, face to the *North, East, West* or *Southwest* these are all good facing stars that will support many opportunities and prosperity. For students, writers, teachers or bloggers, face to the West or North as they have the strongest 'scholarly' energy and indicate success in examinations, accelerating intelligence and accomplishments in literary pursuits.

Stoves, Grills and Fireplaces
The best direction for the stove knobs, buttons or controls is the *North, West, Southwest* or *East*; this applies to outdoor kitchens/grills as well. Fireplaces, either inside or outdoors, can face to the *North, West, Southwest* or *East*; this house can also have a two-way fireplace on the East/West axis; this activates prosperity and romance.

Watchful Eye: *Annual Stars and Three Killings*
This chart has two negative areas to pay attention to that can harm your money, health and household harmony. They are the **Northwest** (2, 5) and the **South** (5, 2). The Northwest becomes more serious in 2023 and 2026 while the South in 2020, 2022 and 2026. No water *(pools, fountains, etc)* or fire *(stoves, fire place/pits or grills)* should be placed in either area, *no matter the year*, it will activate them! Also the Three Killings visits the East in 2025 and 2029. It is taboo to engage in demolition, construction or deep digging. If you must touch this area, use the Great Sun Formula to protect against bad luck.

PERIOD 8

East 2 *(82.6° to 97.5°)* Facing name: **Mao** and the **Rabbit**
East 3 *(97.6° to 112.5°)* Facing name: **Yi**
Chart: **Double Stars Meet at the Sitting** *(Shuang Xing Dao Zuo)*

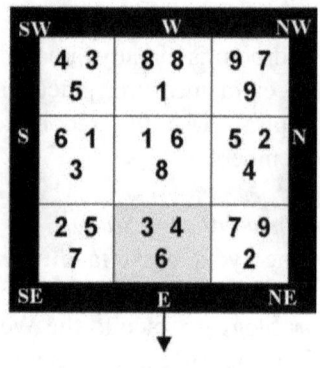

East 2 & 3

Activating the OUTDOORS
Needs Mountain and Water at Back

This property is known as *Double Stars Meet at Sitting* and has the two 8's located at the back of the structure. The East-facing charts can produce righteous, charismatic, loyal, faithful professionals such as doctors, lawyers, and philosophers who are both wealthy and noble. In order to fully energize this chart, you will need a mountain and water in the West (backyard), installing both features is important. Be diligent in creating substantial backing such as a solid fence made of brick, stucco, wood, or any combination thereof. You could create tiered or terraced garden beds in front of the solid fencing to increase the effect. If you have a natural mountain, hill or mound located at the back, you are blessed indeed! Install a beautiful water feature such as a pool, small lake, Koi pond or stream. If you have a pool with a large rock waterfall, the criteria for activating this chart are met if they are located in the center back.

For those living in an apartment, high-rise building, townhome, condominium or a rented space and are not able to install a water feature outdoors, place one indoors in the recommended area. To activate the mountain in the recommended area, use a tall armoire, heavy bookcases or stone statues; these will sufficiently activate the energy.

Period 9 Perks! Install a mountain in the *Northwest* corner of the backyard. The 'mountain' can be higher ground, landscape mounds, elevated brick/stone decking, boulders or any combination. Place water in the *Northeast* area of the front yard such as a fountain.

These Formations are Possible, Not Definite!
For homes facing **East 2** there is a possible *Eight Killings* formation if there is a mountain from the Southwest. A *Peach Blossom Sha* is activated with a road coming from the North famous for causing affairs and sexual misconduct. For homes that face to **East 3,** there is a possible *Eight Roads of Destruction* if there is a road/driveway coming from and exiting from the Southeast direction. There is also a possible *Robbery Mountain Sha* formation if there a jagged cliff, electrical tower, huge dead tree, lamppost, or a broken mountain in the Northeast for *both* East 2 and East 3 homes; they indicate everyone in household getting an unusual disease, hurt by knives and disasters.

Activating the INDOORS
Move your Stuff!

Excellent Doors
Always use and activate doors with excellent facing stars; for this chart they are the *West, Northeast, East* and *South*. This applies to all exterior doors as well as an interior garage door used to enter the house. A Southeast-facing front door (likely an angled door/entrance) is seriously negative. Cure with high quality metal such as brass, bronze, stainless steel, pewter or copper.

Master Bedroom + Family
There are two ways to enhance health, harmony and prosperity in the bedroom and that is location and direction; the *direction* of the bed will give you the most powerful results. Locate the master bedroom in the *South, Northwest,* or *West* as these areas have good mountain stars with great energy. **Bed Directions:** Place the marital/owner's headboard/bed to the *West* or *South*; these directions have a good facing and mountain star combination that will enhance health, prosperity and harmony in the house.

If there are any bedrooms located in either the Southeast or North, take special care. These sectors of the house have very negative energy. In the event the marital/owner's bedroom is already situated there; make sure the bed is not placed to either direction. As an extra measure, place high quality metal in the room and keep the colors soft and neutral. Use the recommended directions when placing the bed for other family members.

Home Office + Study
Place your desk/body to the *West, Northeast, East or South*; these directions have excellent facing stars with auspicious energy. For students, writers, teachers or bloggers, face to the East or South as they have the strongest 'scholarly' energy and indicate success in examinations, accelerating intelligence and accomplishments in literary pursuits.

Stoves, Grills and Fireplaces
The best direction for the stove knobs, buttons or controls is *East, West, South* or *Northeast*; this applies to outdoor kitchens/grills as well. Fireplaces, either inside or outdoors, can face to the *East, West, South* or *Northeast*; this house can also have a two-way fireplace on the East/West axis; this activates prosperity and romance.

Watchful Eye: *Annual Stars and Three Killings*

This chart has two negative areas to pay attention to that can harm your money, health and household harmony; in certain years they become more dangerous. They are the **Southeast** (2, 5) and the **North** (5, 2). The Southeast becomes worse in 2021, 2024, and 2026 while the North in 2021 and 2023. No water *(pools, fountains, etc)* or fire *(stoves, fire place/pits or grills)* should be placed in either area, it will activate them!

Also the Three Killings visits the East in 2025 and 2029. It is taboo to engage in demolition, construction or deep digging. If you must touch this area, use the Great Sun Formula to protect against bad luck.

PERIOD 8
Southeast 1 *(112.6° to 127.5°)* Facing name: **Chen** and the **Dragon**
Very Special Chart: **Pearl String** *(Lin Cu San Poon Gua)*

Activating the OUTDOORS
Needs Mountain in Front, Water at the Back

The *Pearl String* charts are very special and must be energized with a mountain in front and water at the back to fully realize its potential to bring triple good luck! These Southeast-facing properties can produce great talent in all sports, including martial arts. The children of this house may also excel in sciences, especially those requiring technical expertise. To create the *mountain* in front, you may use high ground, landscape mounds, massive boulders (no jagged or pointed edges) or courtyard walls. Keep the mountain a centered as possible in the front yard without blocking the front door. At the back, install a Koi pond, swimming pool, waterfall or large fountain.

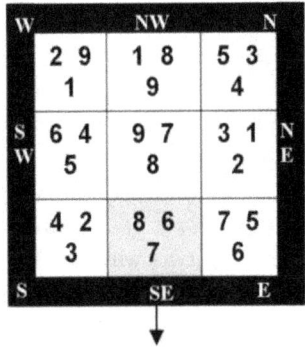

Southeast 1

If you are unable to activate the exterior of your site, install a fountain near the back door inside or outside on the balcony or patio if you have one. Place two stone statues or planters on either side of the front door; tall bookcases or armoire also work well as an internal mountain.

Period 9 Perks! Install a pond, pool or fountain in the *West* corner of the backyard. The water cannot be located between 262.6° to 277.5° or it may activate affairs. *Note:* the 9 mountain star is trapped in the middle and cannot be represented. However, activating the 8 mountain will bring nobility and prosperity.

These Formations are Possible, Not Definite!
An *Eight Killings* formation is possible if there is a mountain bringing energy to the house from the North direction. A *Peach Blossom Sha* is activated with a road coming from the West famous for causing affairs and sexual misconduct. There is also a possible *Robbery Mountain Sha* formation if there a jagged cliff, electrical tower, huge dead tree, lamppost, or a broken mountain in the Northeast; they indicate everyone in household getting an unusual disease, hurt by knives and disasters.

Activating the INDOORS
Move your Stuff!

Excellent Doors
Always use and activate good doors; the best doors for this house are facing the *Northwest, West, Northeast, Southeast* and *Southwest*. This applies to all exterior doors as well as an interior garage door used to enter the house. An interior garage door rates very high because in modern homes this is often the main entry into the house, therefore it is extremely important!

Master Bedroom + Family
There are two ways to health, relationships, and prosperity in the bedroom and that is location and direction; the *direction* of the bed will give you the most powerful results. Locate the master bedroom in the *Southwest, Northwest,* or *Southeast* (second floor) as these areas have good mountain stars. **Bed Directions:** Place the marital/owner's headboard/bed to the *Northwest, Southwest* or *Southeast*; these bed directions have a good mountain *and* facing star combinations with excellent energy. Use the above directions when placing the bed for other family members.

Home Office + Study
Place your desk, face to the *Northwest, Southwest, West, Northeast* or *Southeast*; these directions have excellent facing stars and energy. For students, writers, teachers or bloggers, face to the Southwest as it has the strongest 'scholarly' energy and indicates success in examinations, accelerating intelligence and accomplishments in literary pursuits.

Stoves, Grills and Fireplaces
The best direction for the stove knobs, buttons or controls is *Southwest, Northwest, Northeast* or *West*; this applies to outdoor kitchens/grills as well. Fireplaces, either inside or outdoors, can face to the *Southwest, Northwest, Northeast* or *West*; this house may also have a two-way fireplace on the Northeast-Southwest axis; this activates prosperity and romance.

Watchful Eye: *Annual Stars*
This chart has two negative areas to pay attention to that can harm your money, health and household harmony. They are the **East** *(5 facing star)* and the **South** *(2 facing star)*. The East becomes more serious in 2020, 2023 and 2025 while the South in 2020, 2022, and 2026. No water *(pools, fountains, etc)* or fire *(stoves, fire place/pits or grills))* should be placed in either area, *no matter the year*, it will activate them!

PERIOD 8
Southeast 2 *(127.6° to 142.5°)* Facing name: **Xun**
Southeast 3 *(142.6° to 157.5°)* Facing name: **Su** and the **Snake**
Chart: **Prosperous Sitting Prosperous Facing** *(Wang Shan Wang Shui)*

Activating the OUTDOORS
Needs Water in Front, Mountain in Back

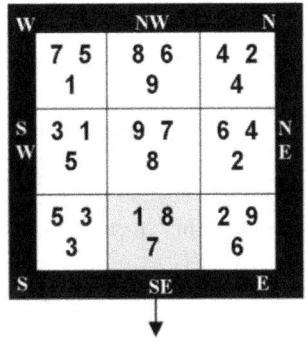

Southeast 2 & 3

These properties are 'lucky for people, lucky for money' and are called *Prosperous Sitting and Facing* (Wang Shan, Wang Shui). This chart can produce those who have high morals, nobility, trustworthiness and the Southeast-facing is suited for philosophers, performers, singer, and artists. In order to fully energize the potential, you will need significant backing with a solid fence made of stone, stucco, bricks, wood or any combination thereof. If there is a natural mountain, hill or mound behind the property, this is very auspicious! Place a beautiful water feature in the front such as a fountain, stream, Koi pond or waterfall.

If you are unable to activate the exterior of your site, install a fountain near the front door (inside or out). Place two stone planters or statues near the back door (inside or out). You may also use a tall armoire or bookcases near the back door; they work very well as an internal mountain.

Period 9 Perks! If you do not already have a water feature in the Southeast, install a fountain in the *East* area of the front yard. *Note:* the 9 mountain star is trapped in the middle and cannot be represented. However, activating the 8 mountain will bring nobility and prosperity.

These Formations are Possible, Not Definite!
There is a possible *Eight Roads of Destruction* if the house faces **Southeast 2** and a road/driveway comes from/exits the South or East. An *Eight Killings* formation is possible for homes facing **Southeast 3** if there is a mountain bringing energy to the house from the West direction. A *Peach Blossom Sha* is activated with a road coming from the South. There is also a possible *Robbery Mountain Sha* formation if there a jagged cliff, electrical tower, huge dead tree, lamppost, or a broken mountain in the East for both facings; they indicate everyone in household getting an unusual disease, hurt by knives and disasters.

Activating the INDOORS
Move your Stuff!

Excellent Doors
Always use and activate good doors; the best ones for this chart are facing to the *Southeast, Northeast, East, or Southwest* directions. This applies to all exterior doors as well as an interior garage door used to enter the house. An interior garage door rates very high because in modern homes this is often the main entry into the house, therefore it is extremely important!

Master Bedroom + Family
There are two ways to enhance health, harmony and prosperity in the bedroom and that is location and direction; the *direction* of the bed will give you the most powerful results. Locate the master bedroom in the *Northwest, Northeast,* or *the Southeast* (second floor) as these have good mountain stars. **Bed Directions:** Place the marital/owner's headboard/bed to the *Southeast, Northwest, or Northeast*; these directions have a good mountain *and* facing star combinations with excellent energy. *Use the above directions when placing the bed for other family members.*

Home Office + Study
Place your desk/face to the *Southeast* or *East, Northwest, Southwest or Northeast;* these directions have very auspicious energy. For students, writers, teachers or bloggers, face to the Northeast as it has the strongest 'scholarly' energy and indicates success in examinations, accelerating intelligence and accomplishments in literary pursuits.

Stoves, Grills and Fireplaces
The best directions for the stove knobs, buttons or controls are *Southeast, East, Northeast* or *Southwest*; this applies to outdoor kitchens/grills as well. Fireplaces, either inside or outdoors, can face to the *Southeast, East, Northeast* or *Southwest*; this house can also have a two-way fireplace on the Northeast-Southwest axis; this activates prosperity and romance.

Watchful Eye: Annual Stars
This chart has two negative areas to pay attention to that can harm your money, health and household harmony; in certain years they become more dangerous. They are the **West** *(5 facing star)* and the **North** *(2 facing star)*. The West becomes more serious in 2020 and 2024 while the North in 2021 and 2023. No water *(pools, fountains, etc)* or fire *(stoves, fire place/pits or grills)* should be placed in either area, *no matter the year*, it will activate them!

CHAPTER SEVEN
The Period 7 Charts and Activation

The Period 7 homes lost much of their vitality beginning February 4th 2004 and they will need to be *re-energized* in very precise and particular ways. No need to wait until Period 9 however, you can capture all the good luck now!

If you moved into your property between February 4, 1984 to February 3, 2003, and have not engaged in any major remodeling, your house is a Period 7. You will need to activate the Period 7 Natal Star Charts with water, mountain, cures and use good doors. In order to proceed and to locate your unique chart and to set things into motion, you'll need the facing direction. If you have not already discovered the facing direction, refer to the section of the book entitled *'How to Determine the Facing'* on page 49. Once you have the degree check the 24 Mountains chart on page 51. Your move-in date determines which Period your house falls into. Draw a floor plan of your home. Divide it up into nine cells and overlay the directions and Star Chart. Place this information outside the floor plan so that you can sketch in possible bed locations, desks, water, and so forth as you read the recommendations. If you are unsure which directions go where, you will find them in the Natal Star Charts in the little black area outside the numbers. Only one chart applies to your home and its unique energy. The rest of the charts serve as great reference material assisting your friends, family, co-workers or if you move into another home. You'll be able to arrange everything perfectly—again!

It does take some time to fully master Flying Stars (not to mention all the other systems for that matter), so the charts have been fully evaluated for you. The recommendations and assessments have made use of the five elements, cosmic trinity, timeliness of the stars, annual stars, proper activation of mountain and facing stars, He Tu, Luo Shu, the two Ba Guas, Eight Mansions, Flying Stars, San Yuan and San He formulas.

Every home has areas where there is negative energy. The *Watchful Eye* is to alert you to pay attention to these areas as in certain years, they can be worse. No fire or water should be located there, no matter the year, as they will be activated. Cure these areas as recommended so that they become neutral. You will also need to be aware of when the *Three Killings* visits the front of your property. It is taboo to engage in deep digging, remodeling or demolition. Use good dates from the *Great Sun Formula* if you must touch this area. These dates will protect you from inauspicious events occurring.

Most Period 7 homes are best brought current to Period 9. Changing the Period of a home and bringing it to the current, most prosperous energy is accomplished through major renovations. What constitutes a major renovation? Removing the entire roof *(and some small percentage must be exposed to the open sky at least for a few hours),* major interior remodeling, renovating the front entrance and door, painting the entire inside and outside at the same time, remodeling kitchen or bathrooms, installing a skylight/s, changing all the floors at the same time, adding on a room or adding an attached garage. All of these things will cause a major shift in energy, and therefore your Flying Star Chart will change. However, if you are not able to change the Period of the property, this chapter is devoted to calming the negative energy of the Period 7 charts and enhancing the good.

PERIOD 7
South 1 *(157.6° to 172.5°)* Facing Name: **Bing**
Chart: Double Stars Meet at Facing *(Shuang Xing Dao Xiang)*

Activating the OUTDOORS
Install Water, Doors, Mountain & Cures

	NW	N	NE	
W	4 1 / 8	8 6 / 3	6 8 / 1	
	5 9 / 9	3 2 / 7	1 4 / 5	E
	9 5 / 4	7 7 / 2	2 3 / 6	
	SW	S	SE	

This chart has the two 7's in the front of the property known as *Double Stars Meet at Facing* and was quite lucky until February 4th, 2004. In general, South-facing structures support people of authority, those who are charismatic, and the family can accumulate lots of property. It can also bring descendants who will achieve high-ranking positions in politics *if* activated accordingly. To re-energize this chart during Period 8 or 9, use the following recommendations:

Water: Install a water feature in the *West* (9 facing star), *Northeast* (8 facing star), or *Northwest* (1 facing star). The water can be a Koi pond, swimming pool, waterfall or large fountain.

Mountain: Simulate a mountain in the *Southwest* (9 mountain star), *North* (8 mountain star) or *East* (1 mountain star). The 'mountain' can be higher ground, courtyard walls, landscape mounds, boulders (no sharp or jagged edges) or any combination (the mountain should be 3 feet or higher). Install a water feature such as a Koi pond, waterfall or stream in the front garden.

Cures: Although the South energy reduces the 7 stars, place a small water feature or bird bath near the front door. Also, paint the door red; these cures will further exhaust the negative energy. If you are unable to activate this chart exterior to your site, then place two stone statues or planters near the back door. Install a tall floor fountain in the Northeast corner. If you are not allowed to paint the front door red on the exterior, then paint the interior side red. For those living in an apartment, high-rise building, townhome, condominium or a rented space and are not able to install a water feature outdoors, place one indoors in the recommended area. To activate the mountain in the recommended area, use a tall armoire, heavy bookcases or stone statues; these will sufficiently activate the energy.

These Formations are Possible, Not Definite!
There is a potential *Eight Roads of Destruction* if there is a road or real water coming from/exiting the Southeast direction; they are notorious for bringing bankruptcy, disease, and divorce. This house also has a potential *Robbery Mountain Sha* formation if there is a jagged cliff, electrical tower, huge dead tree, lamppost, or a broken mountain in the Southwest that indicates being hurt by knives, unusual diseases and disasters.

Activating the INDOORS
Move your Stuff!

Excellent Doors
Always use and activate doors with excellent facing stars; for this chart they are the *North, Northeast, West, East,* and *Northwest*. This applies to all exterior doors as well as an interior garage door used to enter the house. An interior garage door rates very high because in modern homes this is often the main entry into the house, therefore it is extremely important.

Master Bedroom + Family
There are two ways to health, harmony and prosperity in the bedroom and that is location and direction; the *direction* of the bed will give you the most powerful results. Locate the master bedroom in the *North, Northeast, East* or *Northwest* as these areas have good mountain stars. **Bed Directions:** Place the marital/owner's headboard/bed to the *North, Northeast, East* or *Northwest* directions. These bed directions have a good mountain *and* facing star combination with excellent energy.

If there are any bedrooms located in either the West or Southwest, take special care. These sectors of the house have very negative energy. In the event the marital/owner's bedroom is already situated there; make sure the bed is not placed to either direction. As an extra measure, place high quality metal in the room and keep the colors soft and neutral. Use the recommended directions when placing the bed for other family members.

Home Office + Study
Place your desk/body to the *North, Northeast, West, East* or *Northwest*; these directions have great facing stars. For students, writers, teachers or bloggers use the East and Northwest as they have the strongest 'scholarly' energy and indicate success in examinations, accelerating intelligence and accomplishments in literary pursuits.

Stoves, Grills and Fireplaces

The stove knobs, buttons or controls should face to the *Northeast, Northwest,* or *West* directions; this applies to outdoor kitchens/grills as well. This house cannot have fire (kitchen, stove or fireplace) in the center (3, 2) of the house; it can cause serious illness, bickering/fighting and lawsuits. Fireplaces, either inside or outdoors, can face to *the Northwest, West, East or Northeast*; this house can also have a two-way fireplace (in any room) on the East/West axis; this activates prosperity, promotions and romance.

Watchful Eye: *Annual Stars and Three Killings*

Pay special attention to the *Southwest* with the 5 facing star. It becomes more serious in 2019, 2022 and 2024. No water *(pools, fountains, etc)* or fire *(stoves, fire place/pits or grills)* should be placed in the Southwest area, *no matter the year*, it gets activated! The *Three Killings* visits the South in 2020 and 2024.

The Three Killings positions changes locations every year. It is taboo to engage in construction, demolition or deep digging such as a swimming pool. For this home, it visits the front (South) in 2020 and 2024.

PERIOD 7

South 2 (172.6° to 187.5°) Facing Name: **Wu** and the **Horse**
and **South 3** (187.6° to 202.5°) Facing Name: **Ting**
Chart: Combination of Ten *(He Shih Chu)* and
Double Stars Meet at Back *(Shuang Xing Dao Zuo)*

Activating the OUTDOORS
Install Water, Mountain & Cures

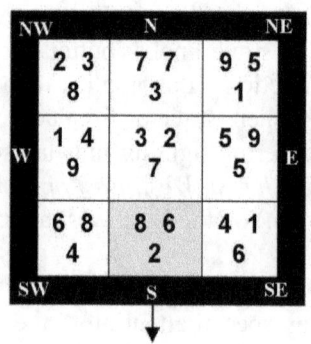

This chart has the two 7's at the back of the property known as *Double Stars Meet at Sitting* and a *Combination of Ten*; which was extremely auspicious until February 4th, 2004 when much of its vitality was lost. However, the South-facing homes support entrepreneurs and success in scholarly pursuits *if* activated accordingly. To re-energize this chart during Period 8 or 9, use the following recommendations:

Water: Install a water feature in the *East* (9 facing star), *Southwest* (8 facing star), or *Southeast* (1 facing star). The water can be a Koi pond, swimming pool, waterfall or large fountain. East water cannot be between 82.6° to 97.5° or it may activate affairs.

Mountain: Simulate a mountain in the *Northeast* (9 mountain star), *South* (8 mountain star) or *West* (1 mountain star). The 'mountain' can be higher ground, courtyard walls, landscape mounds, boulders (no sharp or jagged edges) or any combination (the mountain should be 3 feet or higher). Install a water feature such as a Koi pond, waterfall or stream in the front garden.

Cures: Paint the back door red (North-facing), and place a small water feature such as a bird bath to weaken the negative energy there. If you are unable to activate the chart exterior to your site, place a water fountain in the Southwest corner inside. Install two stone statues or planters on either side of the front door (inside or outside).

For those living in an apartment, high-rise building, townhome, condominium or a rented space and are not able to install a water feature outdoors, place one indoors in the recommended area. To activate the mountain in the recommended area, use a tall armoire, heavy bookcases or stone statues; these will sufficiently activate the energy.

These Formations are Possible, Not Definite!
For homes that face **South 2**, there is a possible *Eight Killing Forces* if there is a mountain located in the Northwest direction. If there is a road coming from the East, it could activate the *Peach Blossom Sha*. These homes also may have a *Robbery Mountain Sha* formation if there is a jagged cliff, electrical tower, huge dead tree, lamppost, or a broken mountain in the Southeast. For homes that face to **South 3,** there is a possible *Eight Roads of Destruction* if there is a road or water coming from/exiting the Southwest direction, it is common for them to bring bankruptcy, disease, and divorce.

Activating the OUTDOORS
Move your Stuff!

Excellent Doors
Always use and activate doors with excellent facing stars; for this chart they are the *South, East, Southeast, West* and *Southwest*. This applies to all exterior doors as well as an interior garage door used to enter the house. An interior garage door rates very high because in modern homes this is usually the main entry into the house, therefore it is extremely important!

Master Bedroom + Family
There are two ways to enhance relationships, harmony and prosperity in the bedroom and that is location and direction; the *direction* of the bed will give you the most powerful results. Locate the master bedroom in the *West, South, Southeast* or *Southwest* as these areas have good mountain stars. **Bed Directions:** Place your headboard/bed to the *South, Southeast, West* or *Southwest*. These bed directions have a good mountain *and* facing star combination with excellent energy. If there are any bedrooms located in either the East or Northeast, take special care. These sectors of the house have very negative energy. In the event the marital/owner's bedroom is already situated there; make sure the bed is not placed to either direction. As an extra measure, place high quality metal in the room and keep the colors soft and neutral. Use the recommended directions when placing the bed for other family members.

Home Office + Study
Place your desk/body to the *South, East* or *Southeast, West* or *Southwest*; these directions have excellent facing stars. For students, writers, teachers or bloggers use the West and Southeast as they have the strongest 'scholarly' energy and indicate success in examinations, accelerating intelligence and accomplishments in literary pursuits.

Stoves, Grills and Fireplaces
The stove knobs, buttons or controls should face *Southwest, Southeast, West* or *East*; this applies to outdoor kitchens/grills as well. This house *should not* have a kitchen or fireplace in the center of the home (3, 2 combination); it can bring serious health issues such as heart attacks and high blood pressure, bickering/fighting and lawsuits.

Fireplaces, either inside or outdoors, can face to *the Southwest, Southeast, West* or *East*; this house can also have a two-way fireplace (in any room) on the East/West axis; this activates prosperity and romance.

Watchful Eye: Annual Stars and Three Killings
This chart has one negative area to pay attention to that can harm your money, health and household harmony. It is the **Northeast** *(5 facing star)* and becomes worse in and 2021 and 2025. No water *(pools, fountains, etc)* or fire *(stoves, fire place/pits or grills)* should be placed in this area, *no matter the year*, it gets activated! The Three Killings visits the front in 2020 and 2024 so no deep digging in these areas.

PERIOD 7
Southwest 1 (202.6° to 217.5°) Facing Name: **Wei** and the **Goat**
Chart: **Double Stars Meet at Facing** *(Shuang Xing Dao Xiang)*

Activating the OUTDOORS
Install Water, Mountain & Cures

This property is known as *Double Stars Meet at Facing* and it has two 7's at the front of the site; this was very auspicious until February 4th, 2004 when much of its vitality was lost. However, the Southwest-facing properties are also known for turning bad fortunes into lucrative opportunities and may also denote the birth of an intelligent, wealthy and prosperous person *if* activated properly. To re-energize this chart during Period 8 or 9, use the following recommendations:

	NE	
6 8 3	4 1 1	8 6 5
2 3 8	1 4 7	9 5 6
3 2 9	7 7 4	5 9 2
	SW ↓	

Water: Install a water feature in the *South* (9 facing star), *North* (8 facing star), or *Northeast* (1 facing star). The water can be a Koi pond, swimming pool, waterfall or large fountain. If you place water in the *North*, the water feature should not touch between 352° to 7° degrees; this will create illicit affairs.

Mountain: Simulate a mountain in the *Southeast* (9 mountain star) or the *East* (8 mountain star). The 'mountain' can be higher ground, courtyard walls, landscape mounds, boulders (no sharp or jagged edges) or any combination (the mountain should be 3 feet or higher).

Cures: The Southwest earth energy strengthens the 7 stars, so place a small water feature or bird bath near the front door. Also, paint the *front* door red; these cures will further exhaust the negative energy. If you are not allowed to paint the front door red on the exterior, then paint the interior side red. Any *Southeast-facing* 'front' door or interior garage door will need to be cured with high quality metal such as brass, bronze, stainless steel, pewter or copper.

For those living in an apartment, high-rise building, townhome, condominium or a rented space and are not able to install a water feature outdoors, place one indoors in the recommended area. To activate the mountain in the recommended area, use a tall armoire, heavy bookcases or stone statues; these will sufficiently activate the energy.

These Formations are Possible, Not Definite!
These homes also may have a *Robbery Mountain Sha* formation if there is a jagged cliff, electrical tower, huge dead tree, lamppost, or a broken mountain in the *Southeast* and a *Peach Blossom Sha* if there is water located in the *North*.

Activating the OUTDOORS
Move your Stuff!

Excellent Doors
Always use and activate doors with excellent facing stars; for this chart they are the *North, Northeast, East* and *South*. This applies to all exterior doors as well as an interior garage door used to enter the house. A Southeast-facing door, in this chart, is seriously negative. If this is a well-used door, you will need to cure it with lots of metal next to or directly on the door. However, these doors can never be fully cured, only *weakened* as the movement/use of it will always keep it activated. For the best luck, use another door.

Master Bedroom + Family
There are two ways to enhance health, harmony and prosperity in the bedroom and that is location and direction; the *direction* of the bed will give you the most powerful results. Locate your master bedroom in the *North, East,* or *Southeast* as these areas have good mountain stars with great energy. **Bed Directions:** Place the marital/owner's headboard/bed to the *North, Northeast* or *East*. These bed directions have a good mountain *and* facing star combination with excellent energy.

If there are any bedrooms located in either the Southeast or South, take special care. These sectors of the house have very negative energy. In the event the marital/owner's bedroom is already situated there; make sure the bed is not placed to either direction. As an extra measure, place high quality metal in the room and keep the colors soft and neutral. Use the recommended directions when placing the bed for other family members.

Home Office + Study
Place your desk/body to the *North, Northeast, East,* or *South*; these directions have excellent facing stars and will active prosperity and promotions. For students, writers, teachers or bloggers use the Northeast as it has the strongest 'scholarly' energy and indicates success in examinations, accelerating intelligence and accomplishments in literary pursuits.

Stoves, Grills and Fireplaces
The stove knobs, buttons or controls should face *North, Northeast* or *South;* this applies to outdoor kitchens/grills as well. Fireplaces, either inside or outdoors, can face the *North, Northeast* or *South*; this house also can have a two-way fireplace (in any room) on the North/South axis; this activates opportunities and prosperity.

Watchful Eye: *Annual Stars*
This chart has two negative areas to pay attention to that can harm your money, health and household harmony; in certain years they become more dangerous. They are the **Southeast** *(9, 5)* and the **West** *(2 facing star)*. The *Southeast* becomes worse in 2021, 2024, and 2026 while the West in 2020 and 2024. No water *(pools, fountains, etc)* or fire *(stoves, fire place/pits or grills)* should be placed in either area, *no matter the year*, it will activate them!

PERIOD 7

Southwest 2 (217.6° to 232.5°) Facing Name: **Kun**
and **Southwest 3** (232.6° to 247.5°) Facing name: **Shen** and the **Monkey**
Chart: **Double Stars Meet at Sitting** *(Shuang Xing Dao Zuo)*

Activating the OUTDOORS
Install Water, Mountain & Cures

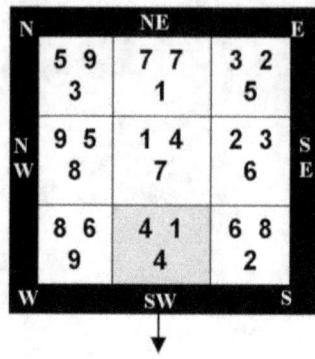

This property has the two 7's at the back of the property called *Double Stars Meet at the Sitting*; this was very lucky for relationships and money until February 4th, 2004 when much of its vitality was lost. However, the Southwest-facing properties are known for turning bad fortunes into lucrative opportunities and may also denote in the birth of an intelligent, wealthy and prosperous person *if* activated properly. To re-energize this chart during Period 8 or 9, use the following recommendations:

Water: Install a water feature in the *North* (9 facing star), *South* (8 facing star), or *Southwest* (1 facing star). The water can be a Koi pond, swimming pool, waterfall or large fountain.

Mountain: Simulate a mountain in the *Northwest* (9 mountain star) or *West* (8 mountain star). The 'mountain' can be higher ground, courtyard walls, landscape mounds, boulders (no sharp or jagged edges) or any combination (the mountain should be 3 feet or higher).

Cures: The Northeast earth energy strengthens the 7 stars, so place a small water feature or bird bath near the back door. Also, paint the door red; these cures will further exhaust the negative energy. Any *Northwest-facing* 'front' door or interior garage door will need to be cured with high quality metal such as brass, bronze, stainless steel, pewter or copper.

For those living in an apartment, high-rise building, townhome, condominium or a rented space and are not able to install a water feature outdoors, place one indoors in the recommended area. To activate the mountain in the recommended area, use a tall armoire, heavy bookcases or stone statues; these will sufficiently activate the energy.

These Formations are Possible, Not Definite!
The **Southwest 2** homes have a possible *Eight Roads of Destruction* if there is a road/water coming from/exiting certain areas of the South and West directions; they are noted for bringing disease, bankruptcy and divorce. These homes also may have a *Robbery Mountain Sha* formation if there is a jagged cliff, electrical tower, huge dead tree, lamppost, or a broken mountain in the South; they indicate everyone in household getting an unusual disease, hurt by knives and disasters.

The **Southwest 3** facing properties may have an *Eight Killing* formation if there is a mountain located in the East. A *Peach Blossom Sha* is activated with a road coming from the West. These homes also may have a *Robbery Mountain Sha* formation if there is a jagged cliff, electrical tower, huge dead tree, lamppost, or a broken mountain in the Southwest.

Activating the INDOORS
Move your Stuff!

Excellent Doors
Always use and activate doors with excellent facing stars; for this chart they are the *North, South, Southwest* and *West*. This applies to all exterior doors as well as an interior garage door used to enter the house. In modern homes, an interior garage door is often the main entry into the house, therefore it is extremely important.

Master Bedroom + Family
There are two ways to enhance relationships, health and prosperity in the bedroom and that is location and direction; the *direction* of the bed will give you the most powerful results. Locate your master bedroom in the *Southwest, South,* or *West*; these sectors of the house have good mountain stars. **Bed Directions:** Place the marital/owner's headboard/bed to the *South, Southwest,* or *West*; these bed directions have a good mountain *and* facing star combination with excellent energy.

If there are any bedrooms located in either the North or Northwest, take special care. These sectors of the house have very negative energy. In the event the marital/owner's bedroom is already situated there; make sure the bed is not placed to either direction. As an extra measure, place high quality metal in the room and keep the colors soft and neutral. Use the recommended directions when placing the bed for other family members.

Home Office + Study
Place your desk/body to the *North* or *South, Southwest,* or *West*. For students, writers, teachers or bloggers face to the Southwest as it has the strongest 'scholarly' energy and indicate success in examinations, accelerating intelligence and accomplishments in literary pursuits.

Stoves, Grills and Fireplaces
The stove knobs, buttons or controls should face to the *South, Southwest* or *North*; this applies to outdoor kitchens/grills as well. Fireplaces, either inside or outdoors, can face the *South, Southwest* or *North*; this house also can have a two-way fireplace (in any room) on the North/South axis; this activates opportunities and prosperity.

Watchful Eye: *Annual Stars*
This chart has two negative areas to pay attention to that can harm your money, health and household harmony; in certain years they become more dangerous. They are the **Northwest** *(5 facing star)* and the **East** *(2 facing star)*. The Northwest is worse in 2023 and 2026 while the East in 2020, 2023 and 2025. No water *(pools, fountains, etc)* or fire *(stoves, fire place/pits or grills)* should be placed in either area, *no matter the year*, it will activate them!

This house should never have fire or water, on the exterior, in the Northwest and East sectors of the house. In certain years, these areas become more serious.

PERIOD 7
West 1 (247.6° to 262.5°) Facing Name: **Geng**
Chart: **Reverse Formation**

Activating the OUTDOORS
Install Water, Mountain & Cures

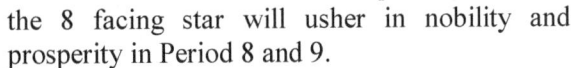

This chart is known as a *Reverse Formation*, and was not particularly auspicious even in Period 7; now it's worse in Period 8 and 9. However, the West-facing properties produce well-educated, intelligent, polite and charming people who can become very wealthy through good business management, or getting involved in politics *if* activated accordingly. To re-energize this chart during Period 8 or 9, use the following recommendations:

Water: Install a water feature in *Southeast* (8 facing star), or *Northwest* (1 facing star). The water can be a Koi pond, swimming pool, waterfall or large fountain. *Note:* the 9 facing star is trapped in the center and cannot be activated. However, placing water on the 8 facing star will usher in nobility and prosperity in Period 8 and 9.

Mountain: Simulate a mountain in the *South* (9 mountain star), *Northeast* (8 mountain star) or *North* (1 mountain star). The 'mountain' can be higher ground, courtyard walls, landscape mounds, boulders (no sharp or jagged edges) or any combination (the mountain should be 3 feet or higher).

Cures: Unfortunately, the front door (West-facing) and back door (East-facing) must be cured or you may be plagued with sickness and robberies. The *front door* will need lots of metal such as brass, copper, bronze, pewter, stainless steel or large metal wind chimes; remove any water feature placed here. Place small water such as a bird bath near the *back door* and paint it red.

For those living in an apartment, high-rise building, townhome, condominium or a rented space and are not able to install a water feature outdoors, place one indoors in the recommended area. To activate the mountain in the recommended area, use a tall armoire, heavy bookcases or stone statues; these will sufficiently activate the energy.

These Formations are Possible, Not Definite!
The house does have a possible *Eight Roads of Destruction* formation if there is a road/driveway coming from and exiting the Southwest direction; noted for bankruptcy, disease or divorce. These homes also may have a *Robbery Mountain Sha* formation if there is a jagged cliff, electrical tower, huge dead tree, lamppost, or a broken mountain in the South; they indicate everyone in household getting an unusual disease, hurt by knives and disasters.

Activating the INDOORS
Move your Stuff!

Excellent Doors
Always use and activate doors with excellent facing stars; for this chart they are the *Northwest, South, Southwest,* and *Southeast*. This applies to all exterior doors as well as an interior garage door used to enter the house. In modern homes, an interior garage door is often the main entry into the house, therefore it is extremely important. A North-facing door, in this chart, is seriously negative. If this is a well-used door, you will need to cure it with lots of metal next to or directly on the door. However, these doors can never be fully cured, only *weakened* as the movement/use of it will always keep it activated. For the best luck, use another door.

Master Bedroom + Family
There are two ways to enhance relationships, harmony and prosperity in the bedroom and that is location and direction; the *direction* of the bed will give you the most powerful results. Locate your master bedroom in the *Northeast, South,* or *Northwest* as these sectors have good mountain stars. **Bed Directions:** Place the marital/owner's headboard/bed to the *Northwest, South, Northeast* and *Southeast* directions. These bed directions have a good mountain *and* facing star combination with excellent energy. Use the above directions when placing the bed for other family members.

Home Office + Study
Place your desk/body to the *Northwest, South* or *Southwest* and *Southeast*. For students, writers, teachers or bloggers face to the South or Northwest as they have the strongest 'scholarly' energy and indicate success in examinations, accelerating intelligence and accomplishments in literary pursuits.

Stoves, Grills and Fireplaces
The stove knobs, buttons or controls should face *Southeast, South* and *Northwest;* this applies to outdoor kitchens/grills as well. This house *cannot* have a kitchen or fireplace in the center of the home (5, 9 combination); it can bring serious health issues such as heart attacks and high blood pressure. Fireplaces, either inside or outdoors, can face to *Southeast, South* and *Northwest*; this house can also have a two-way fireplace (in any room) on the Southeast/Northwest axis; these directions activate wealth.

Watchful Eye: Annual Stars and Three Killings
This chart has two negative areas to pay attention to that can harm your money, health and household harmony. They are the **North** *(5 facing star)* and the **West** *(2 facing star)*. The North is worse in 2021 and 2023 while the West in 2020 and 2024. No water *(pools, fountains, etc)* or fire *(stoves, fire place/pits or grills)* should be placed in either area, *no matter the year*, it will activate them! The *Three Killings* visits the front in 2023 so no deep digging in these areas. If you must touch this area, use the Great Sun Formula and select good dates to protect you from harm.

The Three Killings positions changes locations every year. It is taboo to engage in construction, demolition or deep digging such as a swimming pool. For this home, it visits the front (West) in 2023.

PERIOD 7

West 2 (262.6° to 277.5°) Facing Name: **You** and the **Rooster**
and **West 3** (277.6° to 292.5°) Facing Name: **Xin**
Chart: **Prosperous Sitting and Facing** *(Wang Shan Wang Shui)*

Activating the OUTDOORS
Install Water, Mountain & Cures

NE	E	SE
2 6 1	7 2 5	6 1 6
9 4 3	5 9 7	1 5 2
4 8 8	3 7 9	8 3 4
NW	W	SW

This chart had the two 7's perfectly placed in Period 7 known as *Prosperous Sitting and Facing*; it was very prestigious until February 4th, 2004 when it turned harmful. However, the West-facing properties produce people who can be powerful in the politics, super athletes, and those very accomplished in academia *if* activated accordingly. To re-energize this chart during Period 8 or 9, use the following recommendations:

Water: Install a water feature in the *Northwest* (8 facing star), or *Southeast* (1 facing star). The water can be a Koi pond, swimming pool, waterfall or large fountain. *Note:* the 9 facing star is trapped in the center and cannot be activated. However, placing water on the 8 facing star will usher in nobility and prosperity in Period 8 and 9.

Mountain: Simulate a mountain in the *North* (9 mountain star), *Southwest* (8 mountain

star) or *South* (1 mountain star). The 'mountain' can be higher ground, courtyard walls, landscape mounds, boulders (no sharp or jagged edges) or any combination (the mountain should be 3 feet or higher).

Cures: Unfortunately, the front door (West-facing) and back door (East-facing) must be cured or you may be plagued with sickness and robberies. The *front door* will need small water such as a bird bath and paint it red. The *back door* will need lots of metal such as brass, copper, bronze, pewter, stainless steel or large metal wind chimes; remove any water feature placed here.

For those living in an apartment, high-rise building, townhome, condominium or a rented space and are not able to install a water feature outdoors, place one indoors in the recommended area. To activate the mountain in the recommended area, use a tall armoire, heavy bookcases or stone statues; these will sufficiently activate the energy.

These Formations are Possible, Not Definite!
The **West 2** homes also have a possible *Eight Killing Forces* if there is mountain chi coming from the Southeast. A *Peach Blossom Sha* is activated with a road coming from the South. These homes also may have a *Robbery Mountain Sha* formation if there is a jagged cliff, electrical tower, huge dead tree, lamppost, or a broken mountain in the South. The **West 3** facing homes have a possible *Eight Roads of Destruction* formation if there is a road/driveway coming from and exiting the Northwest direction; these indicate money-loss. This direction also has a possible *Robbery Mountain Sha* in the Southwest.

Activating the INDOORS
Move your Stuff!

Excellent Doors
Always use and activate doors with excellent facing stars; for this chart they are the *North, Northwest, Northeast,* and *Southeast*. This applies to all exterior doors as well as an interior garage door used to enter the house. In modern homes, an interior garage door is often the main entry into the house, therefore it is extremely important! A South-facing door, in this chart, is seriously negative. If this is a well-used door, you will need to cure it with lots of metal next to or directly on the door.

Master Bedroom + Family
There are two ways to enhance health, harmony and prosperity in the bedroom and that is location and direction; the *direction* of the bed will give you the most powerful results. Locate your master bedroom in the *North, Southwest, Northwest,* or *Southeast* as these sectors have good mountain stars with great energy. **Bed Directions:** Place the marital/owner's headboard/bed to the *Northwest North, Southwest,* or *Southeast*; these bed directions have a good mountain *and* facing star combination with excellent energy. *Use the above directions when placing the bed for other family members.*

Home Office + Study
Place your desk/body to the *Northwest, Northeast, North* or *Southeast*. These directions have superb facing stars. For students, writers, teachers or bloggers face to the Southeast or North as they have the strongest 'scholarly' energy and indicate success in examinations, accelerating intelligence and accomplishments in literary pursuits.

Stoves, Grills and Fireplaces
The stove knobs, buttons or controls should face to the *North, Northwest* or *Southeast*; this applies to outdoor kitchens/grills as well This house *should not* have a kitchen or fireplace in the center of the home (5, 9 combination); it can bring serious health issues such as heart attacks and high blood pressure. Fireplaces can face to *the North, Northwest or Southeast*; the house may also have two-way fireplace (in any room) that faces Northwest/Southeast axis and this will activate wealth.

Watchful Eye: *Annual Stars and Three Killings*
This chart has two negative areas to pay attention to that can harm your money, health and household harmony. They are the **South** *(5 facing star)* and the **East** *(2 facing star)*. The South becomes more serious in 2020, 2022 and 2026 while the East in 2020, 2023 and 2025. No water *(pools, fountains, etc)* or fire *(stoves, fire place/pits or grills)* should be placed in either area, *no matter the year*, it will activate them! The Three Killings visits the front in 2019 and 2023, so it is taboo for deep digging and construction.

PERIOD 7

Northwest 1 *(292.6° to 307.5°)* Facing Name: **Xu** and the **Dog**

Chart: **Prosperous Sitting and Facing** *(Wang Shan Wang Shui)*

Activating the OUTDOORS
Install Water, Mountain & Cures

This property is known as *Prosperous Sitting and Facing* and in Period 7, the 'stars' were perfectly placed; money and people luck would have been apparent. However, since February 4th, 2004, the energy has turned somewhat harmful. The Northwest–facing structures are famous for turning almost everything to an advantage; this is especially true involving business *if* they are activated accordingly. To re-energize this chart during Period 8 or 9, use the following recommendations:

Water: Install a water feature in the *Southeast* (9 facing star) or *East* (1 facing star). The water can be a Koi pond, swimming pool, waterfall or large fountain. If you install water in the East, it should not be located between 82.6° to 97.5° as this can attract affairs; the water may be better placed in the Southeast (center of your back garden).

Mountain: Simulate a mountain in the *Southwest* (9 mountain star), *East* (8 mountain star) or *North* (1 mountain star). The 'mountain' can be higher ground, courtyard walls,

landscape mounds, boulders (no sharp or jagged edges) or any combination (the mountain should be 3 feet or higher).

Cures: The Northwest metal energy strengthens the 7 facing star in the front, so place a small water feature or bird bath near the door (still, not moving water and no more than 1-2 gallons). This will continually exhaust the negative energy of the robbery star. Any *Northeast-facing* 'front' door or interior garage door will need to be cured with high quality metal such as brass, bronze, stainless steel, pewter or copper.

For those living in an apartment, high-rise building, townhome, condominium or a rented space and are not able to install a water feature outdoors, place one indoors in the recommended area. To activate the mountain in the recommended area, use a tall armoire, heavy bookcases or stone statues; these will sufficiently activate the energy.

These Formations are Possible, Not Definite!
These homes may have a *Robbery Mountain Sha* formation if there is a jagged cliff, electrical tower, huge dead tree, lamppost, or a broken mountain in the *Southwest*; they indicate everyone in household getting an unusual disease, hurt by knives and disasters. You could also activate a *Peach Blossom Sha* if there is water or road in the *East*.

Activating the INDOORS
Move your Stuff!

Excellent Doors
Always use and activate doors with excellent facing stars; for this chart they are the *South, East, West,* and *Southeast*. This applies to all exterior doors as well as an interior garage door used to enter the house. In modern homes, an interior garage door is often the main entry into the house, therefore it is extremely important!

Master Bedroom + Family
There are two ways to enhance health, harmony and prosperity in the bedroom and that is location and direction; the *direction* of the bed will give you the most powerful results. Locate your master bedroom in the *North, Southwest,* or *East* as these sectors have good mountain stars. **Bed Directions:** Place the marital/owner's headboard to the *East, North* or *West*; these bed directions have a good mountain *and* facing star combination with excellent energy. Use the above directions when placing the bed for other family members.

Home Office + Study
Place your desk/body to the *South, East, West* or *Southeast*; these directions have great facing stars with prosperous energy. For students, writers, teachers or bloggers face to the South as it has the strongest 'scholarly' energy and indicate success in examinations, accelerating intelligence and accomplishments in literary pursuits.

Stoves, Grills and Fireplaces
The stove knobs, buttons or controls should face to the *East, South* or the *Southeast*; this applies to outdoor kitchens/grills as well. Fireplaces, either inside or outdoors, can face to *the East, South* or the *Southeast*; this house should not have a two-way fireplace on the Northeast/Southwest axis (in any room); this activates illness, disease and bankruptcy.

Watchful Eye: *Annual Stars*
This chart has two negative areas to pay attention to that can harm your money, health and household harmony. They are the **Northeast** *(5 facing star)* and the **Southwest** *(2 facing star)*. The Northeast becomes worse in 2021 and 2025 while the Southwest in 2022 and 2024. No water *(pools, fountains, etc)* or fire *(stoves, fire place/pits or grills)* should be placed in either area, *no matter the year*, it will activate them!

Take precautions when renovating areas that have the 5 facing star; in certain years they can be very aggressive. For this house, the Northeast sector of the house becomes more serious in 2021 and 2025. If you must touch this area, use the Great Sun Formula dates and metal to protect against bad luck.

PERIOD 7

Northwest 2 *(307.6° to 322.5°)* Facing Name: **Chien**
Northwest 3 *(322.6° to 337.5°)* Facing Name: **Hai** and the **Pig**
Chart: **Pearl String Formation** *(Lin Cu San Poon Gua)*

Activating the OUTDOORS
Install Water, Mountain & Cures

	SE	
7 6 5	5 7 6	1 3 2
9 2 1	6 8 7	3 5 4
2 4 3	7 9 8	8 1 9
	NW ↓	

(E/NE on left, S/SW on right, N at bottom-left, W at bottom-right)

This special energy, known as a *Pearl String* (aka Continuous Bead), is one of the most unique charts in the Flying Star system; however they are only potent for 20 years. It was very lucky in Period 7 but now has lost much of its vitality since February 4th, 2004. The Northwest-facing properties are famous for turning almost everything to an advantage; this is especially true involving business *if* they are activated accordingly. To re-energize this chart during Period 8 or 9, use the following recommendations:

Water: Install a water feature in the *Northwest* (9 facing star) or *West* (1 facing star). The water can be a Koi pond, swimming pool, waterfall or large fountain. This is the only Period 7 chart with the 9 facing star in the front—very auspicious when activated.

Mountain: Simulate a mountain in the *Northeast* (9 mountain star), *West* (8 mountain star) or *South* (1 mountain star). The 'mountain' can be higher ground, courtyard walls, landscape mounds, boulders (no sharp or jagged edges) or any combination (the mountain should be 3 feet or higher).

Cures: A Southeast-facing *back door* has negative energy, paint it red and place a bird bath or small water feature to exhaust the energy. Any *Southwest-facing* 'front' door or interior garage door will need to be cured with high quality metal such as brass, bronze, stainless steel, pewter or copper.

For those living in an apartment, high-rise building, townhome, condominium or a rented space and are not able to install a water feature outdoors, place one indoors in the recommended area. To activate the mountain in the recommended area, use a tall armoire, heavy bookcases or stone statues; these will sufficiently activate the energy.

These Formations are Possible, Not Definite!
For homes that face **Northwest 2,** there is a possible *Eight Roads of Destruction* if you have a road coming from/exiting from either the West or North directions; they are famous for bringing disharmony, bankruptcy, and divorce. These homes also may have a *Robbery Mountain Sha* formation if there a jagged cliff, electrical tower, huge dead tree, lamppost, or a broken mountain in the North. For the **Northwest 3** facing homes if a mountain is located in the South you could have an *Eight Killing Forces*. These homes also may have a *Robbery Mountain Sha* formation if there is a jagged cliff, electrical tower, huge dead tree, lamppost, or a broken mountain in the West. A *Peach Blossom Sha* is activated with a road coming/exiting from the North.

Activating the INDOORS
Move your Stuff!

Excellent Doors
Always use and activate doors with excellent facing stars; for this chart they are the *Northwest, North, West,* and *East*. This applies to all exterior doors as well as an interior garage door used to enter the house. In modern homes, an interior garage door is often the main entry into the house, therefore it is extremely important!

Master Bedroom + Family
There are two ways to enhance health, harmony and prosperity in the bedroom and that is location and direction; the *direction* of the bed will give you the most powerful

results. Locate your master bedroom in the *South, West,* or *Northeast* as these sectors have good mountain stars. **Bed Directions:** Place the marital/owner's headboard/bed to the *West, South* or *East*; these bed directions have a good mountain *and* facing star combination with excellent energy. Use the above directions when placing the bed for other family members.

Home Office + Study
For the best health, business opportunities, and romance, face your desk/body to the *Northwest, West, East* or *North*. These directions have great facing stars. For students, writers, teachers or bloggers face to the North as it has the strongest 'scholarly' energy and indicate success in examinations, accelerating intelligence and accomplishments in literary pursuits.

Stoves, Grills and Fireplaces
The stove knobs, buttons or controls should face to the *West, North* or *Northwest*; this applies to outdoor kitchens/grills as well. Fireplaces, either inside or outdoors, can face *the West, North* or *Northwest*. This house should not have a two-way fireplace on the Northeast/Southwest axis (this applies to any room).

Watchful Eye: Annual Stars
This chart has two negative areas to pay attention to that can harm your money, health and household harmony. They are the **Southwest** *(5 facing star)* and the **Northeast** *(2 facing star)*. The Southwest becomes more serious in 2019, 2022, and 2024 while the Northeast in 2021 and 2025. No water *(pools, fountains, etc)* or fire *(stoves, fire place/pits or grills)* should be placed in either area, *no matter the year*, it will activate them!

PERIOD 7

North 1 *(337.6° to 352.5°)* Facing Name: **Ren**
Chart: **Double Stars Meet at Sitting** *(Shuang Xing Dao Zuo)*

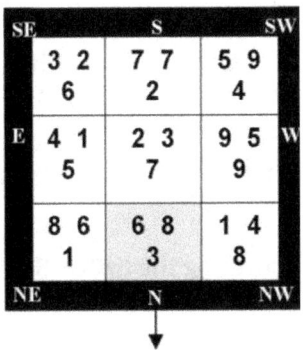

Activating the OUTDOORS
Install Water, Mountain & Cures

This property has the two 7's at the back, called *Double Stars Meet at Sitting* and it was quite auspicious for relationships and people until February 4th, 2004 when much of its vitality was diminished, however, it's the *only* Period 7 chart with the *8 facing star* in the front! The North-facing charts are known to produce those who are charismatic and very successful business people *if* activated accordingly. To re-energize this chart during Period 8 or 9, use the following recommendations:

Water: Install a water feature in the *Southwest* (9 facing star), *North* (8 facing star), or *East* (1 facing star). The water can be a Koi pond, swimming pool, waterfall or large fountain.

Mountain: Simulate a mountain in the *West* (9 mountain star), *Northeast* (8 mountain star) or *Northwest* (1 mountain star). The 'mountain' can be higher ground, courtyard walls, landscape mounds, boulders (no sharp or jagged edges) or any combination (the mountain should be 3 feet or higher).

Cures: In the *South* place a small bird bath and paint any South-facing back door red; these cures will exhaust the negative 7 energy. A grill, fireplace or fire pit also works as great cures for the 7 energy. Any *West-facing* 'front' door or interior garage door will need to be cured with high quality metal such as brass, bronze, stainless steel, pewter or copper.

For those living in an apartment, high-rise building, townhome, condominium or a rented space and are not able to install a water feature outdoors, place one indoors in the recommended area. To activate the mountain in the recommended area, use a tall armoire, heavy bookcases or stone statues; these will sufficiently activate the energy.

These Formations are Possible, Not Definite!
There is a possible *Eight Roads of Destruction* with this facing if there is a road coming from/exiting the Northwest direction; they are famous for bringing money-loss and disasters. These homes also may have a *Robbery Mountain Sha* formation if there is a jagged cliff, electrical tower, huge dead tree, lamppost, or a broken mountain in the West; they indicate everyone in household getting an unusual disease, hurt by knives and disasters.

Activating the INDOORS
Move your Stuff!

Excellent Doors
Always use and activate doors with excellent facing stars; for this chart they are the *Southwest, North, Northwest, East,* and *Northeast*. This applies to all exterior doors as well as an interior garage door used to enter the house. In modern homes, an interior garage door is often the main entry into the house, therefore it is extremely important

Master Bedroom + Family
There are two ways to enhance relationships, harmony and prosperity in the bedroom and that is location and direction; the *direction* of the bed will give you the most powerful results. Locate your master bedroom in the *East, Northwest, North* (second floor*)* or *Northeast* as these sectors have good mountain stars. **Bed Directions:** Place the marital/owner's headboard/bed to the *Northwest, East Northeast* or *North;* these bed directions have a good mountain *and* facing star combination with excellent energy. If there are any bedrooms located in either the Southwest or West, take special care. These sectors of the house have very negative energy. In the event the marital/owner's bedroom is already situated there; make sure the bed is not placed to either direction. As an extra measure, place high quality metal in the room and keep the colors soft and neutral. Use the recommended directions when placing the bed for other family members.

Home Office + Study
For the best health, business opportunities, and romance, face your desk/body the *Northwest, Southwest, East, Northeast*, or *North*. For students, writers, teachers or bloggers face to the Northwest and East as they have the strongest 'scholarly' energy and indicate success in examinations, accelerating intelligence and accomplishments in literary pursuits.

Stoves, Grills and Fireplaces
The stove knobs, buttons or controls should face to the *North, Northwest, East* or *Southwest*; this applies to outdoor kitchens/grills as well. This house *cannot* have a kitchen or fireplace in the center of the home (2, 3 combination); it can bring serious health problems such as heart attacks, extreme tension/stress, reproductive issues and

high blood pressure. Fireplaces, either inside or outdoors, can face *the North, Northwest, East* or *Southwest*.

Watchful Eye: Annual Stars and Three Killings
This chart has two negative areas to pay attention to that can harm your money, health and household harmony. They are the **West** *(2, 5)* and the **Southeast** *(2 facing star)*. The West gets worse in 2020 and 2024 while the Southeast in 2021, 2024 and 2026. No water *(pools, fountains, etc)* or fire *(stoves, fire place/pits or grills)* should be placed in either area, *no matter the year*, it will activate them! The *Three Killings* visits the front in 2022 so it is taboo to engage in deep digging or construction. If you must touch this area, use the Great Sun Formula for good dates to protect you from harm.

The Three Killings positions changes locations every year. It is taboo to engage in construction, demolition or deep digging such as a swimming pool. For this North-facing home, it visits the front (North) in 2022.

PERIOD 7

North 2 *(352.6° to 7.5°)* Facing name: **Tzi** and the **Rat**
North 3 *(7.6° to 22.5)* Facing name: **Kwei**
Chart: **Combination of Ten** *(He Shih Chu)*

SE	S	SW
1 4 6	6 8 2	8 6 4
9 5 5	2 3 7	4 1 9
5 9 1	7 7 3	3 2 8
NE	N ↓	NW

Activating the OUTDOORS
Install Water, Mountain & Cures

This property had the prestigious chart known as the Combination of Ten aka *Sum of Ten*; however, since February 4th, 2004 much of its vitality was diminished.
However, the North-facing charts can produce occupants that can successfully run their own businesses; they also may enjoy good fortune with their career taking them all over the world, *if* it is activated accordingly. To re-energize this chart during Period 8 or 9, use the following recommendations:

Water: Install a water feature in the *Northeast* (9 facing star), *South* (8 facing star), or *West* (1 facing star). The water can be a Koi pond, swimming pool, waterfall or fountain.

Mountain: Simulate a mountain in the *East* (9 mountain star), *Southwest* (8 mountain star) or *Southeast* (1 mountain star). The 'mountain' can be higher ground, courtyard walls, landscape mounds, boulders (no sharp or jagged edges) or any combination (the mountain should be 3 feet or higher).

Cures: In the *North*, install a small bird bath and paint a North-facing front door red; these cures will exhaust the negative 7 energy. Any *East-facing* 'front' door or interior garage door will need to be cured with high quality metal such as brass, bronze, stainless steel, pewter or copper.

For those living in an apartment, high-rise building, townhome, condominium or a rented space and are not able to install a water feature outdoors, place one indoors in the recommended area. To activate the mountain in the recommended area, use a tall armoire, heavy bookcases or stone statues; these will sufficiently activate the energy.

These Formations are Possible, Not Definite!
The **North 2** properties may have a *Robbery Mountain Sha* formation if there a jagged cliff, electrical tower, huge dead tree, lamppost, or a broken mountain in the West. A *Peach Blossom Sha* is activated by real water or a road coming from the West. For homes that face **North 3**, there is a possible *Eight Roads of Destruction* if you have a road/driveway coming from and exiting the Northeast direction. These homes also may have a *Robbery Mountain Sha* formation if there is a jagged cliff, electrical tower, huge dead tree, lamppost, or a broken mountain in the Northeast.

Activating the INDOORS
Move your Stuff!

Excellent Doors
Always use and activate doors with excellent facing stars; for this chart they are the *Southeast, Northeast, West, Southwest* and *South*. This applies to all exterior doors as well as an interior garage door used to enter the house. In modern homes, an interior garage door is often the main entry into the house, therefore it is extremely important!

Master Bedroom + Family
There are two ways to enhance relationships, health and prosperity in the bedroom and that is location and direction; the *direction* of the bed will give you the most powerful results. Locate your master bedroom in the *West, Southeast, South,* or *Southwest* as these sectors have mountain stars with wealth energy. **Bed Directions:** Place the marital/owner's headboard/bed to the *West, Southwest, Southeast* or *South*; these bed directions have a good mountain *and* facing star combination with excellent energy. If there are any bedrooms located in either the East or Northeast, take special care. These sectors of the house have very negative energy. In the event the marital/owner's bedroom is already situated there; make sure the bed is not placed to either direction. As an extra measure, place high quality metal in the room and keep the colors soft and neutral. Use the recommended directions when placing the bed for other family members.

Home Office + Study
Place your desk/face to the *Northeast, West, Southwest, South or Southeast*; these directions have superior facing stars. For students, writers, teachers or bloggers face to the Southeast or West as they have the strongest 'scholarly' energy and indicate success in examinations, accelerating intelligence and accomplishments in literary pursuits.

Stoves, Grills and Fireplaces
The stove knobs, buttons or controls should face *Southeast, South, West* or *Northeast*; this applies to outdoor kitchens/grills as well. This house *cannot* have a kitchen or fireplace in the center of the home (2, 3 combination); it can bring serious health problems such as heart attacks, extreme tension/stress, reproductive issues and high

blood pressure. Fireplaces, either inside or outdoors, can face *the Southeast, South, West* or *Northeast*.

Watchful Eye: Annual Stars and Three Killings
This chart has two negative areas to pay attention to that can harm your money, health and household harmony. They are the **East** *(9, 5)* and the **Northwest** *(2 facing star)*. The East becomes worse in 2021 and 2023 while the Northwest in 2019, 2023 and 2026. No water *(pools, fountains, etc)* or fire *(stoves, fire place/pits or grills)* should be placed in either area, *no matter the year*, it will activate them! The *Three Killings* visits the front in 2018 and 2022 so it is taboo to engage in deep digging or construction. If you must touch this area, use the Great Sun Formula for good dates to protect you from harm.

This type of major remodeling will change the Period of the house. It takes on the energy of the current Period in which the renovations are done. If you moved-in during Period 7 and have engaged in massive reconstruction during Period 9 (2024 to 2044), the house becomes a Period 9 home. Check the Three Killings position and protect that area with metal or use the Great Sun Formula.

PERIOD 7

Northeast 1 *(22.6° to 37.5°)* Facing name: **Chou**
Chart: **Double Stars Meet at Sitting** *(Shuang Xing Dao Zuo)*

Activating the OUTDOORS
Install Water, Mountain & Cures

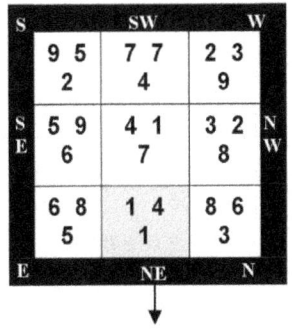

This property has the two 7's at the back known as *Double Stars Meet at Sitting*; it was lucky for relationships/money until February 4th, 2004 when much of its vitality was diminished. The Northeast charts can produce people of noble energy *if* they are activated accordingly. To re-energize this chart during Period 8 or 9, use the following recommendations:

Water: Install a water feature in the *Southeast* (9 facing star) or *East* (8 facing star). The water can be a Koi pond, swimming pool, waterfall or large fountain.

Mountain: Simulate a mountain in the *South* (9 mountain star), *North* (8 mountain star) or *Northeast* (1 mountain star). The 'mountain' can be higher ground, courtyard walls, landscape mounds, boulders (no sharp or jagged edges) or any combination (the mountain should be 3 feet or higher).

Cures: In the *Southwest* place a small bird bath and paint a Southwest-facing back door red; these cures will exhaust the negative 7 energy. A grill, fireplace or fire pit also works as great cures for the 7 energy. Any *Northwest-facing* 'front' door or interior garage door will need to be cured with high quality metal such as brass, bronze, stainless steel, pewter or copper.

For those living in an apartment, high-rise building, townhome, condominium or a rented space and are not able to install a water feature outdoors, place one indoors in the recommended area. To activate the mountain in the recommended area, use a tall armoire, heavy bookcases or stone statues; these will sufficiently activate the energy.

These Formations are Possible, Not Definite!
These sites may also have a *Robbery Mountain Sha* formation if there is a jagged cliff, electrical tower, huge dead tree, lamppost, or a broken mountain in the North; they indicate that everyone in household getting an unusual disease, hurt by knives and disasters. A *Peach Blossom Sha* is activated with a road coming from the South famous for causing affairs and sexual misconduct.

Activating the INDOORS
Move your Stuff!

Excellent Doors
Always use and activate doors with excellent facing stars; for this chart they are the *North, Northeast, Southeast* and *East*. This applies to all exterior doors as well as an interior garage door used to enter the house. In modern homes, an interior garage door is often the main entry into the house, therefore it is extremely important!

Master Bedroom + Family
There are two ways to enhance relationships, harmony and prosperity in the bedroom and that is location and direction; the *direction* of the bed will give you the most powerful results. Locate your master bedroom in the *North, Northeast* or *East* as these sectors have good mountain stars with great energy. **Bed Directions:** Place the marital or owner's headboard/bed to the *North, East* or *Northeast*; these bed directions have a good mountain *and* facing star combination with excellent energy. If there are any bedrooms located in either the Southeast or South, take special care. These sectors of the house have very negative energy. In the event the marital/owner's bedroom is already situated there; make sure the bed is not placed to either direction. As an extra measure, place high quality metal in the room and keep the colors soft and neutral. Use the recommended directions when placing the bed for other family members.

Home Office + Study
Place your desk/body to the *North, Southeast, Northeast or East*; these directions have excellent facing stars. For students, writers, teachers or bloggers face to the Northeast as

it has the strongest 'scholarly' energy and indicate success in examinations, accelerating intelligence and accomplishments in literary pursuits.

Stoves, Grills and Fireplaces
The best direction for the stove knobs, buttons or controls is *East, Southeast,* or *Northeast*; this applies to outdoor kitchens/grills as well. Fireplaces, either inside or outdoors, can face *the East, Southeast* or *Northeast*.

Watchful Eye: *Annual Stars*
This chart has two negative areas to pay attention to that can harm your money, health and household harmony. They are the **South** *(9, 5)* and the **Northwest** *(2 facing star)*. The South becomes worse in 2020, 2022 and 2026 while the Northwest 2019, 2023, and 2026. No water *(pools, fountains, etc)* or fire *(stoves, fire place/pits or grills)* should be placed in either area, *no matter the year*, it will activate them!

The Three Killings changes locations each year. It is taboo to engage in deep digging such as a swimming pool. It may be equally unlucky to dig when a 5 star visits for the year. Protect yourself from bad luck by using the Great Sun Formula for auspicious dates to begin construction.

PERIOD 7

Northeast 2 *(37.6° to 52.5°)* Facing name: **Gen**
Northeast 3 *(52.6° to 67.5°)* Facing name: **Yin and the Tiger**
Chart: **Double Stars Meet at Facing** *(Shuang Xing Dao Xiang)*

	S	SW		W
SE	8 6 2	1 4 4	6 8 9	NW
	3 2 6	4 1 7	5 9 8	
E	2 3 5	7 7 1	9 5 3	N
		NE		

Activating the OUTDOORS
Install Water, Mountain & Cures

This property is known as *Double Stars Meet at Facing* with the once prominent 7's located in the front; since February 4th 2004 this chart has been diminished a great deal. However, the Northeast-facing sites can produce people who can accumulate wealth with a world-wide business *if* they are activated accordingly. To re-energize this chart during Period 8 or 9, use the following recommendations:

Water: Install a water feature in the *Northwest* (9 facing star) or *West* (8 facing star). The water can be a Koi pond, swimming pool, waterfall or large fountain.

Mountain: Simulate a mountain in the *North* (9 mountain star), *South* (8 mountain star) or *Southwest* (1 mountain star). The 'mountain' can be higher ground, courtyard walls, landscape mounds, boulders (no sharp or jagged edges) or any combination (the mountain should be 3 feet or higher).

Cures: With the 7 stars in the facing, place a small water feature or bird bath near the front door. Also, paint a Northeast-facing door red; these cures will further exhaust the negative energy. Any *North-facing* or *Southeast-facing* 'front' door or interior garage door will need to be cured with high quality metal such as brass, bronze, stainless steel, pewter or copper.

For those living in an apartment, high-rise building, townhome, condominium or a rented space and are not able to install a water feature outdoors, place one indoors in the recommended area. To activate the mountain in the recommended area, use a tall armoire, heavy bookcases or stone statues; these will sufficiently activate the energy.

These Formations are Possible, Not Definite!
For homes facing **Northeast 2** there is a possible *Eight Roads of Destruction* if you have a road/driveway coming from and exiting the North and East directions. This formation can harm health, devastate people's lives and kill wealth and harmony! These properties may also have a *Robbery Mountain Sha* formation if there is a jagged cliff, electrical tower, huge dead tree, lamppost, or a broken mountain in the East; they indicate everyone in household getting an unusual disease, hurt by knives and disasters.

For the **Northeast 3** facing properties there is a possible *Eight Killing Forces* if there is a mountain in front of the property on the left-hand side (Northeast). A *Peach Blossom Sha* is activated with a road coming from the South famous for causing affairs and sexual misconduct. There is also a possible *Robbery Mountain Sha* formation if there a jagged cliff, electrical tower, huge dead tree, lamppost, or a broken mountain in the North.

These roads or driveway could create Eight Roads of Destruction depending on their direction in relationship to the door. These formations involve specific 15-degree increments for the door and the 'road'.

Activating the INDOORS
Move your Stuff!

Excellent Doors
Always use and activate doors with excellent facing stars; for this chart they are the *South, Southwest, West,* and *Northwest*. This applies to all exterior doors as well as an interior garage door used to enter the house. In modern homes, this is often the main entry into the house, therefore it is extremely important!

Master Bedroom + Family
There are two ways to enhance relationships, harmony and prosperity in the bedroom, and that is location and direction; the *direction* of the bed will give you the most powerful results. Locate your master bedroom in the *South, Southwest, or West* as these sectors of the house have good mountain stars. **Bed Directions:** Place your headboard/bed to the *South, Southwest* or *West*; these bed directions have a good mountain *and* facing star combination with excellent energy.

If there are any bedrooms located in either the North or Northwest, take special care. These sectors of the house have very negative energy. In the event the marital/owner's bedroom is already situated there; make sure the bed is not placed to either direction. As an extra measure, place high quality metal in the room and keep the colors soft and neutral. Use the recommended directions when placing the bed for other family members.

Home Office + Study
Place your desk/body to the *South, Southwest, West* or *Northwest*; these have great facing stars. For students, writers, teachers or bloggers face to the Southwest as it has the strongest 'scholarly' energy and indicate success in examinations, accelerating intelligence and accomplishments in literary pursuits.

Stoves, Grills and Fireplaces
The stove knobs, buttons or controls should face to the *Southwest, West* or *Northwest;* this applies to outdoor kitchens/grills as well. Fireplaces, either inside or outdoors, can face to the *Southwest, West* or *Northwest*.

Watchful Eye: *Annual Stars*
This chart has two negative areas to pay attention to that can harm your money, health and household harmony. They are the **North** *(9, 5)* and the **Southeast** *(2 facing star)*. The North becomes worse in 2021 and 2024 while the Southeast in 2021, 2024 and 2026. It is also unsafe for health to sleep to the Northwest (5, 9). No water *(pools, fountains, etc)* or fire *(stoves, fire place/pits or grills)* should be placed in either area, *no matter the year*, it will activate them!

PERIOD 7
East 1 *(67.6° to 82.5°)* Facing name: **Jia**
Chart : **Reverse Formation**

Activating the OUTDOORS
Install Water, Mountain & Cures

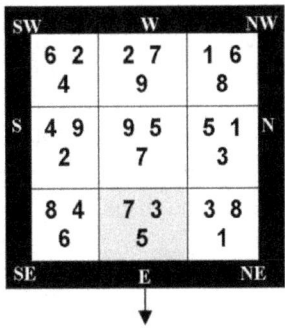

This chart is known as a *Reverse Formation;* this was not considered that auspicious even in Period 7; and has become less so since February 4th 2004. However, the East-facing properties can produce those who excel in the world of academia if they are activated accordingly. To re-energize this chart during Period 8 or 9, use the following recommendations:

Water: Install a water feature in the *South* (9 facing star), *Northeast* (8 facing star), or *North* (1 facing star). The water can be a Koi pond, swimming pool, waterfall or large fountain.

Mountain: Simulate a mountain in the *Southeast* (8 mountain star) or *Northwest* (1 mountain star). The 'mountain' can be higher ground, courtyard walls, landscape mounds, boulders (no sharp or jagged edges) or any combination (the mountain should be 3 feet or higher).

Cures: Unfortunately, the front door and back door are a problem. Paint the *front door* red and place metal wind chimes near it as well. Place small water such as a bird bath near the *back door* and paint it red. This will exhaust much of the negative energy at these important doors; while not considered a total cure, it will mitigate a lot of problems.

For those living in an apartment, high-rise building, townhome, condominium or a rented space and are not able to install a water feature outdoors, place one indoors in the recommended area. To activate the mountain in the recommended area, use a tall armoire, heavy bookcases or stone statues; these will sufficiently activate the energy.

These Formations are Possible, Not Definite!
There is a possible *Eight Roads of Destruction* formation if you have a road/driveway coming from and exiting the Northeast direction; they are notorious for bringing illness, bankruptcy, and divorce. There is also a possible *Robbery Mountain Sha* formation if there a jagged cliff, electrical tower, huge dead tree, lamppost, or a broken mountain in the South; they indicate everyone in household getting an unusual disease, hurt by knives and disasters.

Activating the INDOORS
Move your Stuff!

Excellent Doors
Always use and activate doors with excellent facing stars; for this chart they are the *Northwest, South, Southeast, North* and *Northeast*. This applies to all exterior doors as well as an interior garage door used to enter the house. In modern homes, an interior garage door is often the main entry into the house, therefore it is extremely important.

Master Bedroom + Family
There are two ways to enhance relationships, harmony and prosperity in the bedroom and that is location and direction; the *direction* of the bed will give you the most powerful results. Locate your master bedroom in the *Northwest, South* or *Southeast* as these sectors have good mountain stars with great energy. **Bed Directions:** Place the marital/owner's headboard/bed to the *Northwest, South, or Southeast*. These bed directions have a good mountain *and* facing star combination with excellent energy. *Use the above directions when placing the bed for other family members.*

Home Office + Study
Place your desk/body to the *Northwest or South, North or Southeast, or Northeast; these directions have great facing stars.* For students, writers, teachers or bloggers face to the Southeast or Northwest as they have the strongest 'scholarly' energy and indicate success in examinations, accelerating intelligence and accomplishments in literary pursuits.

Stoves, Grills and Fireplaces
The best directions for the stove knobs, buttons or controls is the *Northeast, South, Southeast* or *North*; this applies to outdoor kitchens/grills as well. Furthermore, this house *cannot* have a kitchen or fireplace in the center of the home (9, 5 combination); it can bring serious health issues such as heart attacks and high blood pressure; it may also indicate hazardous fires in certain years. Fireplaces, either inside or outdoors, can face to the *Northeast, South, Southeast* or *North*; this house can also have a two-way fireplace (in any room) on the North-South axis; this activates prosperity.

Watchful Eye: Annual Stars and Three Killings

This chart has one negative area to pay attention to that can harm your money, health and household harmony. It is the **Southwest** *(2 facing star)* and it becomes worse in 2022 and 2024. No water *(pools, fountains, etc)* or fire *(stoves, fire place/pits or grills)* should be placed in this area, *no matter the year*, it gets activated! The *Three Killings* visits the front in 2021 so it is taboo to engage in deep digging or construction. If you must touch this area, use the Great Sun Formula for good dates to protect you from harm.

The Three Killings positions changes locations every year. It is taboo to engage in construction, demolition or deep digging such as a swimming pool. For this East-facing home, it visits the front in 2021.

PERIOD 7

East 2 *(82.6° to 97.5°)* Facing name: **Mao** and the **Rabbit**
East 3 *(97.6° to 112.5°)* Facing name: **Yi**
Chart: **Prosperous Sitting and Facing** *(Wang Shan Wang Shui)*

SW	W	NW
3 8 4	7 3 9	8 4 8
5 1 2	9 5 7	4 9 3
1 6 6	2 7 5	6 2 1
SE	E	NE

(S on left, N on right; arrow pointing down from E)

Activating the OUTDOORS
Install Water, Mountain & Cures

In the day (Period 7), this was indeed an excellent chart known as *Prosperous Sitting and Facing* and would have been very lucky for money and people; alas, its decline in vitality began February 4th, 2004. However, the East-facing properties are known to produce charismatic, loyal, faithful professionals such as doctors, lawyers, and philosophers who are both wealthy and noble *if* it is activated accordingly. To re-energize this chart during Period 8 or 9, use the following recommendations:

Water: Install a water feature in the *North* (9 facing star), *Southwest* (8 facing star), or *South* (1 facing star). The water can be a Koi pond, swimming pool, waterfall or large

fountain. Water in the North should not be located between 352.6° to 7.5°.

Mountain: Simulate a mountain in the *Northwest* (8 mountain star) or *Southeast* (1 mountain star). The 'mountain' can be higher ground, courtyard walls, landscape mounds, boulders (no sharp or jagged edges) or any combination (the mountain should be 3 feet or higher).

Cures: Unfortunately, the front door (if it faces East) and back door (if it faces West) are a problem. Place small water such as a bird bath near the *front door* and paint it red. Paint the *back door* red and place some metal wind chimes near it as well. This will exhaust much of the negative energy at these important doors; while not considered a total cure, it will help. If you have a North or South-facing interior garage door, use it least 80% of the time to ensure wealth and happy events.

For those living in an apartment, high-rise building, townhome, condominium or a rented space and are not able to install a water feature outdoors, place one indoors in the recommended area. To activate the mountain in the recommended area, use a tall armoire, heavy bookcases or stone statues; these will sufficiently activate the energy.

These Formations are Possible, Not Definite!
For homes facing **East 2** there is a possible *Eight Killings* formation if there is a mountain from the Southwest direction noted for activating blood-related accidents. A *Peach Blossom Sha* is activated with a road coming from the North famous for causing affairs and sexual misconduct.

For homes that face to **East 3,** there is a possible *Eight Roads of Destruction* if there is a road/driveway coming from and exiting from the Southeast direction. There is also a possible *Robbery Mountain Sha* formation if there a jagged cliff, electrical tower, huge dead tree, lamppost, or a broken mountain in the Northeast for *both* East 2 and East 3 homes; they indicate everyone in household getting an unusual disease, hurt by knives and disasters.

Activating the INDOORS
Move your Stuff!

Excellent Doors
Always use and activate doors with excellent facing stars; for this chart they are the *Southwest, North, Northwest, Southeast* and *South*; this applies to all exterior doors as well as an interior garage door used to enter the house. In modern homes, an interior garage door is often the main entry into the house, therefore it is extremely important!

Master Bedroom + Family
There are two ways to enhance relationships, harmony and prosperity in the bedroom and that is location and direction; the *direction* of the bed will give you the most powerful results. Locate your master bedroom in the *Northwest* or *Southeast* as these locations have good mountain stars. **Bed Directions:** Place the marital/owner's headboard/bed to the *North, Southeast* or *Northwest;* these bed directions have a good mountain *and* facing star combination with excellent energy. *Use the above directions when placing the bed for other family members.*

Home Office + Study
Place your desk/body to face the *Northwest* or *Southwest, North, Southeast* or *South*; these directions have good facing stars with benevolent energy. For students, writers, teachers or bloggers face to the Southeast or Northwest as they have the strongest 'scholarly' energy and indicate success in examinations, accelerating intelligence and accomplishments in literary pursuits.

Stoves, Grills and Fireplaces
The best direction for the stove knobs, buttons or controls is the *South, North, Northwest* or *Southwest;* this applies to outdoor kitchens/grills as well. Furthermore, this house *cannot* have a kitchen or fireplace in the center of the home (9, 5 combination); it can bring serious health issues such as heart attacks and high blood pressure; it may also indicate hazardous fires in certain years. Fireplaces, either inside or outdoors, can face to the *South, North, Northwest* or *Southwest*; this house can also have a two-way fireplace on the North-South axis; this activates wealth energy.

Watchful Eye: Annual Stars and Three Killings
This chart has one negative area to pay attention to that can harm your money, health and household harmony. It is the **Northeast** *(2 facing star)* and it becomes worse in 2021 and 2025. No water *(pools, fountains, etc)* or fire *(stoves, fire place/pits or grills)* should be placed in this area, *no matter the year*, it gets activated! The *Three Killings* visits the front in 2017 and 2021 so it is taboo to engage in deep digging or construction. If you must touch this area, use the Great Sun Formula for good dates to protect you from harm.

PERIOD 7

Southeast 1 *(112.6° to 127.5°)* Facing name: **Chen** and the **Dragon**
Chart: **Prosperous Sitting** and **Facing** *(Wang Shan Wang Shui)*

Activating the OUTDOORS
Install Water, Mountain & Cures

	W	NW	N
SW	6 4 / 9	7 5 / 8	3 1 / 3	NE
	2 9 / 4	8 6 / 7	5 3 / 1
S	4 2 / 2	9 7 / 6	1 8 / 5	E
		SE	

In the day (Period 7), this was indeed an excellent chart known as *Prosperous Sitting and Facing* and would have been very lucky for money and people; alas, its decline in vitality began February 4th, 2004. However, the Southeast-facing properties can produce great talent in all types of sports and the children can excel in sciences, especially those requiring technical expertise *if* it is activated accordingly. To re-energize this chart during Period 8 or 9, use the following recommendations:

Water: Install a water feature in the *Southwest* (9 facing star), *East* (8 facing star), or *North* (1 facing star). The water can be a Koi pond, swimming pool, waterfall or large fountain.

Mountain: Simulate a mountain in the *Southeast* (9 mountain star) or *East* (1 mountain star). The 'mountain' can be higher ground, courtyard walls, landscape mounds, boulders (no sharp or jagged edges) or any combination (the mountain should be 3 feet or higher).

Cures: Unfortunately, a Southeast-facing front door and a Northwest-facing back door are very problematic and they must be cured. Paint the *front door* red and place a small bird bath near it; this will help exhaust the energy. The *back door* needs a great deal of high quality metal (brass, copper, or bronze) and is best not used.

For those living in an apartment, high-rise building, townhome, condominium or a rented space and are not able to install a water feature outdoors, place one indoors in the recommended area. To activate the mountain in the recommended area, use a tall armoire, heavy bookcases or stone statues; these will sufficiently activate the energy.

These Formations are Possible, Not Definite!
An *Eight Killings* formation is possible if there is a mountain bringing energy to the house from the North direction. A *Peach Blossom Sha* is activated with a road coming from the West famous for causing affairs and sexual misconduct. There is also a possible *Robbery Mountain Sha* formation if there a jagged cliff, electrical tower, huge dead tree, lamppost, or a broken mountain in the Northeast; they indicate everyone in household getting an unusual disease, hurt by knives and disasters.

Activating the INDOORS
Move your Stuff!

Excellent Doors
Always use and activate doors with excellent facing stars; for this chart they are the *East, West, North* and *Southwest*. This applies to all exterior doors as well as an interior garage door used to enter the house. In modern homes, an interior garage door is often the main entry into the house, therefore it is extremely important

Master Bedroom + Family
There are two ways to enhance relationships, health and prosperity in the bedroom and that is location and direction; the *direction* of the bed will give you the most powerful results. Locate your master bedroom in the *West or East*, or *Southeast* (upstairs) as these sectors all have good mountain stars. **Bed Directions:** Place the marital/owner's headboard/bed to the *East, West* or to the *North* which is acceptable energy. These bed directions have a good mountain *and* facing star combination with excellent energy. *Use the above directions when placing the bed for other family members.*

Home Office + Study
Place your desk/body the *East, West, Southwest* or *North;* these directions have great facing stars. For students, writers, teachers or bloggers face to the West as it has the strongest 'scholarly' energy and indicate success in examinations, accelerating intelligence and accomplishments in literary pursuits.

Stoves, Grills and Fireplaces
The best direction for the stove knobs, buttons or controls is the *East, Southwest, West,* or *North;* this applies to outdoor kitchens/grills as well. Fireplaces, either inside or outdoors, can face to the *East, Southwest, West,* or *North*; this house can also have a two-way fireplace on the East-West axis; this activates prosperity and romance.

Watchful Eye: *Annual Stars*
This chart has two negative areas to pay attention and they are the **Northwest** *(5 facing star)* and the **South** *(2 facing star)*. The Northwest is worse in 2023 and 2026 while the South in 2020, 2022 and 2026.

PERIOD 7
Southeast 2 *(127.6° to 142.5°)* Facing name: **Xun**
Southeast 3 *(142.6° to 157.5°)* Facing name: **Su** and the **Snake**
Chart: **Pearl String** *(Lin Cu San Poon Gua)*

Activating the OUTDOORS
Install Water, Mountain & Cures

This property was a very special star chart called the **Pearl String** aka Continuous Bead; since February 4th, 2004 however, it is no longer prestigious. The Southeast-facing charts can produce those who have high morals, nobility, trustworthiness and the Southeast-facing is suited for philosophers, performers, singer, and artists *if* they are activated accordingly. To re-energize this chart during Period 8 or 9, use the following recommendations:

Water: Install a water feature in the *Northeast* (9 facing star), *West* (8 facing star), or *South* (1 facing star). The water can be a Koi pond, swimming pool, waterfall or large fountain. Water in the South should not be located between 172.6° to 187.5° and may cause extra-marital affairs or sexual misconduct.

Mountain: Simulate a mountain in the *Northwest* (9 mountain star) or *West* (1 mountain star). The 'mountain' can be higher ground, courtyard walls, landscape mounds, boulders (no sharp or jagged edges) or any combination (the mountain should be 3 feet or higher).

Cures: Unfortunately, a Southeast-facing front door and a Northwest-facing back door are problematic and they must be cured. The *front door* needs a great deal of high quality metal (brass, copper, or bronze) and is best not used. Install a small bird bath near the back door as this will help exhaust the robbery energy. It should be still, not moving water, and not more than 1-2 gallons of water.

For those living in an apartment, high-rise building, townhome, condominium or a rented space and are not able to install a water feature outdoors, place one indoors in the recommended area. To activate the mountain in the recommended area, use a tall armoire, heavy bookcases or stone statues; these will sufficiently activate the energy.

These Formations are Possible, Not Definite!
There is a possible *Eight Roads of Destruction* if the house faces **Southeast 2** and a road/driveway comes from/exits the South or East; they indicate sickness, bankruptcy, and divorce. An *Eight Killings* formation is possible for homes facing **Southeast 3** if there is a mountain bringing energy to the house from the West direction; this formation will cause blood-related accidents. A *Peach Blossom Sha* is activated with a road coming from the South famous for causing affairs and sexual misconduct. There is also a possible *Robbery Mountain Sha* formation if there a jagged cliff, electrical tower, huge dead tree, lamppost, or a broken mountain in the East for both facings; they indicate everyone in household getting an unusual disease, hurt by knives and disasters.

Activating the INDOORS
Move your Stuff!

Excellent Doors
Always use and activate doors with excellent facing stars; for this chart they are the *West, Northeast, East,* and *South.* This applies to all exterior doors as well as an interior garage door used to enter the house. In modern homes, an interior garage door is often the main entry into the house, therefore it is extremely important!

Master Bedroom + Family
There are two ways to enhance relationships, harmony and prosperity in the bedroom and that is location and direction; the *direction* of the bed will give you the most powerful results. Locate your master bedroom in the *West, Northwest,* or *East* as these sectors all have good mountain stars. **Bed Directions:** Place the marital/owner's headboard/bed to the *West or East* and *South* is acceptable; these bed directions have a good mountain *and* facing star combinations. *Use the above directions when placing the bed for other family members.*

Home Office + Study
Place your desk/body to the *West, Northeast, East* or *South;* these directions have great facing stars with benevolent energy. For students, writers, teachers or bloggers face to the East as it has the strongest 'scholarly' energy and indicate success in examinations, accelerating intelligence and accomplishments in literary pursuits.

Stoves, Grills and Fireplaces
The best direction for the stove knobs, buttons or controls is the *East, West, Northeast,* or *South*; this applies to outdoor kitchens/grills as well. Fireplaces, either inside or outdoors, can face to the *East, West, Northeast,* or *South*; this house can also have a two-way fireplace on the East/West axis; this activates prosperity and romance.

Watchful Eye: *Annual Stars*

This chart has two negative areas to pay attention to that can harm your money, health and household harmony. They are the **Southeast** *(5 facing star)* and the **North** *(2 facing star)*. The Southeast becomes worse in 2021, 2024 and 2026 while the North in 2021 and 2024. No water *(pools, fountains, etc)* or fire *(stoves, fire place/pits or grills)* should be placed in either area, *no matter the year*, it will activate them!

This type of major remodeling will change it from a Period 7 to the current Period in which the renovations are undertaken. Pay attention if the 5 annual star visits the area of construction or remodeling. If a 5 star visits the area, use Great Sun Formula for good dates.

Glossary of Terms and Feng Shui Chronology

In this glossary, the Chinese to English translations for the official pinyin and the non-standard Wade-Giles method are used. Pinyin is the internationally recognized Roman transliteration of Chinese characters and it was officially adopted by the People's Republic of China in 1979. The Wade-Giles system of transcription, developed by sinologists Thomas Wade and Herbert Giles in the late nineteenth century, served as the Chinese-to-English benchmark for most of the twentieth century. For instance, the word "chi" (pronounced *chee*) is spelled *ch'i* according to Wade-Giles and *qi* in pinyin. A *Feng Shui Chronology* is also included starting 2852 BCE to 2018 AD.

4 Destructions: involves the cardinal directions (N, S, E, W) and incoming road or water that marks a clash of yin and yang energy. These formations bring hassles and no harmony to those in the household.

4 Greatest Masters: The four most influential Feng Shui Masters of all time are *Kuan Lo* (209-256 CE), *Kuo Po* (276-324 CE), *Yang Yun Song* (834-906 CE), and *Tseng Wen-Chan* (854-916 CE).

6 Harms/Clashes: these are direct 'animal' clashes (e.g. Horse and Rat) that involve the door which may be yin energy and the road or water may be yang energy, or vice versa. These formations bring hassles and no harmony to those in the household.

8 Trigrams: The Guas or Trigrams are simply a global perspective of the universe, and they fully express how the Chinese understand energy. Each Gua has three lines, comprised of solid lines (yang energy) or a broken lines indicating yin energy. These three lines also represent the cosmology of heaven, earth and man. The famous Ba Gua is composed of eight trigrams; 'Ba' means *eight*, and 'Gua' means the *result of divination*. The eight Trigrams/Guas are Xun, Li, Kun, Dui, Chien, Kan, Gen, and Chen representing Southeast, South, West, Northwest, North, Northeast and East respectively.

24 Mountains: The most important ring of the Luo Pan divided into 24 sections, each occupying 15° and populated by the eight of the 10 Heavenly Stems, the 12 Earthly Branches and the four diagonal directions represented by the Trigrams Xun, Kun, Gen and Qian. The 24 Mountains ring is used in San Yuan and San He methods to locate certain types of Qi and to read the meaning thereof.

28 Xiu: 28 Constellations divided into the 4 Celestial Animals.

60 Dragon Expanding and Contracting: This is used to assess the energy of the householder to the sitting or mountain to check for compatibility. This is said to be *heaven chi* that supports the occupants. The element of birth may be different using the Na Yin. The Na Yin is the hidden Five Melodic Element that is a result of the pairing up of the Heavenly Stem and Earthly Branch, known as the *hidden element*. The result is that the element might, at times, turn out to be completely different—this is known as the 'received note'' or 'melodic sound'. For example, a person born in 6-21-1954 is Jia (wood) Wu (fire) but = is metal. Another example is a person born 12-31-1958 is Wu (earth) Xu (Dog) = is wood.

60 Equal Division Dragons: Used to assess a mountain behind the site; if the house sits or faces *(ideally both)*, then a 60 Dragon mountain has the 3's and 7's that can ride the chi and support the people. Each dragon occupies 6 degrees of the ring, making a total of 6x60=360.

81 Combinations: There are nine (9) stars and when combine each with the other, they create the famous *81 combinations* or sets (9x9=81). The 81 combinations have a unique description for each set; they are an extraction from various, distinctive Feng Shui classic texts including the Purple White Scripts *(Tzi Bai Jue)*, Ode of Time and Space *(Xuan Kong Mi Zi)*, Heavenly Jade Classics *(Tien Yue Jing)*, and the Time Space Mysticism *(Xuan Kong Jie.)* While each star has a meaning, when they combine they can indicate very specific outcomes and results. However, timing, activation and landforms often determine if these 'descriptions' will actually occur.

60 Earth Penetrating Dragons: The 60 earth-penetrating dragons take into consideration the energy of a hillside or mountain immediately behind the house or building, basically evaluating its quality. The 'dragons' cover only 6 degrees, but all 60 dragons are assessed by one of five types of energy being either auspicious or inauspicious detailed in ancient texts known as the *'Secret Verses'*.

72 Dragons: The 72 Piercing Dragons are similar to the 60 Dragons; they are also used to examine the energy of a mountain; it covers 5-degree increments. However, the 72 Piercing Dragons is mainly concerned with evaluating the *largest* or main mountain at the back of the property. While the 60 Dragons measure closer, more specific energy fed immediately behind the site. The formula for the 72 Dragons is attributed to the famous Master Yang Yun Song who lived during the Tang Dynasty (618 – 907 AD). It also calculates the quality of the mountain into one of five types of energy and the Secret Verses are also used.

120 Gold Divisions (Fen Chin): There are two rings for the 120 Gold Divisions, *heaven* and *earth* plate. These are auspicious dragons for establishing a 'door facing' in order to match a direction that enhances the person's 'element'. The 'facing' element should produce/support the element of the occupants. This ring was added to the Luo Pan around 906-960 CE.

240 Gold Divisions (Fen Chin): in some early Luo Pans, the 240 divisions were common. This ring would allow the practitioner to divide each mountain into 10 divisions of 1.5° each. Some authorities suggest that the 240 Fen Chin came chronologically before the 120 Fen Chin. This ring is located among the Heaven Plate rings and does not appear on modern day standard San He Luo Pans. The purpose is the same as for the 120 Gold Divisions.

A

Acupuncture: is the stimulation of specific acupoints along the skin of the body involving various methods such as the application of heat, pressure, or laser as well as penetration of thin needles; most often used in the treatment of pain.

Advanced Eight Mansions: Dividing the 24 facing directions into 15-degree increments where a negative direction can be used on the 1st and 3rd mountain. For example a 1 Life Gua can use West 1 and West 3 but not pure West which is the middle 15 degrees known as West 2. The same principle applies to the other negative directions except Northeast for East Life people and Southeast for West Life people as they may only use the 3rd mountain of those directions.

After heaven sequence: (known as the Ho Tien in Chinese) this sequence of trigrams denotes motion, transformation, and the interaction of natural and human chi forces. This is the sequence used in Feng Shui applications.

Age of Eight: Also known as Period 8; a twenty-year period of time that affects the luck of mankind and influences the world with its energy. These twenty-year periods were first tracked and recorded by the ancient Chinese in about 2500 BC. They observed that every 180 years the planets in our solar system line up. It was further noted that every twenty years the Milky Way shifts and influences the events of mankind. These periods run from one to nine every twenty years and then start all over again. The current Age of Eight began February 4, 2004. This is part of the Flying Star system (Xuan Kong Fei Xing).

Alchemy, Chinese: Chinese Alchemy mainly focuses on the purification of one's spirit and body with the goal of attaining immortality through the practice of Qigong and/or consumption and use of various concoctions known as alchemical medicines or elixirs, each of which having different purposes. Pao Chi refers to the alchemy of processing Traditional Chinese medicines, such as honey or wine frying and roasting with toxic metals such as mercury, lead, and arsenic. The Taoist' *Quest for Immortality*, had two distinct parts, the classical Tao Chia, which was mystical and stemmed primarily from Lao Tzu and Zhuangzi, and the more popular Tao Chiao, which was the well-loved, magical and alchemical side of Taoism.

Almanac, Chinese: Also referred to as the *Tong Shu*. Since ancient times, this annual publication is of great importance to the people of the Orient. It serves as a useful guide to everyday life, dispensing advice on good days for burials, weddings, and business transactions. Even in modern times, millions of people still consult the Chinese Almanac every day.

Ancient Feng Shui Textbooks: Fei Xing Fu (Ode to Flying Stars); Zang Shu (The Burial Book); Qing Nang Jing (The Green Satchel Classic); Tien Yu Jing (The Heavenly Jade Classic); Han Long Jing (The Classic of Challenging the Dragon); Yi Long Jing (The Classic of Spying the Dragon); Zi Bai Jue (The Secret of the Purple and White Stars); Qing Nang Xu (Preface to the Green Satchel Classic); Qing Nang Ao Yu (Delving into the Green Satchel Classic); Xuan Kong Mi Zhi (Secrets of Time and Space); Xuan Ji Fu (Ode to Mysticism); Du Tien Bao Zhao Jing (A Treatise of Form and Formula; Shen's Xuan Kong Xue (Master Shen's Time-Space Feng Shui School).

Ann Shan: a strong table/flat mountain, or a mountain that is close or in front of the building but separated by a river or a field.

Ann Tan: is a mountain that is hidden from view while *inside* the house. While just the top of the mountain is visible, it feels like someone is "peeping" into the house. This is also known as 'Peeping Tom Sha" energy.
Annual star: a prevailing star, or number that ushers in yearly changes.
Annual stars: Visiting yearly stars to each of the eight palaces in every structure all over the world.
Application: Refers to the information required for the reading to do the analysis.
Arrowana: the Feng Shui fish used in water-features that supposedly represent wealth.
Assistant Star Water Method: A technique used to enhance wealth, health, or relationships with an energy path, such as a road, driveway, or footpath. Real water may also be used.
Auspicious: The Chinese favor the term *auspicious*, meaning something is lucky, and good events will ensue.
Ayurvedic Medicine: is a system of traditional medicine native to the Indian subcontinent and a form of alternative medicine. By the medieval period, Ayurvedic practitioners developed a number of medicinal preparations and surgical procedures for the treatment of various ailments.

B
Ba Bai: the 8-White Star in the nine stars.
Ba Gua Mirror: This mirror (flat, concave, or convex) is surrounded by the eight trigrams and used to deflect negative energy or something in view that is not desirable. This Ba Gua is identified as having three solid lines at the top known as the Chien/Qian trigram or Gua.
Ba Gua: Also spelled as Pa Kua. An octagonal arrangement of the eight trigrams or Guas of Taoist mysticism; used as a basic tool of energy assessment in Feng Shui.
Bai Hu: the White Tiger, one of the Celestial animals, the right side (female) or the West.
Basements: Traditional basements are built at the sub-ground level and into the earth. They often have small windows looking out on the ground level (dirt or earth). The earth level is cold chi or cold energy.
Ba Kong Wang: Eight void/evil lines.
BaZhai: Also spelled Pa Chai, this is the Eight Mansions system. It is also referred to as the East-West System and the Major Wandering Stars.
BaZhai Ming Jing: The *Bright Mirror of Eight Houses* book written by Daoist monk, Ruo-Guan Daoren. His first book, *The Old Fisherman of Xu River* (Xu Jiang Diao Sou) has become a must read for serious students of Feng Shui.
BaZi: means eight characters in Mandarin Chinese. It is a Chinese astrology system also known as the Four Pillars of Destiny.
Bei Dou Xing: the Big Dipper.
Big Dipper Casting Golden Light: Known as *Jin Guang Dou Lin Jing* in Chinese and also spelled as *Kam Kwong Dou Lam King*. This style of Eight Mansions is used by those in Grandmaster Yap's lineage; it is also called the *Golden Star Classic*.

Big Dipper, Northern Dipper, Great Bear: Star Constellation visible in the Northern Hemisphere depicting the Nine Stars (presently there are seven visible stars), used for navigation and seasonal calculations. The ancients said that which is displayed in Heaven is also displayed on Earth *(as above, so below)*.

Bird, Red: Part of the Celestial Animals; a low hill formation at the front of a house or site.

Black Hat Sect: A new school of Feng Shui created in the 1980s. It was brought to the Western world by Professor Thomas Lin Yun, a Buddhist monk of the Black Hat Order of Tibetan Buddhism. Although not considered an authentic system of Feng Shui, Black Hat is the most recognized style in the world except in Asian countries, which are most familiar with traditional schools of Feng Shui.

Black Turtle: aka the *Dark Warrior* is located at the back of a property, part of the Celestial Animals landforms which acts as a protector for the occupants.

Blood of the Dragon: watercourses, rivers, canals and natural wash beds.

Book of Burial: written in the fourth century C.E. by Guo Pu, this is the precursor to Form School of Feng Shui.

Book of Changes: Also known as the *I Ching*.

Book of Nine Elixirs: The *Book of the Nine Elixirs* (Jiudan Jing), written around 649 to 686 BC, is the main extant text of the Great Clarity, the earliest identifiable tradition of Chinese alchemy. It describes the preparation of nine elixirs, paying particular attention to the ritual context and sequencing. The main stages are the transmission from master to disciple, the establishment of the ritual area, the choice of an auspicious time, the compounding of the elixir, its offering to the gods, and its ingestion.

Branches: see Earthly Branches.

Bright Hall: This area is an open space near the front door (interior and exterior) where chi can collect; in Chinese known as the Ming Tang.

BTB Feng Shui: Black Tantric Buddhist Feng Shui also known as Black Hat Sect.

Buddhism: is a nontheistic *(not having a belief in a god)* religion that encompasses a variety of traditions, beliefs and practices largely based on teachings attributed to Siddhartha Gautama, who is commonly known as the Buddha, meaning "the awakened one". According to Buddhist tradition, the Buddha lived and taught in the eastern part of the Indian subcontinent sometime between the 6th and 4th centuries BCE.

Bu Sha Fa: land embrace.

C

Calendar, Solar: a calendar, like the standard Western one, based on the Earth's revolution round the Sun, but more precisely aligned to the seasons.

Canal: An artificial waterway for boats or irrigation. In Feng Shui, canals are considered rivers; they can be particularly ruinous if they run behind a home.

Cardinal directions: Points of geographic orientation—North, South, East and West. The specific and exact points of these directions are 0/360, North; 90 degrees, East; 180 degrees, South; and 270 degrees, West.

Cash: the name for old round Chinese coins with a square hole in the middle.

Castle Gate Theory: Technique to determine whether the Castle Gate is useful to replace the ruling star. It's a wealth-producing formula in the San Yuan school; the Chinese term is *Cheng Men Jue*. There are actually two popular variations of a Castle Gate.

Celestial Animals: Green Dragon, White Tiger, Black Tortoise, Red Bird and Snake in the middle; these are essential landforms meant to support and protect the structure. It also ensures that chi/energy may accumulate so that the occupants can thrive.

Celestial Equator: the circular path the constellations travel perpendicular to an imaginary line joining the celestial North Pole to the earth's North Pole. The Chinese use the celestial equator as a baseline to observe the times when stars will appear directly overhead.

Central Palace: The location of the central stars of a chart and depicts the overall harmony of the chart. The Central Palace also refers to the pole star around which revolves the 28 constellations which mark the four seasons and the four animals.

Chai: house, also spelled Zhai.

Chang Sheng Jue: the 12 growth phases of water; Conceived (Tai); Nurture/Birth (Yang); Growth/Childhood (Chang Sen); Bath (Mu Ye); Hat & Belt/Education (Kwan Tai); Position/Adulthood (Kin Kwan); Prosperous (Wang); Weakening (Sui); Sick/Aging (Ping); Death (Sze); Grave (Mu); and Vanished/Void (Cheuh).

Chao Shan: a rising mountain.

Chasing the Dragon: is a technique of examining the mountain's most powerful point of chi and following that *vein* of energy.

Chen: One of the eight trigrams of the Ba Gua. It represents the eldest son, thunder and spring. In the Later Heaven arrangement of the Ba Gua, the Chen trigram is located in the East.

Chi Distribution: a special San Yuan technique in which to manipulate the energy in a structure via wall locations, room locations and doors.

Chi Kung: a martial art which concentrates chi energy in the body.

Chi: The vital life-force energy of the universe and everything in it; sometimes chi is referred to as *cosmic breath*. It is also spelled *ch'i* or *qi* and is pronounced *chee*.

Chien: One of the eight trigrams of the Ba Gua also spelled as *Qian*. It represents the father, the heavens, and late autumn. In the Later Heaven arrangement of the Ba Gua, the Chien trigram is located in the Northwest.

Chinese Lunar and Solar Calendars: The ancient Chinese used the Solstices and Equinoxes to fix their calendar. 15° Aquarius is exactly half way between the winter Solstice and the spring Equinox (on the Northern Hemisphere). In the past, Chinese Lunar New Year started around the Winter Solstice. In 104 BC Emperor Han Wu Di moved the beginning of the year so that the winter Solstice occurs in the eleventh month. Winter Solstice falls on the 15th day of Zi/Rat month, the middle of the winter, 15° Aquarius is the Sun's position. Whenever the sun reaches that position that is the Chinese Solar New Year. This could be February 3, 4, 5. The Chinese chose the 15° Aquarius as the starting point of the spring season and the New Year. The spring Equinox falls exactly in the middle of the spring season; this is always on the 15th day of Mao/Rabbit month. Lunar calendar defines the lunar month on the first day of the appearance of the New Moon. A Lunar New Year begins on the 1st day of this new "moon". A lunar month is from the new moon to the next new moon. The ecliptic was divided into 12 equal divisions by the ancients. The Chinese Solar year is based on these 24 divisions called 24 solar terms. The year is divided into 24 periods of 15 days. Li Chun is the first of the 24 terms. The names of these divisions date back to the late Chou Dynasty (10450—221BC). The most important of the 24 terms is the New Year. All Feng Shui experts worth their salt use the Solar Calendar as the basis of their practice. This is not to say they don't celebrate the Lunar New Year, in fact, they do; the *Chinese New Year* is extremely popular and important.

Chinese New Year: The Chinese New Year occurs every year on the new moon of the first lunar month, about four to eight weeks before spring. The exact date can fall anytime between January 21st and February 21st. Each year is symbolized by one of 12 animals and one of five elements, with the combinations of animals and elements cycling every 60 years. It is the most important Chinese holiday of the year. For Feng Shui purposes, the New Year begins on February 4th (based on the Solar Calendar). The most common Chinese ways of saying Happy New Year are *Gong Xi Fa Cai* **(Mandarin)** and *Gong Hey Fat Choy* (Cantonese). Even though the pronunciations are a little different, both are written the same way.

Chinese Zodiac: is a system that relates each year to an animal and its reputed attributes, according to a 12-year mathematical cycle. It remains popular in several East Asian countries, such as China, Vietnam, Korea and Japan.

Ching Dynasty: AD 1644-1911.

Chou Dynasty: 1027-221 BCE.

Chor San Kibb Sart: means *Robbery Mountain Sha* (a San Yuan formula) and is based on the sitting of the structure.

Chor Sin: the mountain or sitting star.

Chou I: an old name for the I Ching.

Chou Yao Huang Xiang: Chou means to select, Yao means the line in the Trigram. Huang is change and Shan is image. A technique used in Ba Zhai Feng Shui and Shan Shui Long Fan Gua to change the lines of a Trigram and form a new image/meaning. This method is also known as *flipping the Yao* and for some formulas (e.g. Tan Lang, Five Ghosts Carry Treasure and Assistant Star) it has a specified rhythm. For example, upper-middle-lower-MIDDLE-upper-middle-lower-MIDDLE.

Chu Kai: 'Chaos' in the beginning of time.

Chueh Ming: In the Eight Mansions system, this represents total loss, divorce and bankrupcy. According to Master Yap's numeric representation, it is the -90.

Chung He Luo Pan: Also spelled or referred to as Zong He, Zhung He, or Cheng He. This Luo Pan is an amalgamation of the San He and San Yuan compasses and was designed for practitioners who use both systems. Though some rings have been eliminated for size considerations, all essential/standard rings are in place.

Classic of Changes: see the I Ching.

Classical Feng Shui: Also known as Traditional Feng Shui. It is the authentic, genuine Feng Shui that has been developed and applied for hundreds, even thousands, of years in Asia. Sophisticated forms are practiced in Hong Kong, Taiwan, Malaysia, and Singapore. Classical Feng Shui is still being introduced and practiced in Western countries, and has not reached main stream status. The traditional systems of Feng Shui are the *San He*, meaning three combinations, and *San Yuan* or three cycles. All techniques, methods, and formulas will be under one or the other. Feng Shui masters and practitioners will use both systems as one comprehensive body of knowledge.
Cold chi: A room or home built below the earth's surface or into the ground is considered cold chi; these are *yin,* or dead, environments.
Combination of 10: A wealth-producing chart in the Flying Star system where the stars add to ten in all nine palaces. In Chinese it is translated as *He Shih Chu.*
commercial spaces: Business-related property intended to generate a profit, including shopping centers, office buildings, malls, restaurants, retail shops, boutiques, salons, spas, and hotels.
Compass School: a term invented by Westerners, the Compass School holds that each of the eight directions has a different type of chi. It is very computational method, relying on intellect rather than intuitive insights; also known as Li Qi (patterns of chi school).
Compass, Chinese: See Luo Pan.
Confucianism: based on the sixth century B.C.E. teachings of Confucius, a code of ethics and behavior aimed to cultivate social and moral principles.
Connected Pearl Sequence: Consecutive numbers in each palace aka a Pearl String or Continuous Bead.
Correct Needle: the inner three needles on a San He Luo Pan; the needle is interpreted with reference to the earth plate. The correct needle aligns with magnetic North/South.
Cosmic Trinity: Known in Chinese as *Tien-Di-Ren*. Three categories of luck, specifically Heaven Luck, Man Luck, and Earth Luck. The Chinese believe Heaven Luck is fixed; however, humans have control over Feng Shui (Earth Luck) and personal effort (Man Luck).
Court Official: A technique used to bring status and power to a lawyer, judge, or high official using a building (virtual mountain), door direction, road or real water. It is also known as *Ushering the Officer Water Ring;* a San He water formula.

D
Da Gua Pai: A school of Feng Shui which uses the Xian Tien trigrams, Luo Shu numbers and the Hexagrams.
Dao: also spelled *Tao*, is a Chinese concept signifying the way, path, route, or sometimes known as the doctrine or principle. Within the context of traditional Chinese philosophy and religion, Tao is a metaphysical concept originating with Lao Tzu that gave rise to a religion and philosophy (Taoism). The concept of Tao was shared with Confucianism and Zen Buddhism. Within these contexts Tao signifies the primordial essence or fundamental nature of the universe. In Taoism, Chinese Buddhism and

Confucianism, the object of spiritual practice is to *become one with the Tao* or to harmonize one's will with Nature in order to achieve effortless action; this involves meditative and moral practices.

Daoism: see Taoism.

Death and Emptiness Lines (DEL): Also known as a void, or empty lines, they invite a host of negative events if doors fall on these degrees, which are on the exact cardinal points, 90, 180, 270, and 360/0. Though other DELs exist, the consequences are less severe such as in between the Guas or the 24 mountains. Void lines, especially major ones, are reserved for temples, churches, synagogues, and other places of worship. These degrees can attract or serve as doorways for ghosts or spirits. Also known as *Kong Wang* or *Kun Mang*.

Destructive Cycle: the cycle of the Elements that is ordered: Metal, Wood, Earth, Water, then Fire.

Devil's Door/Gate: the Northeast, sometimes considered a bad direction to face a front door.

Di Li: Means Earth theories or Feng Shui as known in the old days. Now a term for 'geography.'

Di: Earth

Dian Nan Pai: one of the six schools of Xuan Kong.

Direct and Indirect Spirit: This theory restricts the placement of water in four directions in certain Periods. For instance in Period 6, 7, 8, and 9 it suggests that water can *only* be placed in the north, southwest, east or southeast. Southwest would be the 'optimum' position in Period 8 and considered 'direct spirit', in Period 7, it was the east. Master Joseph Yu and other masters refer to this theory as the *Holy 1* and the *Holy 0*. Grandmaster Yap Cheng Hai considers this theory somewhat faulty and not totally accurate.

Direction: one of the 8 main compass points, or in a more specialized sense, the 24 Mountain ring. One of the most important aspects of determining the energy of a site or structure is taking the compass direction. Generally, the direction is read at the main door of the structure.

diving driveway: When land or a driveway slopes to the front door, the energy is said to *dive* toward the house. This is considered sha or negative chi because it is too direct and intense to bring good luck.

Door Facing: The facing direction of the door (usually front door).

Dou Niu Sha: bull-fight sha or the 2, 3 star combination.

Double Stars Meet at Facing: *Shuang Xing Dao Xiang* in Chinese means that two stars in the Flying Star system are in the front of the house or building.

Double Stars Meet at Sitting: *Shuang Xing Dao Zuo* in Chinese means that two stars in the Flying Star system are at the back of the house or building.

Dragon Gate Eight Formula: Known in Chinese as *Long Men Ba Da Ju*, this powerful set of formulas involve the energetic harmony of water, mountains, and designed water exits.

Dragon Gate: the gate through which successful scholars are supposed to pass, metaphorically turning from a mere carp into a dragon.
Dragon, Green: the Form School hills to the left of a house or site (looking out from the front door).
Dragon, Yellow: used to represent the center palace.
dragon: In Feng Shui a dragon is a mountain. Dragon is a term also used for something powerful or curving, as in the mythical body of a dragon. It can apply to land and water. The Chinese so revere the dragon that it is used in multiple applications and meanings.
Dragon's Lair: in Feng Shui, all mountains ranges are called dragons. When the dragon meets the terrain, it is his lair (Long Xue). It is the location in which chi can accumulate.
dragon's vein: The vein of the dragon is an area of chi accumulation, most commonly places of running water. In Feng Shui, mountains and mountain ranges are called dragons. Where the dragon meets the terrain is its *lair*, or the most powerful spot of a site.
drain: An opening in the ground usually covered with a grate, which takes water away from an area. Uncovered drains are rectangular and sometimes seen in subdivisions. In Feng Shui, these are considered *water exits* and can bring wealth or disaster. A drain near a main door of a home or business is always bad. Only exposed drains are important in Feng Shui; underground and invisible formations do not count.
Du Yin Sha: Lone Yin Sha; single tree in front of main external door.

E
Early Heaven Ba Gua: This is the first arrangement of the eight trigrams; known as the *Ho Tien* or *Fu Xi* Ba Gua in Chinese. It can be easily recognized as the Chien trigram (three solid lines) and is always placed on the top. This is the arrangement used in Ba Gua mirrors to deter sha Chi.
Earth Luck: One of the three categories of luck that humans can experience; your luck will increase by using Feng Shui, also known as Earth Luck. The Chinese word for earth is *Di*.
Earth Plate: a ring on the Luo Pan to measure door directions/buildings.
Earthly Branch Chen 辰: The Dragon. One of the 24 Mountains located at 112.5° - 127.5°.
Earthly Branch Chou 丑: The Ox. One of the 24 Mountains located at 22.5° - 37.5°.
Earthly Branch Hai 亥: The Pig. One of the 24 Mountains located at 322.5° - 337.5°.
Earthly Branch Mao 卯: The Rabbit. One of the 24 Mountains located at 82.5° - 97.5°.
Earthly Branch Shen 申: The Monkey. One of the 24 Mountains located at 232.5° - 247.5°.
Earthly Branch Si 巳: The Snake. One of the 24 Mountains located at 142.5° - 157.5°.
Earthly Branch Wei 未: The Goat. One of the 24 Mountains located at 202.5° - 217.5°.
Earthly Branch Wu 午: The Horse. One of the 24 Mountains located at 172.5° - 187.5°.
Earthly Branch Xu 戌: The Dog. One of the 24 Mountains located at 292.5° - 307.5°.

Earthly Branch Yin 寅: The Tiger. One of the 24 Mountains located at 52.5° - 67.5°.

Earthly Branch You 酉: The Rooster. One of the 24 Mountains located at 261.5° - 277.5°.

Earthly Branch Zi 子: The Rat. One of the 24 Mountains located at 352.5° - 7.5°.

Earthly Branches: The Chinese Calendar is based on a combination of 10 Heavenly Stems and 12 Earthly Branches; there are 60 possible combinations equaling a cycle of 60 years. Earthly Branches are commonly known as the 12 Animal signs. When located on the 12 Earthly Branches ring of the Luo Pan, each Earthly Branch occupies 30°. When located around the 24 Mountains ring of the Luo Pan, each Earthly Branch occupies 15°.

East Life Group: In the Eight Mansions system, people are divided into the East or West group. The 1, 3, 4 and 9 Life Guas are part of the East Life Group.

East/West system: the system that divides people and houses into two types, the East Group and the West Group.

Eight House Bright Mirror: In Chinese *Pa Chai Ming Jing*, is one of the eight different styles of the Eight Mansions system. This style uses the sitting direction of the house instead of the facing.

Eight House: This is another name for the Eight Mansions; in Chinese it is *Pa Chai* or *BaZhai*.

Eight Killing Forces: A formation where the door direction and the energy of a nearby mountain are out of harmony; they are serious and will bring disaster to the household.

Eight Life Aspirations: Also known as the *Eight Life Stations*, these stations correspond to a point on the Ba Gua and an aspect of life—South, fame; Southwest, marriage; Southeast, wealth; North, career; and so forth. This is the work of Black Hat Sect founder Lin Yun. Eight Life Stations is not found in classic texts or part of the genuine Feng Shui of ancient practice and principles. It is neither an aspect of the Eight Mansions system nor even a derivative of that system. Some popular Feng Shui books that promote Classical Feng Shui also include the Eight Life Aspirations, which only adds to the confusion.

Eight Roads of Destruction II: This formula is a secondary level of the basic and more powerful Eight Roads of Destruction. The theory behind 8R II is that each of the five elements gives 'birth' in one area and goes to the 'grave' in another. The four 'Graves', which are earthly branches, are the Dog, Dragon, Goat and Ox (NW 1, SE 1, SW 1 and NE 1). Water should exit from these points, not enter.

Eight Roads of Destruction: Also known as the *Eight Roads to Hell*, this formation is based on the egress of a road or driveway from a property in correlation to the front door. Even though the road or driveway is considered virtual water, the direction it exits is called a *water exit*. This unlucky formation can have disastrous results, so remedial measures must be taken.

Eight Wandering Stars (aka Tan Lang): also known as the *Big Wandering Sky*, these stars are matched with the nine stars of the Big Dipper, they are as follows: Tan Lang (*Greedy Wolf* aka *Ravenous Wolf*) is matched with Sheng Chi; Jue Men *(Huge Door* aka

Great Door) is matched with Tien Yi; *Wu Chu (Military Arts)* is matched with Yen Nien; *Tso Fu & Fu Pi (Left/Right Assistant* aka the *Big Dipper's Handle)* is matched with Fu Wei; *Lu Chun (Rewards/Salary)* is matched with Wo Hai; *Lien Zheng (Five Ghosts aka Chastity)* is matched with Wu Gwei; *Wen Qu (Literary Arts* aka *The Scholar)* is matched with Lui Sha; *Tien Kong (Broken Soldier* aka *Destructive Army)* is matched with Cheuh Ming. These nine stars and their unique energy are very important in many Feng Shui systems/formulas. These are the 'secret' names for the 9 stars.

electrical towers: The high-tension towers that bring electricity to an area emit incredibly negative energy. The Swedish government has done extensive research on how these towers affect human beings: children are most vulnerable to this intense energy.

Elements, Five: Wu Xing in Chinese for Water, Fire, Earth, Metal, and Wood.

energy: The Chinese call energy chi (also spelled *qi*) and pronounced **chee**. Our entire universe is energy; there are many types of chi—human, environmental, and heaven (the solar system).

Er He: the 2-Black Star of the nine stars.

esoteric: Knowledge that is available only to a narrow circle of enlightened or initiated people or a specially educated group. Feng Shui is part of Chinese metaphysics and is considered esoteric.

external environment: This covers the terrain and topography, including mountains, water, and other natural formations. It also encompasses man-made features, such as roads, pools, retaining walls, highways, poles, drains, washes, tall buildings, stop signs, fire hydrants, and other structures.

F

facing direction: The front side of the home or building, generally where the front or main door is located and faces the street.

Facing Star: Also known as the water star, this star is located in the upper right-hand corner of a Flying Star chart in all nine palaces or sectors. The facing star is in charge of wealth luck.

Facing: The *yang side* of a building; this is important to establish in Flying Stars.

Fan Gua: Gua changing or Yao changing method, also known as 'flipping the yaos'.

Fan Yin: also known as *Reverse Chant*, when the 5-Yellow Star, flying in a yin (backward) direction, occupies the mountain or water star position of the central palace.

Fang Shih: a master of Taoist magic.

Fang Wei: see Compass School.

Fei Xing: Flying Stars.

Fen yeh: the 12 Provincial divisions of ancient China; Chin Dynasty.

Feng sha: a noxious chi-destroying wind.

Feng Shui master: One who has mastered the skills of Classical Feng Shui and/or has been declared as such by his or her teacher, or both. It is also said that a practitioner becomes a master when his or her clients refer to them as master. Most Feng Shui masters from classic traditions will belong to a lineage of their teachers. This is also known as *a lineage carrier,* meaning the master carries on the teachings and practices of his or her education. A Feng Shui master generally oversees his or her own school as well.

Feng Shui schools: There are two major schools or branches (not physical locations, rather they are systems) of Classical Feng Shui, San He and San Yuan; hundreds of formulas, techniques, and systems serve as sub sets of either school. Those who practice Classical Feng Shui, use the San He and the San Yuan systems as one extensive body of knowledge.

Feng Shui Xing Sheng: a professional practitioner of Feng Shui, aka Feng Shui Jia or Kan Yu Jia.

Feng Shui: *(fung schway)* means "wind water"; the two natural forces that drive chi to a site. Feng Shui is the art and science of determining how your environment and home affect you over periods of time. Known as *Kan Yu* (translated as *the way of heaven and earth*) until about a hundred years ago, the Chinese system of maximizing the accumulation of beneficial chi improves the quality of life and luck of the occupants of a particular building or location. The literal translation is wind and water; however, in Classical Feng Shui wind means *direction* and water means *energy*. Pronounced *fung shway* or *foong shway.*

Feng: The Chinese word for **wind;** pronounced *fung,* although *foong* is a more accurate sound.

Fire Burning Heaven's Gate: The northwest location of your site is known as 'heaven's gate'. The 6 star also represents the heavens. When there is the real element of fire, such as a stove or kitchen, in the northwest sector of the house, it is said that 'fire is burning heaven's gate". This can also happened when the 9 star and the 6 star (of the Flying Star system) come together in *any* palace, but is considered seriously inauspicious when these stars are present in the northwest palace. Either the star combination (6, 9) or, the presence of real fire in the northwest always brings bad luck to the father, president, or the leader.

firemouth: The direction of the stove knobs, a concept that is important in the Eight Mansions system. It is sometimes mistakenly referred to as the oven-mouth.

Five Chinese Metaphysical Arts: Shan (Mountain); Yi (Medical); Po (Divination); Ming (Destiny); and Sow (*Physiognomy/Imagery*). *Mountain* (Shan or Xian Xue): This category encompasses philosophy (including the teachings of the fourth-century B.C. philosophers Lao Zi and Zhuang Zi, Taoism), martial arts, Qi Gong, Tai Chi Chuan, meditation, healing, and diet. This category also encompasses the study of Alchemy—the science of prolonging life through specific rituals and exercises, which are deeply rooted in Taoism. *Medicine* (Yi): The Chinese follow an integrated, holistic, and curative approach to medicine: acupuncture, herbal prescriptions, and massage fall into this category. *Divination* (Po): The Chinese are well-known for their intuitive skills and abilities to read and interpret symbols. The divination techniques of Da Liu Ren, Tai Yi Mystical Numbers, Qi Men, Mei Hua Xin Yi (Plum Blossom oracle) employ numbers to predict everything from wars, to missing persons, to the details of one's past and future. *Destiny* (Ming): Most forms of Chinese augury seek to interpret fate and determine the

timing of life events; the ancient sages devoted much time and research to this study. The most popular methods of Chinese fortune-telling include Zi Wei Dou Shu (Purple Star Astrology) and BaZi (literally means 'eight characters' but is also commonly known as the Four Pillars of Destiny), both of which examine a person's destiny and potential based on their date and time of birth. A complimentary form of Ming is the Science of Divination (Bu Shi), which is analogous to the mathematics of probability.
Physiognomy/Imagery (Xiang Xue): Master Yap refers to this category as *Sow*, and it involves making predictions based on the image, form, and features of the landscape, the human face and palms, architecture, and gravesites. Feng Shui is the fortune-telling of a building by rendering an accurate observation of the structure's appearance, shape, direction, and other surrounding environmental features.

Five Elements (Wu Xing): Five types of chi prevailing one after another-Fire, Earth, Metal, Water, Wood; the basis for all Feng Shui calculations.

Five Ghosts Carry Treasure II: It is a more advanced application of the first method in that it uses specific water exits. This method is allegedly more secret than the more widely known version of Five Ghosts Carry Treasure. This formula does not use the door direction. Rather, it relies on the sitting or back of the property, the incoming and outgoing directions of water or a road, and a mountain or a tall building.

Five Ghosts Carry Treasure: Also referred to as *Five Ghosts Carry Money*, is a secret formula for wealth from Taiwan and a favorite technique among Asian masters. It is powerful and uses mountains and water to support people to accumulate wealth.

Five phases: five physical elements in nature that represent the movement of chi. The concept of the five phases is the backbone of Chinese medicine, acupuncture, and Feng Shui.

Floating Stars: a term used by some masters; see Flying Stars.

Flying Stars: Known as *Xuan Kong Fei Xing* in Chinese, which means *mysterious void* or the *subtle mysteries of time and space.* It is a sophisticated and complex system of analyzing how time and space affect a building. The magnetic orientation of the dwelling, along with the move-in date are important factors that determine the innate character of a house.

Forbidden City: This Beijing landmark served as the Chinese imperial palace for nearly 500 years until 1912. It now houses the Palace Museum.

Form and Configuration School (Hsing Shih): Feng Shui practice that uses landform structure to determine positions of maximum beneficial chi accumulation. Master Yang Yun Sung (840-888 CE) was the Form and Configuration School's most famous master.

Form School: The study of the forms and shapes in the environment based on the Five Elements.

Fortunate Mountain Fortunate Water: *Wang Shan Wang Shui*, if the ruling stars are properly located and represented. Also known as 'lucky for money, lucky for people'.

Four Pillars of Destiny: your personal Chinese horoscope, specifically the eight Chinese characters and their associated elements generated by determining the stem and branch of each of the year, month, day, and hour of your birth date; also known as BaZi.

Four Point Gold: a square or rectangular building is considered very auspicious and 'golden' as the chi is distributed evenly.

Fu Bei: Fu Wei, Left Assistant to the Celestial Emperor, Tso Fu aka the Sun (Tai Yang or the Great yang), and the eight (8) star.

Fu Lu Shou: Popular Chinese deities representing Health; Wealth; Long Life. Also known as the Three Lucky Gods.

Fu Mu San Ban Gua: Has different meanings and structures in different schools of Feng Shui. In Xuan Kong Fei Xing (Flying Stars), whenever the chart structure has the combinations 147, 258, 369 in every palace, it is known as a Parent String or the Three Combinations Chart.

Fu Wie: The direction and location for stability as it applies to the Eight Mansions system. According to Master Yap's numeric representation, it is the +60.

Fu Xi Ba Gua Map: the early heaven arrangement of the trigrams. It is believed that the sage Fu Xi drew the first Ba Gua in a square diagram.

Fu Xi: A sage, king and shaman who was responsible for discovering and arranging the Early Heaven Ba Gua. It is also spelled Fu Hsi.

Fu Yin/Fan Yin: opposite meaning or reversed, known as reiterative chant, when the 5 Yellow Star, flying in a yang (forward) direction, occupies the mountain or water star position of the central Palace.

G

Ganzhi system: using the 10 heavenly stems and 12 earthly branches.

gateway: An opening, often a gap between mountains or buildings, where chi is concentrated and can be used to support certain wealth-producing techniques, such as Five Ghosts Carry Treasure formations.

Gen: One of the eight trigrams of the Ba Gua also spelled as *Ken*. It represents the youngest son, the mountain and early spring. In the Later Heaven arrangement of the Ba Gua, the Gen trigram is located in the Northeast.

Geomancy: an old mistranslation of Feng Shui. In reality geomancy is a completely different Arab system of divination by dots and sand, originating in North Africa in the 9th century AD.

Geopathic Stress: A potentially harmful energy field generated underground and radiating upward by mineral deposits, water streams, geological faults, decayed organic matter, graves, burial or ritual grounds, and man-made or other causes.

Goddess/Warrior of the Nine Heavens: aka the *Mysterious Girl*; an ancient legend that tells of the Yellow Emperor Huangdi (2698 to 2598 BC) being awakened by a bright light from heaven in which the Goddess emerged. She held in her hand a 9 by 8 inch jade box. He opened the box and found that it contained a magic scroll written on dragon skin. It is said that by following the secrets written on the 'dragon scroll' that the Emperor defeated the evil wizard (Chi You) in the famous Battle of Zhuolu; thus began the start of the great Han Chinese civilization.

Goat Blade (aka *Triple Goat Punishment* or *Frightened Goat*): Similar to the *Peach Blossom Sha*, these formations incite divorce, adultery, gambling, alcohol abuse, family break-ups, over indulgence in sex and illegal activities leading to failure in business.

Golden Pill: The Taoist masters tried for centuries to create a *'gold pill'* that would produce spiritual transcendence and immortality.

Golden Star Classic: Translates as *Kam Kwong Dou Lam King* in Chinese—also spelled as *Jin Guang Dou Lin Jing*. It is also known as the Big Dipper Casting Golden Light, the style of Eight Mansions used by those in GMY's lineage.

Grandmaster Datuk Chee Kim Thong: A martial arts teacher of Grandmaster Yap Cheng Hai.

grandmaster of Feng Shui: This person has been practicing and teaching for many years, belongs to a respected lineage of masters, and has at least one master among his or her pupils.

Grandmaster Yap Cheng Hai (GMY) 1927-2014: Master Yap was born and raised in Singapore; although he did live briefly in Xiamen, China for four years. He moved to Kuala Lumpur, Malaysia in 1963 to manage his uncle's business and soon became a citizen. Although his life was full, he pursued two passions, that of Feng Shui and Martial Arts. He began practicing Feng Shui professionally in the early 60's. He has consulted with prominent figures such as members of royalty, ministers, corporations, banks, and developers. His loyal client since the sixties, Paramount Garden consulted him to plan their townships that included SEA Park, Damansara Utama and Bandar Utama. GMY is quite famous in SE Asia for his *Water Dragon* techniques which he learned from Grandmaster Chan Chuan Huai in Taiwan who created several billionaires there. He began teaching in the late 1990's to those wishing to learn authentic, Classical Feng Shui.

gravesites: A burial place for the dead. The first type of Feng Shui practiced in China was known as *Yin Feng Shui*, and it involved the selection of burial locations. This tradition is still active in Asian culture—the perfect arrangement for their deceased is big business. Living next to a cemetery will not bring good luck; it is especially bad for money luck. You may also experience frequent visits from spirits and ghosts.

Great Cycle of 180 years: 9 cycles of 20 years. The current Great Cycle begun in 1864.

Green Dragon: is the left hand side of the property as you look out the front door. This represents the male and is also known as Zuo Star or Deputy.

Gu Yang Sha: Lone Yang Sha; electricity post in front of main external door.

Gua Number: Also referred to as *Ming Gua* (nothing to do with the Ming Dynasty). To determine your personal Life Gua number, use your birthday.

Gua: Alternatively spelled *Kua* and also known as a trigram. It represents one of eight Guas of the Ba Gua, defined by a combination of three solid or broken lines.

Guan Dong Pai: one of the six schools of Xuan Kong.

Guest: The star being treated as the *guest* by the host star and how this energy is affecting or interacting with the Host.

GMY Code: this is a code devised by Grandmaster Yap Cheng Hai to easily identify your good and bad directions in the Eight Mansions system; the +90, +80, +70, +60 are your *good* directions representing wealth, health, relationships/longevity and stability respectively. The code of -90, -80, -70, and -60 represent your *bad* directions that if activated, will cause divorce/bankruptcy, bad health/betrayals, affairs/lawsuits and setbacks respectively.

H

Hai Ho: the accidents and mishaps or mild bad luck location in a house.

Han Dynasty: 206 B.C.–220 A.D.

He Tu Diagram: In the He Tu, 1 and 6 are in the north (at the bottom of the diagram), 2 and 7 are in the south, 3 and 8 are in the east, 4 and 9 are in the west while 5 and 10 are at the centre.

Heart Piercing Sha: Tall post in front of a main external door.

Heaven Luck: One of the three categories of luck that humans can experience. The Chinese believe every human has a destiny and a fate determined by the heavens (tien). This category cannot be changed and is considered *fixed*. See also Tien-Di-Ren.

Heaven Plate: a ring on the Luo Pan in which to measure real or virtual water; also known as the water ring.

Heavenly Heart: Is the central palace of the Luo Shu (*magic square of 15*) and the center of the home or building.

Heavenly Stem Bing 丙: Yang Fire. One of the 24 Mountains located at 157.5° - 172.5°.

Heavenly Stem Ting 丁: Yin Fire. One of the 24 Mountains located at 187.5° - 202.5°.

Heavenly Stem Geng 庚: Yang Metal. One of the 24 Mountains located at 247.5° - 261.5°.

Heavenly Stem Kwei 癸: Yin Water. One of the 24 Mountains located at 7.5° - 22.5°.

Heavenly Stem Ji: Yin Earth. *Not one of the 24 Mountains*. Located in the centre.

Heavenly Stem Jia 甲: Yang Wood. One of the 24 Mountains located at 67.5° - 82.5°.

Heavenly Stem Ren 壬: Yang Water. One of the 24 Mountains located at 337.5° - 352.5°.

Heavenly Stem Mu: Yang Earth. *Not one of the 24 Mountains*. Located in the centre.

Heavenly Stem Xin 辛: Yin Metal. One of the 24 Mountains located at 277.5° - 292.5°.

Heavenly Stem Yi 乙: Yin Wood. One of the 24 Mountains located at 97.5° - 112.5°.

Heavenly Stems: The Chinese calendar is based on a combination of 10 Heavenly Stems and 12 Earthly Branches; there are 60 possible combinations equaling a cycle of 60 years. When located around the 24 Mountains ring of the Luo Pan, each Heavenly Stem occupies 15°.

heuristic: A common-sense rule or set of rules intended to increase the probability of solving a problem. Relating to or using a general formulation that serves to guide investigation. Feng Shui *formulas* are to be viewed as heuristic, not hard science.

Hexagrams: the 64 figures formed by placing one trigram on top of another in every possible combination. A figure made up of eight lines on top of one another, either broken or unbroken. The basis of the I Ching.

Hidden Siren: when the 5 Yellow Star flies forward in sequence; it is a mirror of the Luo Shu.
high-rise building: In the external environment, high-rise buildings and skyscrapers function as *virtual* or *urban mountains*.
Ho Hai: Also known as *Wo Hai*. Part of the Eight Mansions system and can bring mishaps and nothing goes smoothly. According to Master Yap's numeric representation, this is the -60.
Ho Tien Ba Gua: the later heaven arrangement of the eight trigrams. King Wen re-ordered the Ba Gua map and this arrangement of the trigrams contain the *application* of Feng Shui.
Ho: The Chinese word for fire.
Hou Tien: Things acquired or modified after birth, often incorrectly translated as 'Later Heaven'.
Hou: a five day period.
Hsia: pronounced *she-ah*; this is the name for the Chinese Solar Calendar based on the cycles of the Sun. The Solar Calendar regulates agriculture because the *Sun* determines the seasons; also used in all Feng Shui techniques for its accuracy. The solar year begins on February 4th or 5th, there are two possible dates is not because an uncertainly, but due to the fact that the Western calendar 'wobbles' because of the insertion of the extra day during 'leap years'.
Hsiieh: the lair, or site, of the maximum concentration of beneficial chi; can also apply to an acupuncture point.
Hsiu: the 28 Chinese (uneven sized) constellations often found marked on one of the outer rings of a Feng Shui compass.
Hsun: the trigram of wind and the early summer; also spelled as Sun/Xun.
Huai-nan-wang Jianji BaZhai Jing: The *Classic of BaZhai According to the King of Southern Huai* (Jiangsu) book.
Huang Di BaZhai Jing: the *Yellow Emperor's Classic of BaZhai* book.
Huang Shi Gong BaZhai: *The BaZhai of Old Man Yellow Stone* book.
Huo Hai: Misfortune, mishap; one of the Eight Wandering Stars used in Ba Zhai Feng Shui.

I
I Ching Feng Shui: Also known as *Xuan Kong Da Gua*. A San Yuan system of Feng Shui that relies on the sixty-four hexagrams of the *I Ching*. Often referred to as the Big 64 Hexagrams, this method offers various techniques—the most popular is for auspicious date selection.
I Ching: A philosophical and divinatory book based on the sixty-four hexagrams of Taoist mysticism. It is also known as the *Classic of Changes* or *Book of Changes*. This book dates back to antiquity around the 4th Century BC, and was authored by four holy men, namely Fu His, King Wen, the Duke of Chou and Confucius.
imprisoned ruling star: the ruling facing star located/trapped in the central palace.

incoming dragon: The energy of a mountain that comes directly to your home or building. If a mountain range is nearby, the highest peak is measured with a Luo Pan because it has the most powerful energy. An entire science is based on determining the effects of mountain energy on any given site. In Feng Shui, mountains and dragons are used interchangeably.

intercardinal directions: Northwest, southwest, northeast and southeast.

interior environment: The interior environment encompasses anything that falls within the walls of a structure, including kitchen, staircase, master bedroom, fireplaces, bathrooms, hallways, dining room, bedrooms, appliances, furniture, and so on.

Inverse Siren: this is when the 5 Yellow Star flies backward in sequence; all nine stars will be the exact opposite positions of the Luo Shu.

J

Jade Belt: a term used in San He system to describe great wealth luck—the land formation that is shaped like a "belt" around the building.

Jiang Da Hong (Ming-Qing Dynasty): One of the famous Feng Shui masters from the past. He had access to the Prime Minister's library and read all the Feng Shui books, then began advocating the use of Yang House as opposed to Yin House Feng Shui and the use of the Flying Stars (Fei Xing) system. He is often referred to as the *'Father of Flying Stars'*. Famous works include—Gui Hou Lu; Di Li Bian Zheng; Tien Yuan Wu Ge; Tien Yuan Yu Yi; Gu Jing Ge; and Shi Long Jing.

Jiang Liang: Used the books in the Qing Nan Jing to overthrow the Qin Emperor to establish the Han Dynasty.

Jiang Pan: a Luo Pan based on the methods of Master Jiang Da Hong.

Jin Guang Dou Lin Jing: The *Classic of the Dipper Casting its Golden Light* book.

Jiu Chi: the 9-Purple Star in the nine stars.

Jiu Yun: nine 20 year periods, a mega cycle or 180 years.

Ju Men: Huge Door/Great Gate, the Monarch of Sickness, Heavenly Wealth/Money from Heaven (Tien Yi) and the 2 Black star.

Jue Ming: 'Destiny Totally Vanishing.' One of the Eight Wandering Stars used in Ba Zhai Feng Shui, also spelled *Cheuh Ming*.

Jui Gong Fei Xing: Nine Palace Flying Stars.

K

Kan Yu: The way of Heaven and the way of Earth. Together this means the way of time and space. This is an old name for Feng Shui.

Kan: One of the eight trigrams. It represents the middle son, the moon and mid-winter. In the Later Heaven Arrangement of the Ba Gua, it is located in the North; the trigram of Moon and water and mid-winter.

Ken: the trigram of mountain and early spring; also spelled Gen.

Killing Breath: see sha chi.

King Wen: Some say he rearranged the Xian Tien Ba Gua to form the Hou Tien Ba Gua (although others say this was the work of Fu Xi), most agree he attached explanatory statements to the Hexagrams.

Kong Wang: also known as Kun Mang, they are void lines or Death and Empty Line (DEL); they invite a host of negative events if doors are at these degrees.

Kua: means both trigram (3 lines) and hexagram (six lines). Also spelled Gua.

Kun: One of the eight trigrams. It represents the mother, the earth and late summer. In the Later Heaven Arrangement of the Ba Gua, it is located in the Southwest.

Kwei: ghosts, has also been translated "demons."

L

Later Heaven Ba Gua: The second arrangement of the trigrams known as the *Wen Wang* or *Xien Tien* Ba Gua. This is used extensively in the application of Classical Feng Shui.

Li Chun: the commencement of spring, the day the Annual Stars change, the beginning of the Chinese Solar New Year, which begins on February 3rd, 4th or 5th of each year.

Li Ji: The centre of reference, where the Luo Pan is placed.

Li Qi: the qualities of chi/qi/energy.

Li: One of the eight trigrams. It represents the middle daughter, fire and full summer. In the Later Heaven Arrangement of the Ba Gua, it is located in the South.

Lian Zhu San Ban Gua: The second type of San Ban Gua (one is lucky for people, the other lucky for money). Lian Zhu means stringed pearls. In each and every palace, the three numbers are consecutive number. Other names are Pearl String and the Continuous Bead formation.

Liang Yi: Two polarities; referring to yin and yang.

Lien Ching: sharp mountains, these are considered sha chi.

Life Gua Number: a number assigned to people, based on birthday and gender, in the Eight Mansions system (BaZhai).

Life Gua Personalities™: a description of personality types based on the Life Gua number in the Eight Mansion system expanded on and first seen in *Classical Feng Shui for Wealth and Abundance* published by Llewellyn on March 2013.

Lin Cu San Poo Gua: an auspicious and special chart in Flying Stars known as the Pearl String Formation. There are two indications—one for wealth and the other for people luck.

Lineage: The line of transmission of sacred knowledge from a common ancestor who is deemed the founder.

Ling Xing: A card issued by the emperor to his officer in charge giving the holder 'power of attorney' to represent the emperor. Also, a term used for the ruling star of a 20 year cycle.

Liu Bai: 6-White Star in the Nine Stars.

Liu Nian Xing: the current yearly star.

Liu Ri Xing: the current daily star.

Liu Sha: In the Eight Mansions system, it also known as the *Six Killings* (aka the six curses, devils or imps) direction and can bring backstabbing, affairs, and lawsuits. According to Master Yap's numeric representation, it is the -80.

Liu Yue Xing: the current monthly star.

Location: A particular place or position, differing from the concept of *direction*. For example, your living room might be located on the south side of your home (location), but your desk faces north (direction).

Long chi: Energy that runs along an extended road or pathway.

Long Mai: the dragon's veins.

Long Men Ba Da Jua: the San Yuan Dragon Gate Eight formulas.

Long or Lung: the dragon or mountain.

Lu Chun: Wo Hai/Huo Hai, Mishaps, Illuminated Orphan or Solitary Sunlight (Ku Yao), The Lonely Star, Rank or Salary Preserved, The Phantom of Misfortune and the 3 star.

Luck: is considered to be comprised of three components known as Heaven Luck (fate), Earth Luck (Feng Shui), and Man Luck (your own efforts).

Lui Sha: a common incorrect spelling of Liu Sha.

lunar calendar: A calendar based on the cycles of the moon.

Lung Ho Tu: dragon map.

Lung Mei: Dragon Veins, but not the same as ley lines. They are the channels that chi follows through the Earth.

Lung: The Chinese word for dragon (can mean water or mountain).

Luo Pan: The Luo Pan is the quintessential tool of a Feng Shui practitioner. It is a compass that contains four to forty concentric rings of information. The most popular model is approximately ten inches across, square, and often constructed of fine woods. The circle part of the Luo Pan is made of brass and rotates to align with the compass itself, which is located in the center. There are three major types of Luo Pans—the *San Yuan* Luo Pan, the *San He* Luo Pan, and the *Chung He* Luo Pan (also known as *Zong He* or *Zhung He*), which is a combination of the first two. Though Luo Pans have similar basic components, Feng Shui masters do customize their own with secret information for them and their students. See the Goddess/Warrior of the Nine Heavens.

Luo Shu: A square that contains nine palaces or cells with a number in each; it adds to fifteen in any direction. The Luo Shu is also known as the *Magic Square of 15*. Also known as the Luo River Writing or River Map.

M

Magic Square: aka the Magic Square of Three and the Luo Shu; all cells add up to 15, vertically, horizontally and diagonally.

main door: This is usually the front door of the home or business. If the occupants always enter the residence from the garage, this may also be considered a main door.

Man Luck: One of the three categories of luck that a human can experience. This area of fortune is mutable and defined by individual effort, such as hard work, study, education, experience, and good deeds. The Chinese word for man is *Ren*. See Tien-Di-Ren.

Man Plate: a ring on the Luo Pan in which to measure/assess the qi/chi of mountains.

Man: Chinese for the front door which should be big and open.

Martial Arts: are codified systems and traditions of combat practices, which are practiced for a variety of reasons: self-defense, competition, physical health and fitness, entertainment, as well as mental, physical, and spiritual development.

Massage: is the manipulation of superficial and deeper layers of muscle and connective tissue using various techniques, to enhance function, aid in the healing process, decrease muscle reflex activity, inhibit motor-neuron excitability, promote relaxation and well-being, and as a recreational activity.

Metal Cures: the best metals are bronze, copper, brass, pewter, stainless steel and wrought iron to weaken the 2 or 5 star.

Ming Dynasty: A ruling dynasty of China, which lasted from 1368 to 1644.

Ming Gua: destiny trigram, or personal Gua number. The annual Flying Star of the year of birth, in the case of males; determined by your year of birth and gender, your ming (birth) Gua (trigram) is the guardian star (or number) you are born under.

Ming Shu: fate calculation, a form of Chinese astrology.

Ming Tang: bright hall, the courtyard, or the open space in front of a building where ben-eficial ch'i can accumulate.

Ming: life, fate, destiny.

Ming; Yun; Ji Yin De; Du Shu: Fate, destiny; fortune or luck; doing good deeds; education, study of books.

Monk Yi Xing: inventor of the *Eight House Bright Mirror* School; this style of Eight Mansion is not used by GMY's lineage.

Monthly Stars: Visiting monthly stars to each of the eight palaces.

Moon Gate: the omega-shaped gates that reduce the loss of chi from a walled area.

Mountain Star: Star governing health, relationships and personality in the Flying Stars.

mountains: Includes real mountains and virtual mountains, such as tall buildings, landscape mounds, retaining walls, huge boulders, or any object of mass in the environment. See *dragon*.

Mu: Wood.

N

Na Jia: A hidden attribute of the Guas; GMY called these the 4th musketeer and sisters and brothers. They are the fire frame (Yin, Wu, Xu) plus Ren; the water frame (Chen, Tzi, Shen) plus Kwei; the metal frame (Su, You, Chou) plus Ting; the wood frame (Hai, Mao, Wei) plus Geng; Chien & Jia (brothers); Sun & Sin (sisters); Bing & Gen (brother & sister); and Kun & Yi (brother & sister).

Na Yin: used to determine the 'hidden' element of a person based on their birth.

Nanotechnology: aka *nanotech* for short is the manipulation of matter on an atomic, molecular, and supramolecular scale. The earliest, widespread description of nanotechnology referred to the particular technological goal of precisely manipulating atoms and molecules for fabrication of macroscale products, also now referred to as molecular nanotechnology.

Nian Shen Fang Wei: the position of the year gods, such as the Grand Duke (Tai Sui) and Year Breaker (Sui Po).

Nian: the year.

Nien Yen: This is the incorrect spelling of the *Yen Nien* (+70) in the Eight Mansions system; you will see this mistake in many Feng Shui books.

Nine Stars: 9 types of chi represented by the 9 numbers; the living spirits that influence our lives. Nine different types of Qi used in the Form School, Flying Stars and other Feng Shui techniques. Associated with Big Dipper and Luo Shu. Hours, days, months, years, units of 20, 60 and 180 years are all described using the Nine Stars. Chinese also call them spirits. Nine Star timekeeping is mainly used in Feng Shui.

P

Pa Chai: see Eight Mansions.

Pa Kua mirror: a mirror (flat, concave, or convex) surrounded by the eight trigrams in the Former Heaven Sequence designed to reflect sha ch'i.

Pa Kua: literally the eight trigrams, or more specifically, the octagonal arrangement of the Eight trigrams.

Pa Loo Hwang Chuen: The Chinese term for Eight Roads of Destruction.

Pa Sha Hwang Chuen: The Chinese translation of the Eight Killing Forces.

Pa Tzu: translates as Four Pillars but literally means eight characters (BaZi)

Pagoda: a multi-tiered Chinese tower designed as a Feng Shui landmark.

Pai: school.

Palace: This is one of the nine Luo Shu cells that a building is divided into for the purposes of a Feng Shui diagnosis. Each Palace (except the Central Palace) corresponds to one of the eight trigrams/directions. Palaces are usually referred to by their trigram, for example the Kun Palace, or more simply by their compass direction.

Parent String Formation: Known in Chinese as *Fu Mu San Poon Gua* and sometimes referred to as the *Three Combinations*, these are special wealth-producing Flying Star charts. This formation of energy applies to certain structures—which are activated by a mountain in the front of the property and water in the back—on intercardinal directions. They only last for twenty years and are unlucky if not activated properly. In Period 8, the Northeast Parent Strings (Northeast 2 & 3) have the 5 facing star in front and this is inauspicious despite the special chart.

Peach Blossom Sha: a San He formula that indicates bad romance, illicit affairs etc.

Pearl String Formation: Known in Chinese as *Lin Cu San Poon Gua* and sometimes referred to as the *Continuous Bead Formations,* these are special wealth-producing Flying Star charts that only show up in homes that face an intercardinal direction. Though excellent energy for prosperity, this formation only lasts for twenty years and is unlucky if not activated properly.

Period 7: this is part of the Flying Star system; Period 7 began February 4, 1984 and ended February 3, 2004. Each Period is 20 years in duration.

Period 8: this is part of the Flying Star system; Period 8 began February 4, 2004 and will end on February 3, 2024. Each Period is 20 years in duration.

period: This is a twenty-year increment of time that affects the luck of man and influences the world with its energy. These twenty-year periods were first tracked and recorded by the ancient Chinese in about 2500 BC. They observed that every 180 years the planets in our solar system line up. It was further noted that every twenty years the Milky Way shifts and influences the events of mankind. These periods run from one to nine every twenty years and then start all over again. Nine periods comprise a megacycle of 180 years.

Poison arrows: see secret arrows.

Po Chun: Tien Kong, Chueh Ming, Disaster, Defeat/Broken army, Destructive Army, Broken Soldier, The Spirit of Solemnity, and the 7 Star.

praxis: An exercise or practice of an art, science, or skill.

Precious Jewel Line (PJL): Also known as *Gold Dragons*, these are specific degrees that brings precious assets and jewels, wealth luck, and nobility to your life. There are only forty-eight of these degrees out of 360.

Productive cycle: a cycle of balance and creation. Each phase produces or enhances the succeeding phase. Fire-earth-metal-water-wood (5 phases) represents the productive cycle.

Prosperous Sitting and Facing: Known in Chinese as *Wang Shan Wang Shui*; a Flying Star chart that means *lucky for people, lucky for money*. These charts have the perfect placement of the current prosperous stars—the facing star is at the facing (lucky for money), and the mountain star is at the sitting (lucky for people).

Q

Qi Gong: also spelled *Qigong, chi kung,* or *chi gung*; traditional Chinese Qi Gong is a practice of aligning body, breath, and mind for health, meditation, and martial arts training. With roots in Chinese medicine, philosophy, and martial arts, qigong is traditionally viewed as a practice to cultivate and balance qi (chi) or what has been translated as "life energy".

Qi Men Dun Jia (also spelled Chi Men Tun Chia): It literally mean *Mysterious Doorway Hidden Jia* and its an advanced ancient metaphysical secret study reserved almost exclusively for the use by kings, general and ruling class of ancient China. It is sometimes used to supplement other date selection methods such as Xuan Kong Da Gua.

Qi Xing Da Jie: the seven star robbery method of manipulating the chi/qi; not used in GMY's lineage.

Qi Zi: the 7-Red Star of the nine stars.

Qi: *(chee)* the underlying and unifying substance and soul of all things. Both physical and metaphysical, qi is the nourishing force at the heart, growth, and development of the heavens, earth and humanity. It is also called *life's breathe*. Also spelled chi and ch'i. Matter and energy in tangible and intangible form

Qi-mouth: Entry point of qi, usually front door.

Qin Dynasty: 221 BC – 206 BC. The Qin (Chin) emperor unified China for the first time.

Ray Kurzweil: is an American author, inventor, futurist, and a director of engineering at Google. Aside from futurology, he is involved in fields such as optical character recognition (OCR), text-to-speech synthesis, speech recognition technology, and electronic keyboard instruments. He has written books on health, artificial intelligence (AI), transhumanism, the technological singularity, and futurism. In his public talks, he has shared his primarily optimistic outlooks on life extension technologies and the future of nanotechnology, robotics, and biotechnology; he and his work is mentioned in *Classical Feng Shui for Health, Beauty & Longevity* (Denise's third book).

R

Red Phoenix: A Celestial Animal that represents the front edge of your property; also known as *Vermillion Bird*.

Reductive Cycle of the Elements: the Five Elements reducing each other in the cycle order Wood - Water - Metal - Earth - Fire.

Ren: man

Replacement Stars: Alternative stars used when the compass direction of the facing is almost on the boundary between the first and second mountains or third and first mountains, in other words between the Major or Minor Voids. Not used in GMY's lineage.

retaining walls: High walls, at least three to six feet in height, which can be used to secure a site and prevent loss of energy. The more dynamic the landscape, the more walls are needed to protect sloping areas or sharp drop-offs.

Reversed Mountain and Water: Shang Shan Xia Shui, a dwelling that has the ruling water star at the sitting and the ruling mountain/sitting star at the front/facing. Can be very lucky if the landforms support this.

Ri: the day.

road: A route, path, or open way for vehicles. In Feng Shui, roads are *rivers* of energy, or chi and play a huge part in analyzing a site because energy is powerful. These virtual, or urban, rivers are calculated when assessing, designing, enhancing, or implementing counter measures or enhancements for a site.

Robbery Mountain Sha: Known in Chinese as *Chor San Kibb Sart*. It is a formation that takes away or robs energy from the site.

Rules of Flight: Rules for flying the stars in either the forward or backward sequence.

S

Sam Sart (Cantonese), the three killings, see also San Sha.

San Bi: the 3-Jade Star of the nine stars.

San He Luo Pan: this Luo Pan, used for San He formulas and schools, is easily identified by its *three* 24 mountain rings. These rings are used to measure direction, mountains, and water as each of these elements has distinctly different energy; however, these rings also relate to the *three harmonies* associated with this school.

San He Pai: Thee Combinations School of Feng Shui in which formulas are based on the four frames and the stems and branches.

San He: Also known as *San Hup*. One of the two major schools of study in Classical Feng Shui—the other is San Yuan. The San He system, excellent for tapping natural landforms, primarily addresses large-scale projects, land plots, urban developments, city planning, and master-planned communities. The system is extensive and has several practical techniques for new and existing residential spaces as well. When assessing and altering a site or a structure, San He and San Yuan can be blended for maximum results.

San Pan Kua: a configuration where all Palaces of the Flying Star chart contain the combinations of 147, 258, and 369. Reputedly, this structure is auspicious under all circumstances. This is also known as a Parent String or Three Combinations.

San Pao: the three Treasures: Jing (essence), Chi (vitality), Shen (spirit), which have no Western counterpart.

San Sha: Fate Stars called the Three Evils or Three Killings, or literally, the three shas. Other names are Sam Sart *(Cantonese)*, Sarm Sart, Jupiter Calamity, Sui Sart, Kibb Sart, and Coy Sart. Each year the Three Killings changes positions and it is taboo to renovate, dig or do repairs/construction in this area; it involves 75 degrees.

San Yuan Chiu Yun: the three sub-cycles and nine periods.

San Yuan Jiu Yun: three periods and nine sub cycles.

San Yuan Luo Pan: Used in the Flying Stars and the Xuan Kong systems, the San Yuan Luo Pan is readily indentified by the 64 hexagrams of the I Ching ring. It has only one 24 mountain ring. The first ring of this Luo Pan is always the Later Heaven Ba Gua arrangement of trigrams.

San Yuan: One of the two major schools of Classical Feng Shui. The Flying Stars is part of this system; it excels in techniques of timing.

San: means three.

Seam Needle: one of the directional needles on a San He to p'an. The seam needle reads 7.5 degrees behind the correct needle. The seam needle was originally used in yin house Feng Shui as the guideline to locate the sha "sands" and "water."

Secret arrows: cutting ch'i generated by a straight alignment of roads, trees, poles, or adjacent buildings.

sector: An area inside or outside a building: south sector, north sector, and so on.

Sent Mun Kuet: the Castle Gate theory, a special formula in flying stars.

Sexagenary combinations: The 60 combinations of 12 Earthly Branches and 10 Heavenly Stems.

Sha chi: Also known as *shar chi*. extremely negative energy, cutting energy or killing chi. Negative energy carrying inauspicious currents that can influence your well-being and can emanate from a variety of sources.

Sha: There are more than 15 distinct and separate words/characters in Chinese, with different meanings, all of which can be transliterated into English as *sha*. Even when they are pronounced with 4 different tones, many cannot be distinguished except by writing the Chinese character. There are three different sha relevant to Feng Shui: Sha: [1st tone] killing, murder, slaughter, hence sha chi, killing chi. Sha: [1st tone also] sand,

(also small hills used as a geographical term), hence the *sha in front of a site.* Sha: [4th tone] an evil spirit, as in the Fate Stars, the three shas.
Shan Gu: a mountain valley.
Shan Li Long Shen: the current prosperous sitting/mountain star also known as the mountain dragon or the mountain dragon spirit.
Shan Long: mountain or water dragon.
Shan Shui: mountains and water.
Shan Xing: the mountain star.
Shan: mountain in the geographical sense, but also the term for the 24 directions on the major to p'an compass ring.
Shang Shan Hsia Shui: literally *up the mountain and down the water*, a reversed house chart.
Shang Yu Pai: one of the six schools of Xuan Kong.
Shang Yuan: the upper 60 year period or the upper cycle.
Shang: to ascend, up, above.
Shao Yong: he wrote the famous book *The Empirical Yijing* (Huang- Yijing-shi) during the Song Dynasty.
Shao Zu Mountain: the highest mountain between the furthest, back mountain.
Shar: see Sha.
Shen Zhu Reng: One of the famous Feng Shui masters who lived during the Qing Dynasty. He wrote *Shen Shi Xuan Kong Xue* or Master Shen's Xuan Kong Knowledge. He originally studied San He and then changed completely and studied San Yuan, advocating use of the Flying Stars (Fei Xing) system.
Shen: spirit, the governing force that enlivens the flesh.
Sheng Chi: Part of the Eight Mansions system. It can bring life-generating energy, wealth, and opportunities. Using Master Yap's numeric representation, this is the +90.
Sheng: life, growth.
Shi Yuan: When a star is out of cycle.
Shi: two hour period.
Shuai: Weakening, retreating or decaying.
Shuang Ling Xing Dou Xiang: Double Ruling stars meet at the facing.
Shuang Ling Xing Dou Zou: Double Ruling stars meet at the sitting/back.
Shui Li Long Shen: the current prosperous facing star, also known as the water dragon or the water dragon spirit.
Shui Xing: the water star.
Shui: The Chinese word for *water;* pronounced *shway.*
Shuo Gua Zhuan: Descriptions of the Trigrams/Guas.
Si Lu: the 4-Green Star in the nine stars.
Si Qi: Dead qi; usually refers to qi out of its cycle.
Si Xiang: Four images of the celestial animals also known as the four spirits of a site.
Sifu: a master teacher, this refers to a male.
Sitting direction: where a house sits, the opposite of the Facing Direction.

Sitting Star: Also known as the Mountain Star in the Flying Star system. It influences people luck, such as fertility, employees, personality and health.
sitting: In Feng Shui it refers to the back of the house, as if the structure is sitting in a chair on the land or property. It is the heavy part of the house; also consider a mountain.
Six Big Schools of Flying Stars: 1) Wu Chang Pai, founder Zhang Zhong San, 2) Chen Nan Pai, founder Fan Yi Ping, 3) Su Chou Pai, founder Zhu Xiao He, 4) Shang Yu Pai, founder Xu Di Hui, 5) Siang Chuo Pai, founder Yin Yi Shao, and 6) Kuang Tong Pai, founder Chai Min San.
Sky Horse: A technique that speeds up the Feng Shui of a site. It uses roads or pathways as conduits of energy to activate this San He formula.
Small Tai Ji: The centre of an individual room.
Southeast Asia: Countries South of China and East of India, including Thailand, Vietnam, Cambodia, Laos, Myanmar, the Philippines, and Singapore.
Spring-Autumn Period, Chun Qiu: 770 BC – 476 BC (in Eastern Zhou Dynasty). This is the period Confucius lived.
squeezed chi: A phenomenon that happens when a building is extremely narrow and does not allow chi to flow or expand. It will deplete wealth and create debt.
Ssu Chou Pai: one of the six schools of Xuan Kong.
Su Chi: stagnant or torpid chi.
Suco: a master teacher, this is a female teacher.
Sui Po: the Branch known as the Year Clasher, diametrically opposite the Branch of the Year or the Grand Duke Jupiter. This is a spiritual aspect of Feng Shui.
Sui Xing: the planet Jupiter.
Sun: see Hsun trigram, also spelled Xun.
Swastika: A universal symbol generally accepted as a solar emblem. It is derived from the Sanskrit Svastika, meaning lucky, fortunate, well being. The counter-clockwise swastika formed within the Magic Square expresses future time. This symbol is also on Buddhas.

T
Tai Chi Martial Arts: also spelled T'ai chi or Taijiquan, and is nicknamed *'meditation in motion'* for its slow, beautiful movements. It is an internal Chinese martial art practiced for both its defense training and its health benefits. It is also typically practiced for a variety of other personal reasons: namely, longevity. As a result, a multitude of training forms exist, both
Tai Chi: The black and white symbol of Taoist philosophy; a sphere with two semi-circles intertwined showing the division of yin and yang energy. An alternate spelling is Taiji.
Taiji: The vibrant part and the soft part that the universe divided into. The 'Ultimate Greatness'. Also refers to the centre of a building.
Tai Sui: Counter Jupiter, or the Grand Duke Jupiter. It is the direction related to the year, for example, Tiger direction in a Tiger year. The Tai Sui covers 15 degrees.
Tai Wei: The official name of the Red Bird.

Tai Yang Dou San Pan: Great Sun Position Formula, a San Yuan formula for good construction/remodeling dates.
Tai Yang: All yang.
Tai Yang: the Sun.
Tai Yin: the Moon.
Tai Zu: the mountain that is farthest behind the location/site or known as *great ancestor*.
Tan Lang Stars: the 9 stars, also known as the small wandering sky or small sky stars. The Eight Mansions are known as the Big Wandering Stars. See Eight Wandering Stars.
Tan Lang: the Greedy Wolf or Covetous Wolf, The Angel of Sheng Chi,—Sheng Chi or Purple Chi/Breath (Tzu chi), the 1 star. See also Eight Wandering Stars.
Tan Yang Wu, Master: famous master that lived during the Republic Era and who wrote- The Great Xuan Kong's Penetrating Path *(Da Xuan Kong Lu Tou)*; The Great Xuan Kong's True Effectiveness *(Da Xuan Kong Shi Yin)*; A New Explanation to Identify and Correct Errors *(Bian Zheng Tan Shi Xin Jie)*. Master Tan had a famous student named *Master Yao Si Yin*, he lived in Taiwan in the 1960's where upon *Grandmaster Yap Cheng Hai* studied San He and San Yuan from (also famous student) Grand Master Chan Shuan Huai (or spelled Chan Chuan Huay).
Tang Dynasty: 618 – 907 C.E.
Tao: also known as *The Way*, and is core of Taoism (pronounced with a D sound).
tapping the energy or chi: A technique that invites the available energy from the external environment to support the occupants of a structure.
Ten Heavenly Stems: *Jia* (bud, the sign of growth, thumbnail, helmet); *Yi* (sprout, the spread of growth, bursting forth from Mother Earth); *Bing* (concentrated growth, fire in the house); *Ting* (maturity, solidity, heaven's kiss, bee sting); *Wu* (flourishing and nurturing); *Yi* (full bloom); *Geng* (harvesting, abundance, fullness leading to change); *Xin* (dead heading, reformation); Ren (sustenance, supporting life); and Kwei (regenerating roots, preparation for spring).
The Burial Book Classic: a book authored by Guo Pun who was born of the San Xi family lineage in the district of Wen Qi around 276 AD. He specialized in Yin Feng Shui as well as face reading and consulted with royalty. This book had a great impact on ancient Feng Shui masters.
The History of the Former Han Dynasty: one of the first books to reference 'Feng Shui'. The other is known as *The Terrestrial Conformation for Palaces and Houses*; these great works did not survive.
The Yellow Emperor's Dwelling Classic: was authored by Wang Wei and it too had a great impact of ancient Feng Shui masters.
Three Harmony Doorways: a San He formula for wealth and harmony using a door and sidewalk, road or driveway.
Three Imperial Positions: in the days of the Imperial Court, the positions of Zhuang Yuan, Bang Yan and Tan Hua refer to the upper, middle and lower cycle of the San Yan system covering 180 years total.

Three Killings: Also known as *Sam Sart* and *San Sha* in Chinese. This negative energy visits a different direction annually. Digging into the earth can disturb this energy and can bring on calamity, that's why it's also referred to as *calamity sha.*

Three Types of Luck: The Cosmic Trinity. The study of a person's life palace in relation to the house's chart; Heaven Luck, Earth Luck and Human Luck.

Ti: Earth.

Tien Ji Bu Ke Xie Lou: is a famous saying that means *"The secrets of heaven should not be divulged"* which was often quoted by Master Jiang Da Hong.

Tien Pan: the heaven's pool or the center of the Luo Pan with the compass floating in a pool of water.

Tien Yi: Part of the Eight Mansion system. It can bring excellent health and wealth. In Chinese it means *heavenly doctor* or *the doctor from heaven watches over you.* Using Master Yap's numeric representation, it is the +80.

Tien: heaven, or in one sense literally the sky.

Tien-Di-Ren: cosmic trinity, heaven luck, man luck and earth luck.

Tiger Water: is the third level of Eight Roads of Destruction that involves improper water exits based on the door direction.

Tiger, White: the Celestial Animal of the West.

tilting a door: A time-honored tradition used by Feng Shui masters and practitioners to change the degree of a door and the energy of a space. The doorframe and threshold are re-angled toward the desired degree. When the door is re-hung, it is *tilted* on a different degree.

Time Star: Also known as the *Base Star* in the Flying Star system; it is the single star below the mountain and facing star of the chart.

T-juncture: When two roads meet perpendicularly to create a *T*. The formation is toxic when a home or business sits at the top and center of that *T*.

Traditional Feng Shui: Another term for Classical Chinese Feng Shui.

Trigram Dui 兌: Marsh. The youngest daughter. Metal. Located in the South East in the Xian Tien Ba Gua, in the West in the Hou Tien Ba Gua.

Trigram Gen 艮: Mountain. The youngest son. Earth. Located in the North West in the Xian Tian Ba Gua, in the North East in the Hou Tien Ba Gua. One of the 24 Mountains located at 37.5° - 52.5°.

Trigram Kan 坎: Water. The middle son. Located in the West in the Xian Tian Ba Gua, in the North in the Hou Tian Ba Gua.

Trigram Kun 坤: Earth. The mother. Located in the North in the Xian Tian Ba Gua, in the South West in the Hou Tian Ba Gua. One of the 24 Mountains located at 217.5° - 232.5°.

Trigram Li 離: Fire. The middle daughter. Fire. Located in the East in the Xian Tian Ba Gua, in the South in the Hou Tian Ba Gua.

Trigram Qian 乾: Heaven. The father. Metal. Located in the South in the Xian Tian Ba Gua, in the North West in the Hou Tian Ba Gua. One of the 24 Mountains located at 307.5° - 322.5°.

Trigram Xun 巽: Wind. The eldest daughter. Wood. Located in the South West in the Xian Tian Ba Gua, in the South East in the Hou Tian Ba Gua. One of the 24 Mountains located at 127.5° - 142.5°.

Trigram Zhen 震: Thunder. The eldest son. Wood. Located in the North East in the Xian Tian Ba Gua, in the East in the Hou Tian Ba Gua.

Trigram: Another term used for Gua (also spelled Kua). A trigram or Gua represents one of eight Guas of the Ba Gua, defined by a combination of three solid or broken lines.

Tsing San, Ling San: direct and indirect spirit, a formula used for the proper placement of water in the San Yuan School.

Tu: Earth.

Tui Chi: chi that is retreating, advancement is impeded. This chi type has expired, is in a state of decline and is waning; it's lost its strength and the energy is weak.

Tui: Also spelled *Dui*. One of the eight trigrams that represents the youngest daughter, the lake, and mid-fall. In the Later Heaven Ba Gua it is located in the west.

Tung Shu: the Chinese Almanac; also spelled Tung Sing.

Twelve Animals: Rat, Ox, Tiger, Rabbit, Dragon, Snake, Horse, Goat, Monkey, Rooster, Dog and Pig; part of the Chinese Zodiac and used extensively in Classical Feng Shui and Chinese Astrology.

Twelve Earthy Branches: Tzi (Rat) young shoot of a plant, gate of yin and yang; Chou (Ox) young plant supported by a stick; Yin (Tiger) celebration of spring and New Year; Mao (Rabbit) life springing forth, spring equinox; Chen (Dragon) pregnant and timid, Easter, estrogen; Su (Snake) 7 months pregnant, with fully formed embryo; Wu (Horse) summer solstice, height of yang cycle and beginning of yin; Wei (Goat) big tree with solid branches; Shen (Monkey) expansion; You (Rooster) harvest and celebration; Xu (Dog) clearing and preparation; and Hai (Pig) conception, mating of yin with yang.

Twenty-four mountains: not real mountains, but the 24 possible facing directions of a structure. It is the 8 directions divided into 15 degree increments creating 24 directions. Every luo pan has at least one ring of the 24 mountains. The 24 mountains is used in both the San He and San Yuan Feng Shui formulas to assess the environment and the structure. Also known as Er Shi Si Shan.

U

Up the Mountain, Down the River: Also known as *Shang Shan Xia Shui* in Chinese. The
prominent stars of the period are in reversed positions. The mountain star is in the front where the facing star should be and the facing star is at the back where the mountain should ideally be placed.

V

virtual mountains: High-rise structures, such as apartments, office buildings, and skyscrapers, are considered virtual, or urban mountains and will influence the energy of nearby structures accordingly.

virtual water: Roads, sidewalks, driveways, low ground, highways, and other similar formations that are purveyors of chi.

W

Wan: Ten thousand.
Wang Chi: Prosperous chi; it is fortunate and timely.
Wang: Prominent or vibrant.
Wang: Prosperous or vigorous.
Warring States Period: 476 BC – 221 BC (in Eastern Zhou Dynasty); after Spring-Autumn Period.
washes: In the external environment, these natural and man-made channels whisk away water from a site.
Water Dragons: Also known as billionaire's Feng Shui. These formulas create extreme wealth with specific water flows and exits. It is a highly specialized area of Feng Shui for which Grandmaster Yap Cheng Hai was famous. It is a San He wealth/water formula.
water exits: The location or direction where water leaves a site. Water exits are used in Feng Shui to bring good results, but if they are not placed well, disaster can ensue.
Water Star: Also called the *Facing Star* in the Flying Star system; it is in charge of wealth luck.
water: In Feng Shui, water is the secret to enhancing wealth, prosperity, longevity, nobility, and relationships. The Chinese word is *Shui,* and it represents energy and life force. Water, according to Feng Shui, is the most powerful element on the planet.
waterfalls: Used to enhance wealth luck; the direction of the waterfall is important.
waxing moon dates: the dates are approximately two weeks between the new moon and full moon; this is when chi is growing. This window of time can be used to augment Feng Shui adjustments. These will line up with Farmer's Almanac.
Weeping Condition: when a star chart has a 5 star (either in the facing or mountain position) that flies either forward or backwards in sequence; known as Fan Yu Yin.
Wen Qu: Academic Path, Literary Arts, The Clever and Indecent Nymph, Liu Sha, Six Killings, Six Curses, Sweep Away (Sao Tang), Civil Career, and the four (4) star.
Wen Wang Ba Gua: another term for the later heaven Ba Gua arrangement of the trigrams.
West Life Group: In the Eight Mansions system, people are divided into the East or West group. The 2, 6, 7, and 8 Life Guas are part of the West Life Group.
Western Feng Shui: In addition to the Black Hat Sect, other schools cropped up that incorporated the principles, but not the rituals, associated with Lin-Yun's followers. As the masters of Classical Feng Shui started to teach around the world, some of the most well-acclaimed instructors and authors of Western Feng Shui began to learn Classical Feng Shui. Unwilling to give up the Western-style Feng Shui that made them famous, they mixed the old with the new, thereby adding to the confusion over authentic Feng Shui. More than half of the Feng Shui books written about the subject include a hodgepodge of both theories.

White Tiger: the right hand side of the building/home as you are looking out the front door. Represent the female, and the West.
Wong, Grandmaster: lived about 600 years ago, little is known except he created numerous formulas such as Five Ghosts Carry Treasure, Sky Horse and several more. He was an important master with no children or students.
Wu Chang Pai: one of the six schools of Xuan Kong; the lineage of Grandmaster Yap Cheng Hai and his students.
Wu Chi: the void or nothingness. Also known as the Great Void in which all things spring.
Wu Chu: Yen Nien, Yan Nien, Golden Water (Chin Shui), and the six (6) star. One of the Eight Wandering Stars used in Ba Zhai Feng Shui.
Wu Gwei: Part of the Eight Mansions system that can attract lawsuits, bad romance, and betrayals. Using Master Yap's numeric representation, it is the -70. This is also known as the *Five Ghosts* direction.
Wu Huang: the 5-Yellow Star of the nine stars.
Wu Ji Da Sha: Yang Earth and Yin Earth, and the Great Sha; the 5 Yellow Star. When the annual 5 Star flies to a direction, do not disturb the earth there. Putting metal in between helps but may not be good enough depending on how serious the disturbance is. This affects everyone, no matter what the four pillars indicate.
Wu Ji: In the beginning there was nothing, the 'Ultimate Void'.
Wu Kwei: Lien Chen or Lien Zheng, Five Ghosts, Honesty, Purity, Chastity, and the 5 Yellow Star.
Wu Qu: Military Path, Military Arts, the Angel of Gallantry, and the 6 Star in the Flying Stars.
Wu Xing: Also known as the five elements of Feng Shui: wood, fire, earth, metal, and water; five phases of qi, the five elements of fire, earth, metal, water and wood.

X

Xia Yu: The great emperor who cured the flooding of the Yellow River.
Xia Yuan: the lower cycle of the flying stars.
Xiang Chu Pai: one of the six schools of Xuan Kong.
Xiao Wei: The official name of the White Tiger.
Xiao Yin: Young yin.
Xie: means too leak out, drain, vent, scatter, disperse, dissipate, or to reveal.
Xien Tien Ba Gua: the early heaven trigram arrangement, also known as the Fu Xi Ba Gua map.
Xing Fa: An approach to assessing form and shape in the environment; form and shape techniques in Feng Shui.
Xu Shui: empty or virtual water or a water space.
Xuan Kong Da Gua: School of Feng Shui based on the 64 Hexagrams of the Yijing; mysterious void wind & water school; aka I Ching Feng Shui and the Big 64 Hexagram Feng Shui.
Xuan Kong Liu Pai Gai Shuo: the six Flying Stars Schools.

Xuan Kong Mi Zi: means *Mysterious Space Secret Decree*, a Chinese Classic on Xuan Kong Feng Shui.
Xuan Kong Shui Fa: time space water method.
Xuan Kong: a School of Feng Shui that includes Flying Star; literally *dark palace*.
Xuan Kong: mysterious void, also time and space school
Xuan Wu: Black Tortoise, located at the back of a building, the most yin side.
Xuan Wu: the main mountain peak.
Xuan: dark, obscure, rather than profound, secret, mysterious, void.
Xue Xin Fu: *Snow Heart Song*; the most important Feng Shui classic book on landforms.
Xue: Dragon's den or lair, cave, den, hole, site with an accumulation of qi, where energy converges; location of a good site.
Xun: One of the eight trigrams of the Ba Gua, also spelled as *Sun*. It represents the eldest daughter, the wind and early summer. In the Later Heaven arrangement of the Ba Gua, the Xun trigram is located in the Southeast.
Xun Long: to seek the dragon by Feng Shui rules; belongs to and surrounds a gravesite.

Y
Yan Shou Gong: is a style of martial arts for longevity devised by Grandmaster Yap Cheng Hai and his teacher, Grandmaster Datuk Chee Kim Thong that is easy to use and master. Grandmaster Yap has written a trilogy of books on the techniques to master.
Yang Chai: the houses of the living.
Yang Feng Shui: Feng Shui was first practiced for the selection of a perfect gravesite, or what is commonly known by the Chinese as Yin Feng Shui—Feng Shui for the dead. Later, techniques were developed to increase luck and opportunities for houses of the living.
Yang Zhai Ai Yiang Pian: *A Comparison for Yang Houses* book.
Yang Zhai Cuo Yao: The *Yang Houses Abstract* book.
Yang Zhai Da Cheng: The *Great Achievements of Yang Houses* book.
Yang Zhai Ji Cheng: The *Complete Anthology of Yang Houses* book.
Yang Zhai San Yao: the *Three Requirements of Yang Houses* book.
Yang Zhai Shi Shu: The *Ten Books of Yang Houses* book.
Yang Yun Song: One of the most respected Feng Shui masters who lived during the Tang Dynasty (AD 840-circa 888). He was the founder of the Form School (landform assessment) and was known as the 'Savior of the Poor' because he used Feng Shui to the help the less fortunate. . He wrote at least six, famous books: 1.) The Heavenly Jade Classic; 2.) Jade Ruler Classic; 3.) Secret Meanings of the Universe; 4.) Classic of the Moving Dragon; 5.) Doubtful Dragon Classic and 6.) The Twelve Stave Method. He also contributed to the creation of many rings on the Chinese Luo Pan including the *Heaven Plate* (Water Ring) in which water is measured and evaluated.

Yang: Alive, active and moving energy; considered the male energy of the Yin-Yang symbol. Represents the active principle in nature exhibited as light, heat, and dryness. On a human level, yang represents masculinity and the positive side of our emotions. Also, yang represents the realm of the living.

Yao: the single line of a trigram or hexagram. The broken line is known as yin Yao, and the solid line is yang Yao.

Yellow Emperor aka **Yellow Lord:** Huangdi (2697-2597 BC), perhaps the greatest of the legendary emperors. Not to be confused with Chin Shih Huang Ti who was the first Chin emperor who burned the books during 221 B.C.

Yellow Spring: A term used by the Chinese to describe Hell or the underworld.

Yen Nien: Part of the Eight Mansions system that can bring longevity, good relationships, and love. Using Master Yap's numeric representation, it is the +70. It is a common mistake to spell this term as Nen Yien.

Yi Bai: the 1-White Star of the nine stars.

Yi Jing, see I Ching.

Yi: short for Yijing.

Yijing or I Ching: Book of Changes; ancient Chinese book of divination using the 64 Hexagrams.

Yin Chai: literally *dark house*, meaning tomb or grave site.

Yin/Yang symbol, see t'ai chi.

Yin: Female energy, passive, and dead; the perfect complement is yang energy. Represents the passive principle in nature exhibited as darkness, cold, and wetness. On a human level, yin symbolizes femininity and inertia. Also, yin represents the realm of the dead.

You Bi: Right Assistant, the Angel of Vigor, Fu Bei or Fu Wei, Right Assistant to the Celestial Emperor, Yu Pi and the 9 Star. It is also spelled Yu Pi.

Yu: space, geographical space.

Yuan Chen Shui: water source, or the water in front of the site.

Yuan: Period of 60 years.

Yue: the month.

Yun Xing: the period star or the timely star.

Yun: a sub cycle or a 20 year period in the San Yuan flying stars.

Z

Zen: A school of Mahayana Buddhism that originated in Japan. It involves the practice of harmony and peace. For homes or buildings, a Zen design includes clean lines and austere spaces. The overall design is calming to the mind.

Zhang Zhung Shan, Master (Qing Dynasty): famous for commentaries on Jiang Da Hong's works, they are as follows; A Straight Explanation of 'Ti Li Distinguishing the Correct' *(Di Li Bian Zheng Shi Jie)*; Yin Yang Both Houses: A Record of Experiments *(Yin Yang Er Zhai Lu Yan);* Intelligently Indicating the Important *(Xin Yan Zhi Yao);* Heaven Yuan: Explaining the Meaning of the Five Poems *(Tien Yuan Wu Ge Chan Yi);*

Xuan Kong's Secret Decree *(Xuan Kong Mi Zhi Pi Zhu)*; Two House Xuan [Kong] Key Points *(Er Zhai Xuan Ji);* Guide to Arriving at the Xue *(Lin Xue Zhi Nan)*
Zhao Shen: a mirror spirit or the secondary auspicious star aka as indirect spirit.
Zhen Wu: a structure intended to ward off evil influences, such as pagoda or even Foo dogs/stone lions.
Zhong Yuan: the middle cycle of the flying stars system.
Zhou Dynasty: 1122BC – 256BC.
Zhou Fu: Left Assistant, The Angel of Wealth and Happiness, and the 8 Star.
Zhou Yi: an old name for the I Ching.
Zhu Jue: Crimson Bird, located at the front of a building, the most yang side.
Zi Bai Jue: Purple White scroll.
Zi Wei Dou Shu: a form of Chinese astrology, different from 4 pillar astrology. Purple Constellation Fate Computation translated in English. This system analyzes from 36 to 157 stars in accordance with your birth information. It uses the Chinese lunar calendar.
Zong Miao: a Royal ancestral temple.
Zou Shu: a written report or written memorial presented to the emperor or one of auspicious spirits.
Zi Wei: The Emperor in Heaven.

Chinese Dynasties and Feng Shui Chronology

Traditional Emperors and Dynasties	Date/Years	Significant Feng Shui Event	
Fu Xi	2852-2737 BCE	Invented the Eight Trigrams, the He Tu (dragon-horse), and Early Heaven Sequence.	
Huang Di	2697-2597 BCE	*Goddess of the Nine Heavens* presents Huangdi a compass. Traditional invention of the calendar, based on the 60-year cycle.	
Yao	2356-2255 BCE	Sets up astronomical observations to regulate the calendar.	
Shun	2255-2205 BCE	Attempted, but failed, to regulate the rivers.	
Yu	2205-2197 BCE	Discovered the Lo Shu (giant turtle), Later Heaven Sequence, and regulated the flooding rivers.	
Xia	2150-1557 BCE	The Hsia (Solar) calendar is devised.	
Shang	1557-1027 BCE	The 60 day jia-tzi cycle is devised from the 10 heavenly stems and 12 earthly branches. Oracle bones divination used, writing was invented and a sundial was used to measure time.	
Chou	1027-221 BCE	King Wen (1122 BCE) arranged the 64 hexagrams. His son Duke of Chou wrote commentary which became the I Ching.	Chan Pu used to find the site of Luo Yang (1027 BCE).
	770-476 BCE *Spring and Autumn Period*	Confucius edited the *I Ching* and wrote the Teng Wings (550 BCE). Lao Tzu wrote the *Tao Te Ching*.	
	476-221 BCE *Warring States Period*	Chou Yen (350-270 BCE) mentions the 5 elements.	
Chin	221-206 BCE	China is unified; burning of the books by Emperor Chin Shih Huang Ti who creates a tomb with at star map on the ceiling and a map of the rivers in his domain in flowing mercury on its floor, and creates the terra cotta warriors discovered in the 1970's. Spoon compass was used.	
Han	206 BCE to 220 CE	The Luo Pan) in use, using the 28 constellations, 10 heavenly stems 12 earthly branches but not the trigrams. Kan Yu becomes a profession. Books on Feng Shui come out: *Golden Kan Yu Thesaurus* and *Green Satchel* (aka the Azure Bag).	

		24 mountains established with earth stems (not trigrams) at the corner positions of Luo Pan.
		Kan Yu becomes a profession.
		Ching Wu, Master Blue Raven wrote *Cannon of Burials* (only fragments have survived).
		Wang Ching wrote the *Fifty Original Groundstones* about burials and building practice.
		Ching Fang (79-37 BCE) established
	220-265 CE Three Kingdoms Period *(Wei, Shui, Wu)*	Chu Ko Liang (181-234) a military strategist invents/uses Chi Men Tun Chia style military magic.
		Kuan Lo (209-256) writes the classic Feng Shui text *Kuan Shih Ti Chih Meng*.
		Guo Pu (276-324) writes the *Burial Classic* where the first mention of 'Feng Shui' occurs. Gets the Book of Blue/Green Satchel/Bag.
Southern & Northern	420-589 CE	Wang Wei (415-443 CE) writes *Huang Ti Chai Ching*, with a square Earth Plate and 24 Mountains. A Feng Shui practitioner was called *Qin Wu Shu*; other names were Kan Yu expert and Yin-Yang expert.
Sui	589-618 CE	A dozen Feng Shui titles appear including *The Water Dragon Classic*. Some *famous masters* between 581-960 CE were Qiu Yan Han, Liu Ziang Dong, Si Ma Tou Tuo, Yang Yun Song, Ceng We Chan, Ceng Wen Di, He Pu, He Ling Tong, and Liao Yu.
Tang	618-906 CE	Yang Yun Song (834-906 CE) established the Heaven Plate and the 72 Dragons ring and writes several books. Copper mirror found. There were over 120 different schools of Feng Shui.
5 Dynasties & 10 Kingdoms	906-960 CE	The 240 Fen Chin ring is developed by Master Yang Yun Song.
		Flying Star Charts found in the Dunhuang monastery manuscripts (928 CE).

Northern Song	960-1127 CE	Shen Kuo (1031-1095) works on declination, the magnetic poles, magnetism, spherical trigonometry, and calendar reform. Some *famous masters* of this time period were Wu Jing Luan, Cai Yan Ding, Cai Ji Tong, Lai Bu Yi, Lai We Jun and Lai Feng Gang.
Northern Kin and Southern Sung	1127-1279 CE	Tsai Shen Yu invents the 60 Dragons ring.
Yuan (Mongol)	1271-1368 CE	Chao Pang (1319-1369 CE) uses the term Lo Ching and states that its practitioners radiated out from the Fukien Province.
Ming	1368-1644 CE	Emperor Chu Yuen (ruled 1368-1398) kills Taoist Feng Shui master & issues false Feng Shui books.
		Yellow Springs (8R & 8K) and RMS rings devised.
		Dry mounted needle becomes the norm.
		Wu Wang Kang edits Lo Ching Chieh, the Ming standard text on the Lo Pan, with 38 rings.
		Master Jiang Da Hong (1620-17 CE) begins to use the San Yuan method.
		Chang Ping Kin writes four San He classics—The Water Dragon Classic; The Original Eight Mansions Formula; The Key San He Feng Shui Formulas and The Mountain Dragon.
		Emperor Qian Long rectifies the calendar and Feng Shui practice with *Hsieh Chi Pien Fang Shui* (1741)
		De Groot and Eitel (missionaries) bring Feng Shui to the West (around 1873).
		Some *famous masters* during 1368-1644 were Liu Ji, Liu Bo Wen, Zhang Jiu Yi, Jiang Yao, Shen Zhu Reng, Shen Shao Xun, Ceng Zheng Ping, Mu Jiang Shi, Leng Qian, Jiang Da Hong, Jiang Ping, Zhang Zhong Shan, Ma Tai Qing and Ma Qing E.
Qing (Manchu)	1644-1911 CE	Jo Kuan Tao Ren's Eight Mansions classic *Pa Chai Ming Ching* (1790).
		Chang Chung Shan founded Wu Chang Pai.
		Shen Chu Reng (1849-1906) writes classic books on Flying Stars.

Republic of China	1912-1949 CE	*Imperial Board of Rites* is disbanded, removing standardization of Astrology and Feng Shui.
		Tan Yang Wu (1891-1945) opens a school in Shanghai, the source of the Wu Chang Pai in Malaysia in 1922. Other *masters* of this time period (now deceased) are You Xi Yin, Rong Bai Yun, Kong Zhao Su, and You Xue Xing.
People's Republic of China	1949-present	Feng Shui is suppressed in mainland China, many masters move to Singapore, Taiwan, Hong Kong and Malaysia.
		The Cultural Revolution closes down most Feng Shui practice in People's Republic of China.
Feng Shui around the World	1962-2018 AD	Important works such as the *Science and Civilization of China* by Joseph Needham (1962); *Chinese Geomancy* by Stephen Feuchtwang (1974); *Living Earth Manual of Feng Shui* by Stephen Skinner (1976); Professor Lin Yun & Sarah Rossbach introduce BTB in 1983; *Chinese Astrology* by Derek Walters (1987); and Lillian Too *(the most prolific author on Feng Shui, 1995 to present)* who co-authored several books with Grandmaster Yap Cheng Hai—all started the Feng Shui movement worldwide. Master Larry Sang started the first Classical Feng Shui school in America in 1991. Master Pun-Yin is selected to 'Feng Shui' Trump Towers in 1998. Grandmaster Yap, along with Joey Yap creates *Yap Cheng Hai Feng Shui Center for Excellence* that lasted from 1999 to 2003. Joey Yap started the Mastery Academy in 2003 (ongoing). Various Classical Feng Shui conferences take place in SE Asia & Europe from 2000 to 2016. Grandmaster Yap Cheng Hai, one of five of the world's grandmasters, passed away in June 2014. Living *Grandmasters* are Larry Sang, Raymond Lo, Joseph Yu, Stephen Skinner (nominated by his peers in 2016) and Eva Wong.

Appendix *(Xuan Kong Lineage since 1686)*

Grandmaster Yap Cheng Hai (GMY) has several hundred, authentic masters scattered around the globe, including his own children: *Master Yap Boh Heong; Master Yap Boh Hian; Master Yap Hwee Boon* (the only daughter); and *Master Yap Boh Chu*. Master Yap Boh Chu has taken directorship of Grandmaster Yap's school after his passing in June of 2014. Master Joey Yap (not a relative) was a former business partner and protégée of GMY (1999-2003). Lillian Too was a life-long friend; she used Grandmaster Yap as a source for some of her earlier books.

Appendix
How to Take a Compass Direction

Some masters take the door degree from *inside* the building. Grandmaster Yap taught his students to take the compass direction—outside, face the door, and at waist level, and placing the Luo Pan directly on it. This results in a very accurate compass reading. A traditional hiking compass may vary a few degrees from a Luo Pan and a Smartphone may vary even more. Purchase a good app that aligns with GPS as phones do not contain a magnet like a regular compass. When using a Luo Pan or hiking compass, place it at waist level and remove all metal belts and jewelry. Take several compass readings to ensure accuracy. Review *How to Determine the Facing* on page 49.

If using a traditional Luo Pan, stand outside the door and face it. Line up the head of the needle between the two red dots. Look at the 6:00 position near your waist and see the degree.

Using your Smartphone to take a compass direction, put your back to the door and it will give you a digital read out similar to this image.

When using a traditional hiking compass, follow the manufacturer's directions.

Appendix
Typical Cures and Enhancements Used in Classical Feng Shui

Classical Feng Shui approaches cures and enhancing energy very differently than the Western styles. Those styles use symbolic and Chinese objects such as bamboo flutes, paintings, coin-chocked frogs, crystals, mirrors, green plants, painting walls the colors related to the Ba Gua, lighting and a host of other things that are not really doing much to the energy. Here are some ideas for practical application to capture the best energy for Period 9, 8 and 7 homes.

Metal Cures: Metal is used to cure the negative 2, 3 and 5 facing stars. Metal may also be used to enhance/strengthen a 6 facing star. Use high quality metals such as bronze, brass (white or yellow), copper, pewter, and stainless steel. While wrought-iron is metal, it does not vibrate high enough; neither does aluminum. Patio furniture made of metal is not sufficient as a cure either. Wind chimes, while aluminum, move with the wind and is considered a good metal cure. Metal clocks that chime are also are good. Metal art and objects make good cures. Stoves, which are always metal, can never be considered as a cure. Stoves, automobiles and lawn furniture--while metal--are not considered or used as metal cures.

Appendix
Typical Cures and Enhancements Used in Classical Feng Shui

Fire Cures/Enhancements: Fire is used to *cure* the 3 and 7 facing stars. It's also used to *enhance* the 8 and 9 facing stars. Real fire should be used such as grills, stove tops, ranges, ovens, fire pits, outdoor and indoor fireplaces, stove knobs/control direction, pizza ovens, torches, and two-way fireplaces (activates both directions). Where real fire cannot be used near a door, paint it a fire color (reds, purple, pink and orange) as your cure. If you use fire to enhance the 8 or 9 facing star, make it important looking, and both can have a combination fire-water feature.

Appendix
Typical Cures and Enhancements Used in Classical Feng Shui

Water Enhancements/Cures: Water is the most powerful of all the elements and will activate and magnify energy—good or bad. Big water features should be placed on good facing stars such as the 8, 9, and 1. Small, still water such as a bird bath or small fountain can be used to reduce the evil 7 facing star. In Period 7 homes, the 7 facing star will appear either in the front or back. Whether the home is a Period 7 or Period 8, the 8 facing star requires water at this time. When we enter Period 9, the 9 facing star will require water. The water can be a pool, pond, lake, water fall, or fountain. Water may be placed on a 3 facing star for lawyers/solicitors; this ensures they continue to get clients who need their skills. However, the 8 facing star and 8 mountain star must be activated as well, and ideally first. If the current prosperity stars are not activated *(the 8 stars)*, the lawyer may get sued or not paid for services.

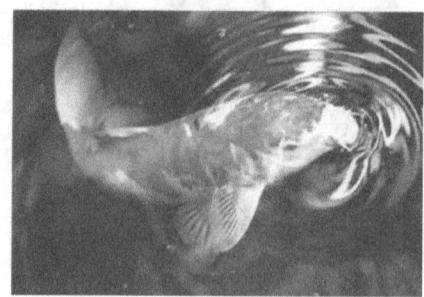

Appendix
Typical Cures and Enhancements Used in Classical Feng Shui

Retaining walls: used at the edge of your property in the front to capture energy/chi from falling into the road or at the back of the property where land slopes away taking the chi with it.

Mountains: this is not a term very familiar to those who read Feng Shui books. However, they are very important in activating great energy at your site. Some Flying Star charts are not fully activated without creating a 'mountain' such as the special charts of Parent and Pearl Strings. Currently, the 8 mountain star in *any* chart should have a mountain currently. When we enter into Period 9, the 9 mountain should be activated. Inside, objects that will activate a mountain star (good or bad) are heavy, tall bookcases, armoire, stone/brick fireplaces, or other heavy and tall items. Landscape mounds, boulders, heavy planter pots, brick/stone walls, basalt pillars, and courtyard walls all serve as a great 'mountain' (all shown here).

Appendix
Typical Cures and Enhancements Used in Classical Feng Shui

Colors and Using Paint Color: In Classical Feng Shui, color and paint color are used gingerly as it counts only about 10% of the overall Feng Shui energy. The ancients did not have paint available; however they did have colored fabrics and textiles (rugs). In modern times we have it readily accessible. While not as strong as the real elements of water, fire, or metal—they can be helpful in an area in question. Fire colors will have the strongest affect; they are reds, purples, pinks and oranges. An over-use of these colors in a bedroom is often too stimulating for a restive sleep. However, bright colors in a baby's or child's room are fine. Colors that represent water are black and blues; they are not strong cures or enhancements. Metal colors are silver, gold or copper with the metallic paints giving the best results. This should be supported by real, actual metal objects as well. While color in a home or office design will most definitely affect our mood, they are not the first choice in cures/enhancements.

Appendix
Typical Cures and Enhancements Used in Classical Feng Shui

Door Tilts or Re-angling: This technique is very common in Southeast Asia. It is used to take a door out of negative energy (a bad facing star, Eight Killings, Peach Blossom Sha or Eight Killings) or to change the star chart—sometimes both. Remember, doors rate extremely high as to whether you will enjoy good Feng Shui or not. Note: Door tilts never change the Period of a house, other actions are required.

Bibliography

Bruun, Ole. *An Introduction to Feng Shui.* Cambridge, UK; Cambridge Press, 2008

Cheong, Hung Hin. *Xuan Kong Purple White Script: An English Translation with Commentaries*. Kuala Lumpur, Malaysia, JY Books Sdn. Bhd, 2009

Choy, Howard. From the article, "*A Brief History of Flying Star Feng Shui*". http://howardchoy.wordpress.com/2012/12/05/a-brief-history-of-xuan-kong-fei-xing-feng-shui/

Huang, Alfred. *The Numerology of the I Ching: A Sourcebook of Symbols, Structures, and Traditional Wisdom*. Rochester, Vermont: Inner Traditions, 2000.

Skinner, Stephen. *Guide to the Feng Shui Compass*. Golden Hoard Press, 2008.
Feng Shui History: the Story of Classical Feng Shui in China and the West from 221 BC to 2012 AD". Singapore, Golden Hoard Press, 2012.
    Flying Stars Feng Shui: Change Your Energy, Change Your Luck. Boston, Massachusetts, Tuttle Publishing, 2003.

Swetz, Frank J. *Legacy of the Luoshu: The 4,000 Year Search for the Meaning of the Magic Square of Order Three.* Wellesley, Massachusetts, A. K. Peters, Ltd. 2008

Too, Lillian. *Flying Stars Feng Shui for Period 8.* Kuala Lumpur, Malaysia, Konsep Lagenda Sdn Ghd, 2003
    Lillian Too's Flying Stars Feng Shui. Kuala Lumpur, Malaysia, Konsep Lagenda Sdn Ghd, 1999
    Secrets of Your House Charts: the little BIG everything book on Feng Shui. Kuala Lumpur, Malaysia, Konsep Lagenda Sdn Ghd, 2013
    Flying Star Feng Shui Made Easy. Kuala Lumpur, Malaysia, Konsep Lagenda Sdn Ghd, 2007
    Lillian Too's Flying Stars Feng Shui for the Master Practitioner. Kuala Lumpur, Malaysia, Konsep Lagenda Sdn Ghd, 2002
    Total Feng Shui: Bring Health, Wealth and Happiness Into Your Life. San Francisco, California, Chronicle Books, 2004

Moran, Elizabeth, Master Joseph Yu, and Master Val Biktashev. *The Complete Idiot's Guide to Feng Shui.* Indianapolis, Indiana; Alpha (A Pearson Education Company), 2002.

Twicken, David. *Flying Stars Feng Shui Made Easy.* Lincoln, Nebraska, Writers Club Press, 2002.

Wong, Eva. *Feng-shui: The Ancient Wisdom of Harmonious Living for Modern Times.* Boston, Massachusetts; Shambala Publications, Inc., 1996.

Yellow Emperor Huang Ti, *The Twelve Principles of Yin and Yang*, given 2698-2598 BC

Worldwide Classical Feng Shui Schools and Consultants

The following is a list of Classical Feng Shui teachers around the world who, in addition to Feng Shui training, also offer consulting services, books, and other products. There are a number of excellent Feng Shui masters around the world that offer classes on one or more of the Five Chinese Metaphysical Arts. You can receive training on Classical Feng Shui (*San He* and *San Yuan*), Face Reading (*Mian Xiang*), Chinese Astrology (*BaZi* also known as *Four Pillars of Destiny* and *Zi Wei Dou Shu*), and Oriental medicine (acupuncture, herbology).

Matriculating from a respected lineage is desirable, but this alone should not determine the master you choose to study with. Select one with whom you resonate. I do not personally know every teacher/consultant I have listed, and you will need to do your own due diligence in selecting a qualified professional teacher or consultant.

The American College of Classical Feng Shui (ACCFS)
Dragon Gate Feng Shui International Consultants
Master Denise Liotta Dennis
Houston, Texas USA
Phone: 713-897-1719
Email: denise@dragongatefengshui.com
Website: www.dragongatefengshui.com

We offer consulting services internationally, long-distance consulting and training, books, free lectures, and live training classes.

Feng Shui Training Programs

There are several ways to learn more about Feng Shui. The following programs are suitable for Feng Shui enthusiasts, real estate agents, architects, interior designers, self-taught Feng Shui practitioners, builders and Feng Shui professionals seeking to deepen their knowledge, and those aspiring to a career in Feng Shui.

3-Day Intensive: Professional Certification
In this course you will learn sophisticated techniques to accurately analyze a home or business that will prepare you to be a sought-after consultant. You will learn how to simultaneously use Eight Mansions and Flying Stars, the two most important systems for interiors. Our classes are amazing, exciting and very effective, in just three days you'll know how to apply your new or years of knowledge to create impressive results. Can be scheduled at any time; Fee $3699.

3-Day Intensive: Master Certification

The demand for skilled consultants who can produce results has far outstripped the supply. Here you will learn the most advanced techniques of Classical Feng Shui. Experienced practitioners are often hired for large projects for the development of master-planned communities, office buildings, shopping centers, hotels, and casinos. Can be scheduled at any time; Fee $4999.

Private Mentoring: FENG SHUI MASTER Program

This is the traditional method of learning Feng Shui mastery and not for everyone. It is a 1-year program (36 Modules) taught twice a month live or via Skype or Zoom; Saturday or Sunday is an option if needed. The mentoring program is taught monthly and provides the most personalized, comprehensive program we offer. Fee: $1800 per month.

Certifications are offered for all the above classes through *The American College of Classical Feng Shui (ACCFS).*

Yap Cheng Hai Academy Sdn. Bhd.
Master Yap Boh Chu
Suite 11-01, 11th Floor
Wisma Hangsam
1 Jalan Hang Lekir
50000 Kuala Lumpur, Malaysia
Phone: +603 2070 8009
Email: info@ychacademy.com
Website: www.ychacademy.com
Started by Grandmaster Yap Cheng Hai (1927-2014)
Offers books, consulting services, software, consulting and training on Classical Feng Shui, primarily in Kuala Lumpur. Possibly sells, traditional Chinese Luo Pans as well.

Lillian Too's World of Feng Shui
Lillian Too, Feng Shui Master
Kuala Lumpur, Malaysia
Phone: 603-2080 3488
Email: courses@wofs.com
Website: www.lillian-too.com
Offers books, magazines, products, Luo Pans, and live classes on Classical Feng Shui in Kuala Lumpur

Feng Shui Research Center
Grandmaster Joseph Yu
26 Betty Roman Blvd.
Markham, Ontario L6C 0A4
Canada
Phone: 905-604-0998
Phone: 416-721-7094
Email: josephyu@astro-fengshui.com
Website: www.astro-fengshui.com
Offers books, Luo Pans, live classes worldwide and correspondence courses on Chinese Astrology and Classical Feng Shui

The America Feng Shui Institute
Grandmaster Larry Sang
111 N. Atlantic Blvd., Ste. 352
Monterey Park, CA 91754
Phone: 626-571-2757
Email: fsinfo@amfengshui.com
Website: www.amfengshui.com
Offers books, Luo Pans, live classes in California, and online courses on Classical Feng Shui, Chinese Astrology, and Face Reading

Mastery Academy of Chinese Metaphysics Sdn. Bhd.
Master Joey Yap
19-3, The Boulevard, Mid Valley City
59200 Kuala Lumpur, Malaysia
Phone: +603-2284-8080
Email: enquiry@masteryacademy.com
Website: www.masteryacademy.com
Offers books, all traditional style Luo Pans, videos, live classes worldwide, and online training on Classical Feng Shui, Chinese Astrology, and Face Reading

Raymond Lo Feng Shui Research
Grandmaster Raymond Lo
Rm. 1233A, Star House
Tsimshatsui, Kowloon, Hong Kong
Phone: + (852) 2736 9568
Phone: + (852) 9024 9438
Email: raymond@fengshui-lo.com
Website: www.raymond-lo.com
Offers books, Luo Pans, and live classes worldwide on Classical Feng Shui and Chinese Astrology

Feng Shui Dragon Enterprises
Master Gayle Atherton
PO Box 886
Double Bay, NSW 1360
2028, Australia
Phone: 02 9362 8089
Email: inquiries@fengshui.com
Website: www.fengshui.com.au
Offers consulting services, Chinese Astrology, books, free mini-seminars on her website and a Feng Shui Kit

The Imperial School of Feng Shui and Chinese Horoscopes
Grandmaster Chan Kun Wah
59 Pettycur Road
Kinghorn, Fife, KY3 9RN, Scotland
Phone: + 44 (0) 159 289 1682
Email: pam@masterkwchan.com
Website: www.masterkwchan.com
Offers correspondence and live training worldwide on Classical Feng Shui and Chinese Astrology

The International School of Feng Shui
Master Ken Lai
PO Box 2124
Maple Grove, MN 55311
Phone: 763-218-1484
Email: kenlai93@yahoo
Website: www.kenlaifengshui.com
Offers live training courses world-wide on Classical Feng Shui and Chinese Astrology

Healing Qi
David Twicken, Feng Shui Master
Email: david@healingqi.com
Website: www.healingqi.com
Offers books, e-books, correspondence and live courses internationally on Classical Feng Shui, Qi Gong, Oriental Medicine, and Chinese Astrology

Singapore Feng Shui Centre
Master Vincent Koh
10 Ubi Crescent #04-66 Ubi Techpark
Singapore 408564
Phone: (65) 6747 8226
Email: singfc@fengshui.com.sg
Website: www.fengshui.com.sg
Offers books, software, and live training courses on Feng Shui and Chinese Astrology

Pak Hok Ming Metaphysic Institute
Master Pak Hok Ming
8/F, Bangkok Bank Building
490-492 Nathan Road, Kowloon, Hong Kong
Phone: (852) 2388 6878
Email: fengshui@hongkong.com
Website: www.hokming.com
Offers books, products, compass/Luo Pan tools, and courses on Feng Shui and Chinese Astrology.

Feng Shui College
Howard Choy, AIA, Feng Shui Master
Sydney, Australia
Phone: 49 30 2838 5855
Email: info@fengshuicollege.ac
Website: www.arqitektur.com
Offers books and training course internationally on Classical Feng Shui.

The School of Chinese Metaphysics (SCM)
Master Peter Leung
102 Allanford Road
Toronto, ON M1T 2N5
Phone: (416) 288-9238
Email: info@fengshuisos.com
Website: www.fengshuisos.com
SCM offers books, software, live training courses on Classical Feng Shui.

Central Academy Of Feng Shui (CAFS)
Master Francis Leyau
169-1, Jalan Sarjana, Taman Connaught,
Cheras, 56000
Kuala Lumpur, Malaysia
Phone: 60 3-91320199
Email: enquiry@fengshuimastery.com
Website: www.fengshuimastery.com
CAFS offers books, products, and live training courses on Feng Shui and Chinese Astrology.

Feng Shui 100
Master Mas Kehardthum
31st Floor of the State Tower, Silom Road
Bangkok, Thailand
Phone: 668-1431-4011
Email: info@fengshui100.com
Website: www.fengshui100.com
Offers live Feng Shui training classes in Thailand, correspondence courses, books, and software.

Feng Shui That Works
Alan Stirling, Feng Shui Master
16 Ash Road, ME2 2JL UK
Phone: 44 (0)203 0114938
Email: alan888@btinternet.com
Website: www.fengshuithatworks.co.uk
Offers live and correspondence courses on Feng Shui, 9 Star Ki (Japanese Astrology), Dowsing, and Chinese Astrology

Feng Shui masters who teach through books but may also consult with clients are: **Grandmaster Dr. Stephen Skinner** (www.sskinner.com); **Master Val Biktashev,** and **Master Elizabeth Moran** (www.aafengshui.com).

These Feng Shui Masters also offer consulting services: Jennifer Bonetto, Newport Beach, California; Katherine McClerkin, Little Rock, Arkansas; Nathalie Ekobo, Barbara Harwell, Kristy Coup, Marianne Kulekowskis, Peggy Lanese, Kristie Yeckel, and Jillian Rothschild-Scholar, of Phoenix, Arizona; Peg Burton, Chicago, Illinois; Sudarika Mitchell of Texas; Angel Thomas, Apopka, FL; Amanda Finch, Fort Collins, CO (*all master graduates of ACCFS*); Jennifer Bartle-Smith, Australia; Maria Santilario, Spain; Bridgette O'Sullivan, Ireland; Cynthia Murray, Colorado; Jayne Goodrick; England; Di Grobler and Christine McNair, South Africa; Nathalie Mourier and Helen Weber, France; and Petra Coll-Exposito, Nicole Zoremba, and Eva-Maria Spöetta, Germany.

Bio of Denise A. Liotta-Dennis
Feng Shui Master, Speaker, Teacher, International Author, and Home Stager

She's known as the "fast-talkin' Texan" -an interesting and delightful oxymoron an interesting and delightful oxymoron. Denise is one of less than 100 genuine Feng Shui masters in North America. With 25+ years of experience, she's the founder and president of *Dragon Gate Feng Shui International Consultants* and *The American College of Classical Feng Shui*. She's been interviewed on television and radio and is the most published Feng Shui author in America.

Born to a Houston entrepreneurial family, Denise, who possesses a quarter century of business ownership experience, is among a rare breed of Feng Shui consultants. Denise not only resonates with all things spiritual, she talks the language and walks in the shoes of business people. Growing up in the shadow of her father's construction and real estate development companies, Denise discovered early in life an innate love of business lifestyles and entrepreneurship. Her work with Feng Shui is also an outgrowth of a natural affinity for interior design. In fact, Denise has more than twenty years' experience working in interior design, including residential and commercial projects.

With a rapid-fire delivery that keeps audiences spellbound, wide-eyed, and on the edge of their seats, Denise—a gifted educator and speaker on Feng Shui and business topics—offers high-energy, content-rich presentations. Peppering her talks with a quaint Southwestern humor, Denise's stories are couched in the real-life foibles of entrepreneurs and those seeking a spiritual path. She shares the spiritual side of life with a practical commercial bent not found among the more esoteric practitioners common to Feng Shui. Denise has studied with four noted Feng Shui Masters from China, Malaysia and Australia, including Grandmaster Yap Cheng Hai and belongs to his 400- year Wu Chang Feng Shui Mastery lineage. She has traveled much of the world; South America, Western Europe, Malaysia, Taiwan, Canada, South Africa, Japan and Mexico.

Denise is the author of 15 other books which are sold in fine bookstores in the United States, Canada, the United Kingdom, Australia, New Zealand, and Singapore. They are offered online at Walmart, Target, Barnes and Noble, Amazon, and are housed in hundreds of libraries including the *Library of Congress*. International online booksellers in Sweden, Germany, France, Poland, Japan, Italy and Denmark sell her books in English.

Dragon Gate Feng Shui International Consultants
The American College of Classical Feng Shui
Houston, Texas USA
713-897-1719 (phone and text)
Email: denise@dragongatefengshui.com
Website: www.dragongatefengshui.com
Facebook: https://www.facebook.com/denise.liottadennis?ref=bookmarks
Twitter: https://twitter.com/deniseannette
LinkedIn: https://www.linkedin.com/pub/denise-liotta-dennis/9/3bb/820
Author Central (Author's Page on Amazon) https://authorcentral.amazon.com/gp/profile

Classical Feng Shui for Wealth & Abundance
By Master Denise Liotta Dennis
ISBN 978-0-7387-3353-1
$17.99

Unlock the full wealth potential of your home or office using the potent formulas and wisdom of Classical Feng Shui. Written by a Feng Shui master, *Classical Feng Shui for Wealth & Abundance* reveals authentic techniques for success with money, business, and career. In this book, beginners and advanced students will learn:

- The two most popular Feng Shui systems: Eight Mansions and Flying Stars
- Easy-to-use Get Rich Keys and your personal Life Gua number for money luck
- Wealth building formulas such as Five Ghosts Carry Treasure, Dragon Gate, and Water Dragons
- How to identify and eliminate killing chi like Eight Roads of Destruction, Robbery Mountain Sha, and Eight Killing Forces

Whether you're buying a house, creating a home, or managing a business, these ancient and powerful techniques are exactly what you need to capture prosperity and success.

Purchase this book at Barnes&Noble.com, Amazon.com and Llewellyn.com. It is also available at Barnes & Noble brick and mortar locations.

Classical Feng Shui for Romance, Sex & Relationships
By Master Denise Liotta Dennis
ISBN 978-0-7387-4188-8
$19.99

Harness the ancient power and wisdom of Classical Feng Shui to enhance all of your relationships, from romantic pursuits to day-to-day interactions with friends, family, and coworkers. Explore real-life stories of men and women's struggles with love and relationships and how Feng Shui enabled them to overcome their obstacles. Whether you are a beginner or advanced student, Master Denise Liotta Dennis provides you with step-by-step instructions on:

- The two most popular Feng Shui systems: Eight Mansions and Flying Stars
- How to heal your house of detrimental formations that will repel romance and cause negative relationships
- Never-before-seen insights on the Life-Gua Zodiac, which helps you assess personality matches

Classical Feng Shui for Romance, Sex & Relationships is filled with effective methods for attracting love, prosperity, and even your soul mate. Use this comprehensive guide to improve not just the energy of your living space today, but also your happiness for many years to come. **Purchase this book at Barnes&Noble.com, Amazon.com and Llewellyn.com. It is also available at Barnes & Noble brick and mortar locations**

Classical Feng Shui for Health, Beauty & Longevity
By Master Denise Liotta Dennis
ISBN 978-0-7387-4900-6
$21.99

Improve your wellness, extend your longevity, and secure a healthy environment with the ancient power and wisdom of Classical Feng Shui. This comprehensive guide reveals ancient and modern techniques for lasting health and beauty that both beginners and advanced students can use. Providing step-by-step instruction, Feng Shui Master Denise Liotta Dennis teaches you:

- The two most popular Classical Feng Shui systems: Flying Stars and Eight Mansions
- Feng Shui's Taoist roots and a variety of health modalities from ancient and modern times
- Profound secrets of the "Heavenly Doctor" position and its importance in enhancing health
- Ways to protect your body and mind from detrimental formations, devices, and environments

With well-researched information, period charts, astoundingly accurate health predictions, and much more, *Classical Feng Shui for Health, Beauty & Longevity* will help you be happier and healthier. P*raise:* "Denise Liotta Dennis has done a great job of clearly expressing [the application of feng shui to health], going into great detail."—Grand Master Dr. Stephen Skinner
Purchase this book at Barnes&Noble.com, Amazon.com and Llewellyn.com. It is also available at Barnes & Noble brick and mortar locations.

Feng Shui That Rocks the House
By Master Denise Liotta Dennis
ISBN-13: 978-1986762892
$28.95

This book explains how to use the simple, yet profound Eight Mansions system. It is a more personalized Feng Shui. Learn your own Magic Life-Gua number and unlock the mysteries to a better life. While it is a compass-based formula, it is easy, effective and powerful. Designed to improve relationships, health and prosperity, you will learn the secretes passed down from Grandmaster Yap Cheng Hai from the famous Golden Star Classics. This book will teach you how to 'rock' your home and business—and finally get the life you want!

Purchase this book at Amazon.com

Hollywood's Fatal Feng Shui
By **Master Denise Liotta Dennis** & **Master Jennifer Bonetto**
ISBN-13:978-1986981965
$29.95

This is the first book to do a critical assessment of the tragic homes of Marilyn Monroe, Michael Jackson, O.J. Simpson, Nicole Brown Simpson, Phil Hartman, Anna Nicole Smith, Sharon Tate, Phil Spector, Lyle and Erik Menendez, and Brittany Murphy using Feng Shui. These famous Hollywood stories still haunt us today. These celebrities' homes attracted illicit affairs, drug abuse, lawsuits, murder, sexual scandals, greed, bankruptcy, cult-driven murders, loss of reputation, and fatal illness.

Feng Shui can explain why the energy of these gorgeous properties created the perfect storm and turned their lives upside down! The book took over a year of digging through public records locating accurate floor plans and land surveys. Along with other research, this allowed for a comprehensive assessment of each property. Classical Feng Shui systems, formulas and methods are explained so the reader may appreciate how it *all* went so wrong. You'll learn about disastrous formations such as the Peach Blossom Sha (illicit affairs, fatal attractions), Eight Roads of Destruction/Hell (bankruptcy, divorce), Eight Mountain Killing Forces (murder and crimes of passion), Robbery Mountain Sha (being hurt by knives), deadly Flying Star combinations and much, much more. **Purchase this book on amazon.com**

How to Start and Grow a Feng Shui Business
By Master Denise Liotta Dennis
ISBN 13: 978-1726468718
$19.95

How to Start and Grow a Feng Shui Business is for Classical Feng Shui practitioners and professionals who desire to begin their studies, near completing or have completed. The first book of its type to guide you in every aspect of creating a successful consulting business. Some topics discussed:

- How to conduct an assessment step-by-step
- Generating a professional report and delivering results
- Classical Feng Shui cures and enhancements
- Fees, checklist, charts, and more
- How to generate a constant flow of clients
- Lecturing to realtors, interior designers and other groups
- Sample Feng Shui reports
- Creating a brand and marketing materials
- Going public—TV, Radio Talk Shows, Vloging and YouTube videos
- Writing books and blogging
- Organizing a professional consulting book
- 100+ photos of Denise's studies with Grandmaster Yap in Germany, Malaysia, South Africa and Sedona

Purchase this book at Amazon.com

The Secrets to Mastering Flying Stars Feng Shui
By Master Denise Liotta Dennis
ISBN-13: 978-1985760127
$38.95

Flying Stars is the most popular, intriguing and misunderstood Feng Shui system in the world. Whether you're a practitioner or a novice, you'll be able to master and deepen your understanding of a method used for 'superior living'. This book delivers a detailed explanation of how *time* and *space* will affect all categories of Feng Shui, that of prosperity, relationships and health.

A fully illustrated, comprehensive and systematic home-study course that is designed for anyone who wants to put Flying Stars Feng Shui to personal, professional or practical use. With over 20 years experience, Master Liotta Dennis reveals the best tricks-of-the-trade. Step by step you are guided to shake up the energy and make-over your home or office while simultaneously learning the profound secrets of Flying Stars.

Purchase this book at Amazon.com

Real Estate Agents' Feng Shui Handbook
By **Barbara Harwell** and **Denise Liotta Dennis**
ISBN: 9781704068367
$19.99

Finally, a Feng Shui book that a Realtor® can use! *Real Estate Agent's Feng Shui Handbook* reveals practical solutions to selling a property quickly. Moreover, it explains the difference between mainstream, faux and genuine Feng Shui. Today it's more important than ever to be informed about how Feng Shui works, and why builders and developers are incorporating it into their projects. While there are savvy Asian buyers investing in America and other countries, non-Asian buyers also use the Ancient Chinese principles of Feng Shui.

The book goes into detail about how to identify good homes, why homes sit on the market, how to cure them, how to help your buyer or seller, and how to use lucky numbers to price homes. This book is a must-read for professional Realtors® and will serve as a handbook for all your property transactions.

This book will be available for purchase at Amazon.com

Printed in the USA
CPSIA information can be obtained
at www.ICGtesting.com
LVHW080002020824
787174LV00011B/298